COVER PICTURE: Tyseley-based GWR 4-6-0 No. 5043 *Earl of Mount Edgcumbe* passes Narroways Junction with 'The Bristolian' on 17 April 2010. Phil Waterfield.

GWR 175
A celebration of 175 years of the Great Western Railway
Created by Isambard Kingdom Brunel

Author: Robin Jones

Design: Mark Aston

Production editor: Janet Richardson

Production manager: Craig Lamb

Brand manager: Sarah Downing

Publisher: Dan Savage

Commercial director: Nigel Hole

Advertising: Carol Woods

Business development director: Terry Clark

Managing director: Brian Hill

Published by:
Mortons Media Group Ltd,
Media Centre, Morton Way,
Horncastle, Lincs LN9 6JR.
Tel: 01507 523456

Printed by:
William Gibbons & Son,
Wolverhampton
ISBN 978-1-906167-52-3

A HERITAGE RAILWAY PUBLICATION

© Mortons Media Group Ltd. All rights reserved. No part of this publication may be reproduced or transmitted in any form or by any means, electronic or mechanical, including photocopying, recording, or any information storage retrieval system without prior permission in writing from the publisher.

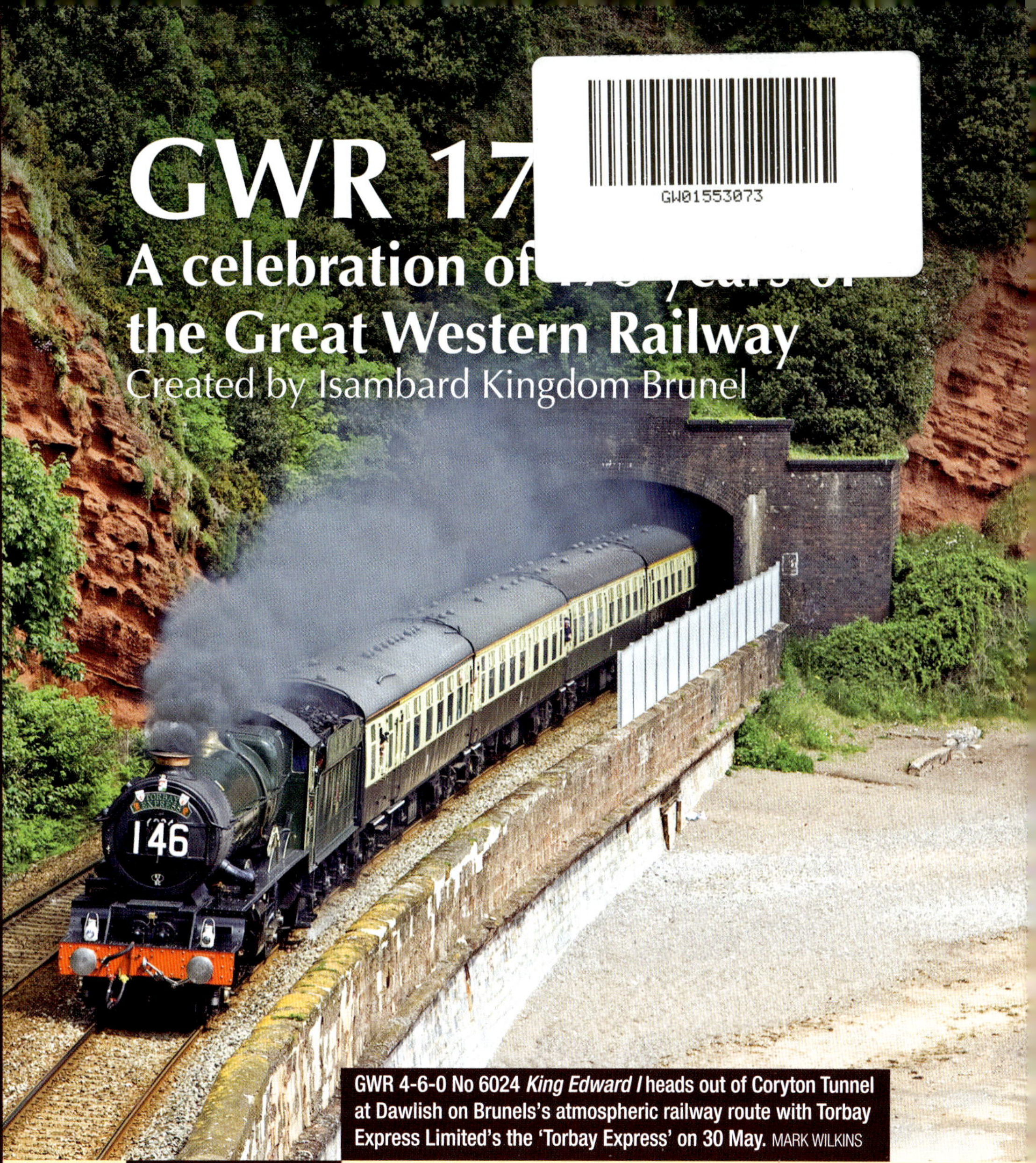

GWR 4-6-0 No 6024 *King Edward I* heads out of Coryton Tunnel at Dawlish on Brunels's atmospheric railway route with Torbay Express Limited's the 'Torbay Express' on 30 May. MARK WILKINS

Chapters

6	IN THE BEGINNING.	78	THE HOLIDAY LINE.
10	GOD'S WONDERFUL RAILWAY IS BUILT.	84	ANTIQUE MAP OF THE GWR SYSTEM IN THE 1930s.
16	WESTWARDS TO PENZANCE.	86	A WORLD WITHOUT STEAM.
26	COPPER DOMES AND STOVEPIPE CHIMNEYS: THE BROAD GAUGE YEARS	92	THE HALCYON TWILIGHT YEARS OF STEAM
34	SWINDON: THE HUB OF THE EMPIRE.	98	THE BLUE PULLMAN.
42	THE EMPIRE OF THE WEST.	100	PRESERVATION: REVIVAL OF THE COUNTRY BRANCH LINE.
48	STEAMING INTO THE 20TH CENTURY.	106	SCRAPMAN SAVES THE GWR!
54	*CITY OF TRURO*: THE 'RELUCTANT' LEGEND.	110	EVERY SCHOOLBOY'S DREAM.
58	TRAINS AND BOATS AND PLANES…AND BUSES TOO!	112	GWR STEAM BACK ON THE MAIN LINE.
64	PADDINGTON: THE GREAT TERMINUS.	118	THE RETURN OF GREAT WESTERN.
66	COLLETT, KINGS, CASTLES AND MUCH MORE.	124	THE SPIRIT OF BRUNEL LIVES ON!
74	A TRICKLE TO A TORRENT.	128	GWR ENGINEERING? IT NEVER STOPPED!

There are many who state that the Great Western Railway came to an abrupt end on 1 January 1948, when the Labour government nationalised Britain's railways.

Don't believe a word of it.

No, I'm not going to try to sound clever by telling you that the Great Western Railway company was not formally wound up until 23 December 1949, although that fact is in our unique GWR timechart which runs throughout this volume.

Never mind the paperwork and the legal document, for the Great Western Railway has never come to an end!

This year, many preservation venues are celebrating GWR 175 – the 175th anniversary of the company and its engineer Isambard Kingdom Brunel being given the powers to build a steam-powered railway from London Paddington to Bristol Temple Meads.

Just as Brunel's magnificent and world-beating 7ft 0¼in broad gauge system and its wonderful express locomotives with the monstrous driving wheels and oversize copper steam domes had to give way to 4ft 8½in in the cause of standardisation, so the glorious steam age of Stars, Castles and Kings moved aside for dieselisation.

Nationalisation, however, had little initial effect on the 'go it alone' spirit of the Paddington/Swindon empire. Indeed, after the brief experiment by British Railways of painting express passenger locomotives blue, they all carried GWR Brunswick green – even the mighty LNER and LMS Pacifics.

The Western Region reintroduced the much-loved chocolate and cream coaches and just as Brunel defied the rest of the county with broad gauge, so it chose diesel hydraulic traction as opposed to diesel electrics.

Following the vast pruning of the national rail network from the fifties onwards, the affection felt by so many to the great days of steam, when the GWR regularly broke records, both officially and otherwise, gave much impetus to the preservation movement, and the reopening of closed branch lines and cross-country routes largely by volunteers for heritage purposes. The busy branch lines so beloved of summer holidaymakers like Minehead and Kingswear are again thriving, while the idyllic GWR country branch line as epitomised by Chinnor, Buckfastleigh, Bodmin, Cranmore or Lydney Town, can be readily experienced. Not to forget the Severn Valley Railway, one of the world's leading centres for railway preservation, or Didcot Railway Centre, which has amassed the biggest collection of GWR locomotives and stock and even runs regular broad gauge trains.

If the powers that be thought in August 1968 that they had seen the last of steam, they had to think again three years later, when GWR icon No 6000 *King George V* ended the British Rail steam ban and paved the way for today's flourishing main line charter scene, in which Tyseley Locomotive Works as a maintenance and restoration depot that has specialised in GWR classic, both express locomotives and tank engines, has in this respect inherited the Swindon mantle.

The GWR today is by no means just about nostalgia for the past and preservation.

Much of Brunel's west of England empire is now served by First Great Western, named in February 2010 as Train Operator of the Year.

The Class 125 Inter-City High Speed Trains trialled on the Western Region where they debuted in the seventies are still very much with us today, having given more than a third of a century of sterling service. Brunel, who tried replacing steam in the 1840s, long before it has realised anything like its true potential, would have been delighted by them.

Tyseley also runs regular timetabled services, in the form of the steam-hauled 'Shakespeare Express' between Birmingham and Stratford-upon-Avon.

Many of Brunel's classic structures have survived the test of time on the national network and remain as a monument to his ingenuity – Maidenhead bridge, Box Tunnel, Paddington the Royal Albert Bridge.

It is planned to electrify the routes from Paddington to Bristol and South Wales, ensuring that the Great Western still plays an integral role in Britain's transport network for the foreseeable future.

So do not lament the passing of the GWR when there is so much of it to see and enjoy today. In GWR 175, we are not celebrating just the rich legacy of the past, but exactly what the logo says – 175 glorious years, with many, many more to come!

Robin Jones

Tyseley Locomotive Works-based GWR 4-6-0s No 4965 *Rood Ashton Hall* and No 5043 *Earl of Mount Edgcumbe* accelerate Vintage Trains 'The Cornishman' away from Parsons Tunnel towards Teignmouth on a glorious sunny 15 May 2010 morning in Devon. ADRIAN TAYLOR

In the Beginning

First mooted in 1800, it was inevitable that a railway would one day be built from London to Bristol. The Stockton & Darlington Railway had led the way with the world's first adoption of steam by a public railway in 1825, and Stephenson's *Rocket* firmly established the superiority of the steam locomotive over all other forms of traction at the Rainhill Trials in 1829.

That event preceded the opening of the Liverpool & Manchester Railway, the world's first inter-city line…upon which a young inventor named Isambard Kingdom Brunel not only rode, but also decided that he could improve on its design.

Railways were not new in the 1820s: there is evidence to suggest that the concept was in use in ancient Greece. By and large, they were short horse-drawn affairs built to take the produces of mines and factories to the nearest canal or river wharf or sea port. It was Cornishman Richard Trevithick who invented the steam railway locomotive and first publicly demonstration one in 1804, to a world that at first was slow to take up on the idea. It was only because of the shortage of horses in the industrial north-east caused by the endless supply needed for the Napoleonic Wars that colliery owners in the north east revisited Trevithick's concept and began building steam locomotives of their own.

From then on, the concept mushroomed as each improved design pushed the basic steam locomotive technology forward. So, whereas in the 1800s, we had horse-drawn plateways, a third of a century later, Britain boasted what was – and very much still is – one of the most magnificent railways in the world.

Let me briefly draw a parallel with rock 'n' roll here. In June 1953, US group The Crows had what many claim was the first hit in the genre, *Gee*, a variation on a fairly basic doo-wop song. Yet just 13 years later, we have the dazzling complexity of the Beach Boys' *Pet Sounds*, followed shortly by the Beatles and *Sergeant Peppers' Lonely Hearts Club Band*, thanks to a few geniuses on the way. Switching this idea back to transport, for Bill Haley, Elvis Presley, Buddy Holly, Phil Spector, Bob Dylan et al, read William Hedley, George and Robert Stephenson, Marc Seguin.

Yet there was one figure who took the steam railway concept to the accepted limits of his day – and went a few miles further. A man who rarely counted the pennies, and spared no expense in bringing his technological dreams to fruition, accepting nothing less than what he believed was the best. A giant of a figure who believed that railways were much more than purely functional, and in his many ground-breaking designs, married the products of the Industrial Revolution and the scientific advantages of his time with the style and harmony of the neo-classical painter.

Isambard Kingdom Brunel. The founder of the Great Western Railway.

Ironically, Isambard Brunel did not set out to be a great champion of the

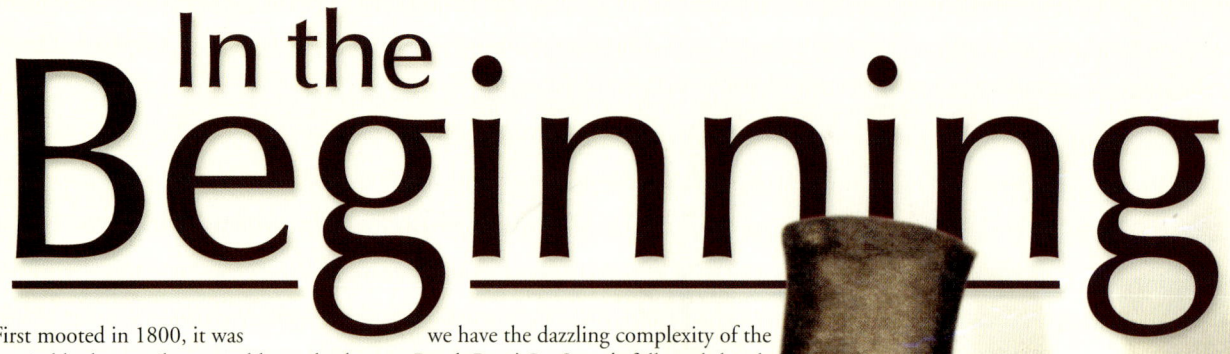

The famous photograph of Isambard Brunel standing next to the chains of his *SS Great Eastern*. BRUNEL 200

Birthplace of the GWR: the offices of Gibbs & Sons in Lime Street, London. GWR

steam age. While Hackworth and the Stephensons were busy developing the steam engine, Isambard and his father Marc were busy looking to an alternative that would better it.

Father and son were friendly with another Cornishman, Sir Humphrey Davy, a chemist who, with his assistant Michael Faraday, discovered that several gases could be liquefied by a combination of low temperature and very high pressure. In 1823, Marc Brunel became convinced that their discoveries could form the basis of a more efficient type of engine to rival the steam variety. Marc and Isambard spent many years experimenting with pressurised carbonic gas in a bid to develop what they named the Gaz Engine, but despite spending £15,000 on the project, it could not be made to work.

In 1824, the Thames Tunnel Company was formed, with Marc Brunel as engineer, and work began when a shaft was sunk at Rotherhithe on 2 March 1825.

In April 1826, Isambard was appointed acting resident engineer, before being given the job permanently on 3 January the following year, when he was just 20!

After many problems, not least of all the illness and loss of life among workmen during floods and cashflow problems, the Thames Tunnel was finally opened amidst much fanfare on 25 March 1843. It was immediately hailed as the eighth wonder of the world. It is considered to be the modern world's first public tunnel to run beneath a river.

While the Thames Tunnel inspired the later creation of the London Underground and indeed became part of it, it had nothing to do with the Great Western Railway… apart from a chance series of events that led Isambard from its murky depths to the great sea port of Bristol.

Isambard narrowly escaped death when the sewage-laden Thames water burst into the tunnel again on 12 January 1828. A timber beam trapped his leg as the floodwaters filled the great black cavity; and although he managed to free himself, to his horror, Isambard saw that the workmen's stairs were blocked by miners panicking to escape, so he turned and headed for the separate visitors' stairs instead.

Before he could reach them, a tidal water swept through the tunnel and swamped him. He did not drown, but was carried right up to the top of the 42ft Rotherhithe shaft on the south bank and safety. However, six workmen, including two who had been working with Isambard when the flood occurred, died.

Having suffered extensive injuries, Isambard was set to recuperate in the Regency seaside resort of Brighton, clearly as much a fun place in those days as today.

He suffered a major relapse during his convalescence by the sea – and his biographers summed up the reason in three words.

"Exertions with actresses."

In a bid to speed up his recovery, Isambard, still only 22, was sent first of all to a relative's house in Plymouth and then on to the genteel Bristol 'resort' of Clifton above the awesome Avon Gorge, which he found as inspirational as the charms of the ladies of Sussex.

The coat of arms of the Great Western Railway, which includes the shields of Bristol and Bath. ROBIN JONES

A simple chain of events had been set in motion which would reshape not only the gorge, but also the whole of the West of England, and indeed, much of the world's transport technology.

In 1753, William Vick, a local alderman, left £1000 to be invested until such time as it had grown into £10,000 – and then it was to be spent on a bridge spanning the great limestone gorge.

By 1829, it had grown to £8000, and the Clifton Bridge Committee was established not only to raise the remaining £2000 but to hold a competition to find the best design, with a prize of 100 guineas for the winner.

Isambard was in the right place at the right time.

Clifton Suspension Bridge, which was completed by Isambard Brunel's friends and admirers in 1864, five years after his death. ROBIN JONES

GWR TIMELINE

1800
Dr John Anderson plans horse-drawn tramroad from Bristol to London.

1804
21 February: Richard Trevithick's first public demonstration of a steam locomotive.

1806
9 April: Isambard Kingdom Brunel born in Portsmouth.

1820
Isambard Brunel, 14, sent to finish his schooling at the College of Caen in Normandy.

1822
August: Isambard, apprenticed under Louis Breguet, the world-famous maker of clocks, chronometers and other scientific instruments, returns to England.

1824
Thames Tunnel Company was formed, with Marc Brunel as engineer. Roadbuilder John McAdam promoted the London & Bristol Rail Road Company.

1827
3 January: Isambard Brunel appointed resident engineer on Thames Tunnel.

1829
Isambard Brunel submits first plan for Clifton Suspension Bridge.

1830
10 June: Isambard Brunel elected a Fellow of the Royal Society.

1831
21 June: Launch ceremony for Clifton Suspension Bridge.

1832
August: Four Bristol businessmen resurrect the idea of a railway to London.

1833
21 January: first meeting of the Bristol Committee which launched the Great Western Railway.
7 March: Brunel appointed as the railway's engineer.
30 July: Bristol Committee's first public meeting.
19 August: The title Great Western Railway adopted by the London and Bristol committees.

He was only too happy to provide the committee with a choice of four designs, all involving a suspension bridge; and great canal and bridge builder Thomas Telford was called in to judge all 22 entries. Telford dismissed them all, including Isambard's design, arguing that his proposed span was too long – and Telford was then invited to draw up a suspension bridge scheme of his own.

Beside himself with rage, Isambard decamped to the north of England looking for work, but was turned down for the post of engineer to the Newcastle & Carlisle Railway.

Nonetheless, on 10 June 1830, he was elected a Fellow of the Royal Society, in recognition of his work on the Thames Tunnel, his plans for the Clifton bridge and his experiments with the Gaz Engine.

Making a U-turn, the bridge committee announced on 16 March 1831 that Isambard's scheme had won a second contest, and he was given a free hand to design the final product. A launch ceremony for the bridge was held on 21 June 1831 –but soon afterwards the committee announced that they did not yet have enough funds to build it.

Isambard then designed Monkwearmouth's North Dock, and on his return south, he visited the Stockton & Darlington Railway, and experienced his first trip on a steam train on 5 December 1831 on the Liverpool & Manchester Railway, but was not impressed.

In 1832, Isambard was given the job of making improvements to Bristol's Floating Harbour, and finally, on 27 August 1836, the foundation stone for Clifton Suspension Bridge was laid by the Marquis of Northampton, president of the British Association for the Advancement of Science. However, financial problems led to the scheme being abandoned in 1853.

The first plan for a railway (horse drawn) from Bristol to London was put forward by Dr John Anderson in 1800. Twenty-four years later, roadbuilder John McAdam promoted the London & Bristol Rail Road Company, which would have run through Mangotsfield, Wootton Bassett, Wantage and Wallingford, with an eastern terminus at Brentford. Francis Fortunes came up with the plan for a General Junction Railroad in 1825, but it too came to nothing.

Four Bristol businessmen, John and William Harford, Thomas Guppy and George Jones took up the idea in 1832. Bristol merchants were desperate to maintain their city as the second port of the country and the chief one for American trade, at a time when the increase in the size of ships and the gradual silting of the River Avon had boosted Liverpool as a better alternative… especially as it had a rail link to London being built…

What was needed was a railway from

Isambard Kingdom Brunel, as painted by his brother-in-law JC Horsley in 1833.

A contemporary cutaway diagram of the Thames Tunnel being constructed. A flooding disaster led to Isambard Brunel being sent to convalesce in Brighton. BRUNEL 200

Bristol that would outperform the lines being constructed to the north-west.

On 21 January 1833, a meeting was held between the Merchant Venturers, who had supported Isambard over the Clifton bridge project, Bristol Corporation, the Bristol Dock Company, the Chamber of Commerce and the Bristol & Gloucestershire Rail Road Company to look at the prospect of building a line to London.

Isambard, along with several rivals, was invited to survey a route, with the winner being chosen on the basis of whichever project would be cheapest.

Isambard tore up the competition rules at the outset.

He told the railway committee that he would only survey a route that was the best, not the cheapest. He gambled with his reputation – and won by far his largest contract to date.

The committee confirmed his appointment, with WH Townsend, a local engineer who had designed the horse-drawn Bristol & Gloucestershire Railway which ran from coal mines at Coalpit Heath to the River Avon at Cuckold's Mill, as his assistant.

Isambard was told to survey the route within a month, and set out on horseback.

He made two controversial decisions. First to use a broad gauge of 7ft 0¼in – as opposed to the 4ft 8½in which was rapidly becoming the norm elsewhere – to allow the possibility of large wheels outside the bodies of the rolling stock which could give smoother running at high speeds; and second to take a route, estimated cost £2,800,000, north of the Marlborough Downs, which had no major towns but which offered potential connections to Oxford and Gloucester.

The project was formally launched at the Bristol Guildhall on 30 July 1833, when it was decided that a company should be formed to build the line, comprising directors from both Bristol and London. The first joint meeting of the 'London & Bristol Railroad' was held at the offices of Gibbs & Sons in Lime Street, London, on 22 August 1833… and when the prospectus was issued soon afterwards, the name Great Western Railway appeared for the first time.

In March 1834, the Great Western Railway Bill was passed in the House of Commons by 182 votes to 92, but had then to go to committee stage.

The committee, chaired by Lord Granville Somerset, met on 16 April – and then sat for 57 days to discuss the bill!

Objectors argued that passengers would be "smothered in tunnels" and "necks would be broken", and that the water supply for Windsor Castle would be destroyed, while the provost of Eton College said the railway would be "dangerous to the morals of the pupils."

The House of Lords rejected the bill by 47 votes to 30 on 25 July 1834; but bolstered by rapidly growing public support, the company issued a new prospectus in September 1834, and after parliament ruled that the line should not go within three miles of Eton, it received royal assent on 31 August 1835. Building work began within a month.

A £2 coin issued in 2006 to mark the bicentenary of Brunel's birth.

A 2007 mural created by artist David Powers and community group art+power for train operator First Great Western now decorates a wall at Bristol Temple Meads station. ROBIN JONES

The modern-day plaque which marks the spot where Isambard Kingdom Brunel was born in Portsea. PORTSMOUTH HISTORIC DOCKYARD

1834
25 July: First GWR Bill rejected by House of Lords.

1835
31 August: Great Western Railway Act received the Royal Assent.
29 October: Decision by GWR Board to adopt broad gauge.

1836
Building of the GWR begins
Taff Vale Railway obtained its Act.
3 March: The first meeting of a new Great Western Steamship Company.
5 July: Isambard Brunel married Mary Horsley, brother of accomplished painter John Horsley, in Kensington church.

1837
3 July: Act obtained for London terminus at Paddington.
18 August: Gooch became GWR Superintendent of Locomotive Engines.

1838
15 January: *North Star* steamed for the first time.
4 June: GWR opened between Paddington and Maidenhead.

1839
April: Electric telegraph in operation as far as Hanwell by April. the GWR pioneered telegraphic communication, and code words came to be used to represent various carriage types.
1 July: Maidenhead-Twyford section opened.

1840
First section of the Taff Vale Railway opened.
Building of the first royal carriage.
Disc and crossbar signals adopted.
Third class introduced: passengers could be conveyed by the slow goods trains in open wagons.
30 March: Twyford-Reading section opened.
1 June: Reading-Steventon section opened.
20 July: Steventon-Faringdon Road section opened.
21 August: Trial trip between Bristol and Bath.
31 August: Bristol-Bath section opens.
6 October: Decision made about choice of Swindon for locomotive works.
25 October: First reported GWR accident, at Faringdon Road engine shed.
17 December: Faringdon Road-Wootton Bassett section opened.

God's Wonderful Railway takes shape

One of two bridges across the River Avon taking the railway through Bath. BRUNEL 200

The Great Western Railway chose a rural village called Paddington, which lay on the outskirts of the city of London, for its terminus.

The first contract for the building of the line was in September 1835. Giving a taste of many magnificent structures to come in the decades that followed, it was the construction of a stupendous eight-arch 891ft-long brick viaduct at Hanwell across the River Brent in Ealing. It was named in honour of Lord Wharncliffe, who had helped the GWR bill through the House Lords, and his coat of arms is still emblazoned on it today.

Putting many 20th-century structures to shame, Isambard designed the viaduct to an Egyptian style, blending the best in contemporary bridge-building technology with neo-classical architecture. Indeed, Brunel structures seem designed to appear as if the Romans had never left Britain in 410 AD and had finally laid railways between their temples, villas and amphitheatres in a new golden age!

Jim Hurst became the GWR's first engine driver at the age of 26 and operated the inaugural service out of Paddington. ROBIN JONES COLLECTION

Splendid as it was, in aesthetic terms, Hanwell viaduct was easily eclipsed by Isambard's magnificent semi-elliptical twin-span bridge across the Thames at Maidenhead. Because the river commissioners would not allow any obstruction of the barge traffic that the GWR would later kill off, he had to design a bridge with only one support in the middle. For his part, Isambard refused to break the super-smooth 1-in-1320 ruling gradient between Paddington and Didcot by raising the height of the line to cross the river.

He devised a completely new type of bridge which his critics said would never hold. The biggest brick feature on the London-Bristol line, it is still carrying main line trains today.

While he was busy building the line, Isambard paid less attention to the adequacy of the rolling stock being brought in to run it. Indeed, it is fair to say that there were experts in the steam locomotive field with far greater knowledge.

Maidenhead Bridge, and the plaque which records Isambard Brunel's extraordinary feat in building it. ROBIN JONES

The 19 engines he bought were of middling quality, and magnificent though his railway and its infrastructure might be, it could be only as good as the trains that ran on it.

Cometh the hour, cometh the man – in the form of 20-year-old Daniel Gooch, who wrote to Isambard about the position of locomotive engineer on the GWR.

Isambard, who had taken on a key position with the building of the Thames Tunnel at a similar age, was prepared to listen.

Young Daniel had worked as a teenager at Robert Stephenson's Vulcan Foundry in Newton-le-Willows and had aided his brother, TL Gooch, in surveying the London & Birmingham and Manchester & Leeds railways. He had also gained some experience of locomotive engine building in Gateshead.

Isambard was immediately impressed, and gave him the job at £300 per annum. In turn, Gooch was impressed by the prospect of Isambard's 7ft 0¼in gauge, but was aghast at the locomotives bought to run on it.

He soon saw that only six of the locomotive ordered by Isambard were capable of running.

In stepped *Rocket* builder Robert Stephenson, who supplied *North Star*, a 2-2-2 locomotive built for the 5ft 6in gauge New Orleans Railway before the order had been cancelled. Gooch, who claimed to have aided its design, ordered it to be regauged to 7ft 0¼in.

It had to be brought in by March, and waited at Maidenhead from the end of November 1837 until the line arrived there in May 1838.

North Star was so successful that a sister locomotive, *Morning Star*, was ordered, followed by another 10.

Because Maidenhead Bridge was still being built, the inaugural 24-mile section of the line stopped short of the town, at Taplow. It was opened to paying passengers on 4 June 1838, after a directors' special had run five days before, taking 300 VIP guests to a banquet at Maidenhead.

On 1 July 1939, Maidenhead-Twyford section opened.

By 1839, the passenger service was extended over Maidenhead Bridge to Twyford, and records showed that in the first year, the GWR had carried 606,396 passengers.

Gooch was told to come up with locomotives capable of tackling this longer run, so at first he modified the Stars by introducing the large haystack-style firebox so typical of broad gauge engines, along with outside sandwich frames, a domeless boiler covered in wooden planks and inside cylinders.

The first of this new type of broad gauge 2-2-2 locomotive was called *Fire Fly*, and GWR directors were so impressed by its outstanding performances that they ordered a further 61 members to be built. They became known as the Firefly class, and by now it was clear that in Brunel and Gooch, the GWR had a perfect partnership.

The GWR main line ploughed on westwards – through the major obstacle of a hill at Holme Park next to the village of Sonning to the east of Reading. Forsaking

Hanwell or Wharncliffe Viaduct in Ealing. ROBIN JONES

The original GWR terminus at Paddington, portrayed on the day that it opened. ROBIN JONES COLLECTION

A portrait of GWR Locomotive Engineer Daniel Gooch in the National Railway Museum at York, along with a miniature 2-2-2 locomotive which he owned. ROBIN JONES

A plaque recalling Daniel Gooch's boyhood home in Bedlington, County Durham. ROBIN JONES

early thoughts of a mile-long tunnel because the GWR board feared passengers might be too scared to ride through it, Isambard ordered a gigantic chasm to be hewn out of the earth by a team of 1200 navvies aided by 200 horses during summer 1838.

The end result was Sonning Cutting, which was nearly two miles long and up to 60ft deep, and took until the end of 1839 to complete.

Laying broad gauge track took longer than a conventional railway with sleepers. The 30ft 'baulks' laid between each cross-member at 15ft intervals and packed with ballast to form a firm foundation for the base used far more manpower and raw materials. Because it was so labour intensive, this system of laying track, and indeed, its design, was not adopted elsewhere in Britain.

Fire Fly proudly headed a special directors' train from Paddington to Reading on 14 March 1840, prior to the first public services running on 30 March.

The section from Reading to Steventon on the Oxford turnpike road opened on 1 June 1840, allowing the university city to be reached by a road coach link.

Two more classic bridges spanned the Thames on this section, Basildon Bridge west of Pangbourne and Moulsdon Bridge just before Cholsey. Also, the short branch from Slough to Windsor includes the 203ft span wrought-iron bowstring Thames Bridge.

On 20 July 1840, services extended to Faringdon Road (later Challow), 63½ miles from Paddington, while at the other end of the line, the first test run between Bristol and Bath ran on 21 August followed by its opening to passenger trains 10 days later.

On 17 December 1840, the first public services passed through a small village called Swindon to reach Hay Lane, a temporary terminus later named Wootton Bassett Road. At this point, the GWR issued its first proper passenger timetable. From Swindon, a branch line to Cheltenham and Gloucester opened on 31 May 1841.

Sonning Cutting was one of the greatest earthworks on Britain's early railway network. ROBIN JONES

A 20-year project to built a replica of Daniel Gooch's ground-breaking 2-2-2 Fire Fly *was completed 2005. The locomotive and replica coaches run along a section of broad/mixed gauge track at the Great Western Society's Didcot Railway Centre.* FRANK DUMBLETON/GWS

The interior of Bath station as built. The trainshed roof has long since gone. BRUNEL 200

Swindon station was opened on 17 July 1842, built by contractors J&C Rigby at their expense in return for the right to operate the refreshment rooms on the ground floor and a hotel on the upper ones. To the annoyance of passengers, the GWR agreed that all trains should stop there for 10 minutes so refreshments could be sold.

The GWR route from London to Swindon was nicknamed 'Brunel's billiard table' because of its above-mentioned gentle ruling gradient; but the line to the west had to cross the southern Cotswold Hills, necessitating major earthworks, beginning with the huge incline at Wootton Bassett.

At Chippenham, Isambard constructed a delightful yellowstone station building, and to take his railway over a valley to the immediate south, built the 90-yard Cotswold stone Chippenham Viaduct, also known as the Western Arches, which are also Grade 2 listed.

A two-mile stretch required an embankment to reach the biggest obstacle of all, Box Hill, an outlier of the Cotswolds. Here, Isambard's engineering design skills were pushed to the limits and beyond.

He shocked his contemporaries by building a two-mile tunnel between the villages of Corsham and Box. Critics argued that because of the 1-in-100 gradient, trains would run out of control in the darkness if their brakes failed, and if a mishap occurred, the passengers would suffocate.

Isambard would hear none of it. He and his resident engineer William Glennie began work on

Box Tunnel's fabulous neo-classical western portal, as drawn by JC Bourne. BRUNEL 200

1841
31 May: Wootton Bassett-Chippenham section opened. Broad gauge Cheltenham & Great Western Union Railway from Swindon Junction to Cirencester opens.
14 June: Opening of Bristol & Exeter Railway between Bristol and Bridgwater.
30 June: GWR line from London to Bristol completed.

1842
The world's first railway refreshment rooms opened at Swindon.
13 June: The first railway journey by a reigning monarch made when Victoria travelled from Slough to Paddington, with Daniel Gooch driving his locomotive *Phlegethon*.
1 July: Bristol & Exeter extended to Taunton.
29 September: First excursion train from Bristol to London.

1843
Bristol & Exeter extends to Beambridge.
2 January: Swindon Works brought into use.
1 July 1843: GWR acquires Cheltenham & Great Western Union Railway, the first takeover by the company.

1844
The Railway Regulation Act made it a legal requirement that the GWR and all other UK railways, had to serve each station with trains which included third-class accommodation at a fare of not more than one penny per mile and a speed of at least 12 mph. GWR starts carriage building at Swindon.
1 May: Bristol & Exeter linked to Exeter.
12 June: Branch opened from Didcot Junction to Oxford.

1845
16 January: Territorial agreement reached between GWR and LSWR.
12 May: Kemble-Standish section opened to provide GWR access to Gloucester via Bristol & Gloucester Railway.
4 August: Oxford, Worcester and Wolverhampton Railway authorised.
16 December: Broad versus narrow gauge locomotive trials begin.

digging the tunnel in September 1836, using up to 1200 navvies working in shifts around the clock for five years and a team of 100 horses to take away the 247,000 cubic yards of spoil. It has been said that the primitive working conditions cost the lives of 100 labourers.

The excavations from the two ends finally met in early spring 1841, and so accurate were Isambard's calculations that the side walls lined up within an inch and a half. The 9636ft tunnel, then the longest on any railway in Britain, reached the stage where one out of two tracks could be used by trains on 30 June 1841, completing the entire route, as the length from Bristol eastwards to the tunnel had by then been finished. Fears of claustrophobia, however, did not immediately pass into history: at first, some passengers left the train before the tunnel and rejoined it on the other side, having journeyed round by road. The first through train was a directors' special which left Paddington at 8am and arrived in Bristol four hours later; before then, a stagecoach would take days to make the trip.

The section of line between Bristol and Bath had opened to the public on 31 August 1840, 10 days after Isambard

No 2 Tunnel on the section between Bristol and Bath. BRUNEL 200

Rain, Steam, and Speed – The Great Western Railway, an oil painting by JMW Turner, depicts an early broad gauge train, probably at Maidenhead Bridge. The painting was first exhibited at the Royal Academy in 1844.

privately treated some of the Bristol directors to the first train trip over the section, behind Firefly locomotive *Arrow* – riding on the locomotive footplate as no carriage was available.

In Bath, a section of the Kennet & Avon Canal at Sydney Gardens, a city pleasure park, needed to be diverted. Isambard designed a 27ft high retaining wall 5ft thick to create a barrier between his railway cutting and the canal. Again, with style to the fore, he built a stone and an ornamental cast-iron bridge to link the two halves of the park, which had been bisected by both railway and canal, along with a skewed stone bridge to carry Sydney Road.

Countering objections from city fathers who feared that the grandeur of Regency Bath could be spoiled by a railway running through the middle, Isambard took his railway to the south of the city centre, following the canal and the River Avon, crossing the river twice, either side of Bath station, with an acutely skewed stone bridge on the western side. Adding to the splendour of the spa resort so beloved by Jane Austen, he designed the splendid two-storey frontage of Bath Spa station to a Jacobean style.

The Bristol terminus, Temple Meads, was even more impressive. Isambard designed the frontage in a dramatic neo-Tudor style to screen the engine and train sheds, which in turn were supported by 44 massive brick flattened arches. A 74ft single-span wooden hammerbeam roof, a direct copy of Westminster Hall, covered the 220ft-long trainshed and its five tracks.

The GWR's Bristol committee had expressed dismay at the very basic original Paddington terminus and insisted that Isambard provided something that was far more grandiose, and Isambard was only too pleased to provide it.

By 1845, the timing for an express train from Paddington to Bristol Temple Meads had been reduced to just three hours.

The West Country would never be quite the same again, but for the Great Western Railway, nicknamed by many 'God's Wonderful Railway', Paddington to Bristol was just the beginning, albeit a truly magnificent one.

The frontage of the original Temple Meads station today. ROBIN JONES

Brunel's Chippenham station and Western Arches. ROBIN JONES

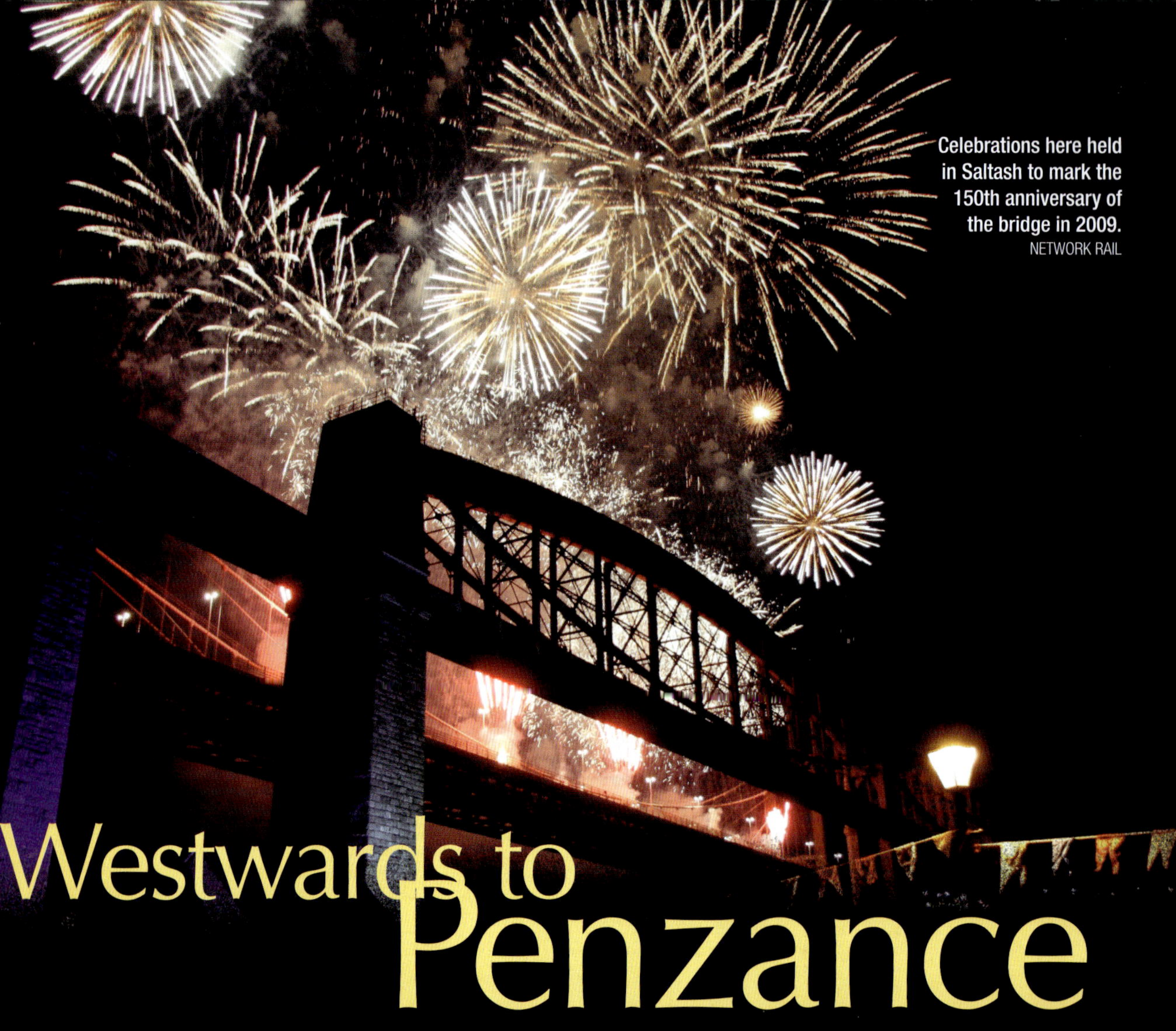

Celebrations here held in Saltash to mark the 150th anniversary of the bridge in 2009. NETWORK RAIL

Westwards to Penzance

Whenever the name Great Western Railway is mentioned, one thought immediately comes to mind: Paddington to Penzance.

Yet while Isambard Brunel and Daniel Gooch were pushing back the frontiers of transport technology on a daily basis – and even leaping too far beyond them, as was the case in south Devon; it took another 18 years from the time when the first train from Paddington pulled into Bristol Temple Meads for one to go all the way through to Penzance, the westernmost extremity of Britain's railway network.

As soon as the Great Western Railway Bill received the royal assent in 1835, Bristol merchants immediately began campaigning for the line to be extended to Exeter.

Approval of the scheme was granted the following year, and the first meeting of the Bristol & Exeter Railway Company was held on 2 July 1936.

Isambard was the clear choice to be appointed engineer, and he grabbed the opportunity to take his GWR broad gauge concept one giant step further, with the development of the passenger express.

In 1839, it was decided to build the line to 7ft 0¼in gauge, and lease it to the GWR, which would provide rolling stock and run the services. The first passengers were 400 invited guests carried on a private train from Bristol to Bridgwater in one hour and 45 minutes, behind Firefly class 2-2-2 *Fireball*, on 1 June 1841.

This northern half of the line opened to the public on 14 June, along with its branch to Weston-Super-Mare, where councillors at first insisted on the trains being pulled from the junction station by horses because they did not want dirty steam engines in their genteel resort, which had developed from a humble fishing village into a new destination for the patrons of the Regency spa resort of Bath.

Steam was eventually allowed into Weston, and the branch and its station were replaced in 1884 by the present-day Weston loop line.

There were comparatively few major engineering feats on the lines of the GWR main line, although there were deep cuttings at Ashton and Uphill, the latter bridged by Brunel's 'flying' Devil's Bridge. An attempt to build a bridge over the River Parrett near

Bristol & Exeter Railway locomotive superintendent James Pearson, who worked under Brunel on the South Devon Railway, devised locomotives with massive 9ft driving wheels for use on expresses, including the legendary 'Flying Dutchman'. Built by Rothwell & Co at Bolton, this is one of eight 4-2-4Ts, numbered 2002 following the Bristol & Exeter's's takeover by the GWR, seen at Bristol. GWT COLLECTION

Bridgwater with an arch that was even flatter than the one at Maidenhead was not successful, and it was replaced with a timber version in 1843 after the foundations moved. Despite the modern myths surrounding him, Isambard was not perfect.

The largest engineering feat on the Bristol & Exeter was the 1092-yd brick-lined Whiteball Tunnel.

The section from Bridgwater to Taunton opened on 1 July 1842. The magnificent Grade 2*-listed Bridgwater station building, designed and built by Brunel, has a distinctive Georgian white stuccoed front which has changed little with the passage of time. It was given a major facelift in 1994.

The completed 76-mile main line from Temple Meads was opened throughout to Exeter St David's on 1 May 1844. To mark the occasion, Firefly class locomotive *Actaeon* ran the 388 miles from Paddington and back, driven by none other than Gooch himself.

The average speed for the outbound five-hour journey, inclusive of stops, was 39mph, and on the way back cut 20 minutes off the scheduled time, averaging 41½mph.

Such speeds were aided by the flattish nature of the line, crossing the fen-like Somerset Level for long periods, allowing high speeds to be more easily attained.

The net result was locomotive performances of a magnitude which the world has never seen before.

Five-hour Exeter expresses began on 10 March 1845, and even when an extra stop was added at Bridgwater, a further five minutes was cut off the journey.

Among the 9.50am Exeter-Paddington expresses, which ran between 1847 and 1852, was the fastest train in the world, nicknamed the 'Flying Dutchman' after the racehorse that won the Derby and the St Leger in 1849.

'Stoking the Dutchman' became a term for hard physical work among engine crews.

The Grade 2* listed Bristol & Exeter Railway's headquarters offices, designed by SC Fripp and built in 1852. ROBIN JONES

The flat nature of the line led to the rare case of it being built for less than the original estimate of £2-million, despite Brunel's reputation for going well over budget.

One big social benefit brought by the railways was the standardisation of time. Before the railway age, individual towns and villages would often have their own local time zones. When the Bristol & Exeter arrived in the latter city, an extra minute hand was added to a clock in Fore Street in order to show both railway time and local time.

Tourism by train to Exeter became big business from 1850 onwards, and paved the way for the GWR to open up the south west as Britain's premier home destination for summer holidays. Among the first tourists to arrive by train were the elderly Marc Brunel and his wife Sophia, carried there by their son's latest railway.

When the GWR's lease on the line ran out in 1849, the Bristol & Exeter decided to run its own trains. A fleet of broad gauge locomotives was

The curving trainshed of Bristol Temple Meads dates from the 1870s. ROBIN JONES

1846

GWR takes over Birmingham & Oxford, Berks & Hants, Monmouth and Hereford and Birmingham, Wolverhampton & Dudley railways and leases South Wales Railway.
Cardboard tickets adopted.
Cloakrooms introduced.
February: *Premier* becomes the first Swindon-produced locomotive.
April: Locomotive *Great Western* emerges from Swindon Works.
30 May: Exeter-Teignmouth line opened by South Devon Railway,
18 August: Gauge Regulation Act passed following the report by Gauge Commission which favoured standard gauge.
30 December: South Devon Railway extends to Newton Abbot.

1847

29 April: *Iron Duke* trial run took place on the Duke of Wellington's birthday.
20 July: Newton Abbot-Totnes on South Devon Railway opened. Atmospheric traction introduced between Exeter and Newton Abbot.
23 October: GWR trains reached a new station at St James Square, Cheltenham.
21 December: Reading-Hungerford branch opened.

1848

South Devon Railway abandoned Brunel's atmospheric system.
Shrewsbury & Chester line opened.
5 May: South Devon Railway SDR reached Laira Green near Plymouth.
5 September: Thingley Junction to Westbury section opened by Wilts, Somerset & Weymouth Railway.
1 November: Southcote Junction-Basingstoke opened.
18 December: Newton Abbot-Torre opened.

1849

'Flying Dutchman' introduced.
2 April: South Devon Railway extended to Plymouth (Millbay) .
May: Bristol & Exeter took back the operation of its line in May.
May: Cheap day tickets excursion tickets first issued
October: Windsor branch opened.

GWR | 17

This disused transhipment shed at Exeter St David's station was the place where goods were transferred from broad gauge wagons to standard gauge counterparts on the London & South Western Railway. ROBIN JONES

A surviving section of the vacuum pipe from Isambard Brunel's atmospheric railway, for decades used as a stormwater outfall at Goodrington Sands, is now preserved at Didcot Railway Centre in the middle of a section of broad gauge track. ROBIN JONES

The only surviving Bristol & Exeter Railway broad gauge coach side, part of the Bristol Industrial Museum collection. Built in 1849 by Bristol horse-drawn coach builder John Perry, the vehicle's 'stagecoach' design clearly reflects the similarity to road vehicles of the day, showing that while the road and rail concepts may have diverged, they were not fully divorced. A six-wheeler clerestory coach, it had four first-class compartments with seating for eight people in each and a central luggage compartment. The coach was sold off for use as a house and the side was recovered from a cottage at South Cerney near Cirencester by the museum in 1966. ROBIN JONES

ordered, 10 built by Stothert & Slaughter of Bristol and another 10 by Longridge & Co of nearby Bedlington, all smaller versions of Gooch's hugely successful GWR Iron Duke class.

In September 1854, the Bristol & Exeter opened its own locomotive workshops at Temple Meads, and five years later turned out the first of 23 broad-gauge engines of its own. The works later became known as Bristol Bath Road, and would become a famous steam depot in the century to come.

In its first three decades, the Bristol & Exeter paid a very reasonable dividend of 4.5 per cent to shareholders, and opened further branches to Clevedon, Tiverton, Yeovil, Chard, Portishead, Wells via Cheddar, Barnstaple and Minehead.

In 1845, the Bristol & Exeter built its own station at right angles to the GWR station and an 'express platform' on the curve linking the two lines so that through trains no longer had to reverse. A grand headquarters was built for the Bristol & Exeter on the west side of its station in 1852-54 to the Jacobean designs of Samuel Fripp.

On 29 May 1854, the Midland Railway laid a third rail along its tracks from Bristol to Gloucester so both broad and standard gauge trains could run. With three railways running into Temple Meads, a scheme to redevelop the station to greatly increase capacity saw it rebuilt between 1871-78. A new three-platform through station with curved wrought iron train shed was built on the site of the GWR express platform, while the Bristol & Exeter station was closed and the site used for a new carriage shed.

The Bristol & Exeter capitalised on its proximity to the Bristol Channel by developing two harbours served by its main line, at Dunball, between Highbridge and Bridgwater.

In the 1860s, it was involved in a scheme to turn the limestone promontory of Brean Down into a major transatlantic port served by the railway, but after a foundation stone was laid on the seabed on 5 November 1864, the buoy to which it had been attached was seen floating off down the Bristol Channel the next day, dragged away by the merciless channel currents, and the vastly over-ambitious plans were ditched.

Royal assent to build a 14-mile branch from Taunton to Watchet was granted on 17 August 1857 – again to broad gauge and with Isambard as engineer.

The front of Exeter St David's station. ROBIN JONES

The line opened on 31 March 1862; its owner, the West Somerset Railway Company, leasing it to the Bristol & Exeter. It was extended to Minehead on 16 July 1874, and was the last new Bristol & Exeter-operated route before the company was finally absorbed by the GWR in 1876.

The 24-mile Minehead branch is today Britain's longest standard gauge heritage line, the West Somerset Railway.

After completing the successful Bristol & Exeter, Isambard looked to extend his broad gauge all the way to Penzance, but he was concerned at the amount of stiff gradients which would be needed to cross the hilly terrain of south Devon en route to Plymouth.

He settled for a route with inclines at places to the west of Newton Abbot like Hemerdon, Dainton and Rattery, all of which were later to become legendary in terms of proving locomotive and crew performances, but he was not sure that the steam locomotives of his day would be adequate.

BR Standard 4MT 2-6-4Ts Nos 80079 and 80080 emerge from Whiteball Tunnel with a charter to Barnstaple on 1 May 1994. DAVID HOLMAN

The atmospheric railway pumping station at Dawlish as painted by Condy, with the vacuum pipe running between the rails. Few illustrations of the atmospheric railway survive.
ELTON COLLECTION, IRONBRIDGE GORGE MUSEUM TRUST

GWR 4-6-0 No 7011 *Banbury Castle* approaches Teignmouth with a southbound express September 1955. COLOUR-RAIL

No 5051 *Earl Bathurst* crosses Cockwood harbour with Past-Time Rail's 'Mayflower' trip from Plymouth to Taunton on 26 March 2005. DAVID HOLMAN

Since his failed experiments with the Gaz Engine, Isambard had always had a conviction that somewhere out there, a better form of traction than the steam locomotive existed.

In September 1844, he and Gooch witnessed a demonstration by inventors Samuel Clegg and Jacob Samuda of a new type of train on the one-and-a-half-mile-long Dalkey & Kingstown Railway which linked Kingstown Harbour with the Dublin & Dalkey Railway.

Clegg, a gas lighting pioneer, and Samuda, a marine engineering expert, had patented what was know as the atmospheric system of propulsion on 3 January 1838. Basically, it worked on the vacuum cleaner principle: no engines, but a pipe between the rails would pull the train along.

The cast-iron tube was sealed by airtight valves at each end. A piston linked to the bottom of a carriage was pushed past the valve into the tube, and stationary steam engines built on the side of the railway-powered pumps to take the air out of the tube, creating a vacuum ahead of the piston.

The greater pressure of the atmosphere behind the piston would force it along the tube and pull the carriage with it, without the need for a locomotive.

Brunel was very impressed. Clean, silent and fast, there were no locomotives to shower passengers in the open trucks of the day with dust and cinders, and the trains would be lighter and more efficient, meaning that the track could be built more cheaply. Stiff gradients could be tackled without having to bring in extra locomotives and crews, for all that would be needed would be another pumping station close by.

His enthusiasm for the atmospheric system was shared by Prime Minister Sir Robert Peel, who wanted to see all railways converted to the method.

After the Dublin & Kingstown Railway came the London & Croydon in 1846, eventually running seven-and-a-half miles from Croydon to New Cross in London, and the 1.4-mile Paris & St-Germain Railway from Bois de Vezinet to St-Germain in Paris in 1847.

The fourth would be the South Devon Railway, which received its royal assent on 4 July 1844 and duly appointed Isambard as its engineer. He recommended atmospheric propulsion for the entire 52-mile route from Exeter to Plymouth – despite the protestations of Gooch, who claimed that a locomotive would run the Kingstown line more cheaply, and joined forces with none other than *Rocket* builder Robert Stephenson to argue the case against the new technology.

However, because of Isambard's promise of huge savings, the South Devon directors unanimously approved his plan.

The route from Exeter to Teignmouth clung to the foot of the wave-lashed sandstone and created a stunningly picturesque route through a series of tunnels linking romantic red-sand beaches and coves.

The construction of this section of the line may today be viewed either as another Brunellian engineering marvel, or plain barking mad.

GWR 4-6-0s No 6024 *King Edward I* and No 5051 *Earl Bathurst* approach the summit of the 1-in-42 of Hemerdon bank at 18mph with the Railway Touring Company's 'Great Britain' trip from Penzance to Thurso on 7 April 2007. After a late departure from Plymouth, the train had a clear road through to Exeter and covered the difficult 62 miles in 63 minutes. BRIAN SHARPE

Today it is the most expensive part of the national rail network to maintain due to marine erosion and rock falls, with regular stoppages and delays.

Nine huge Italianate engine houses were built at three-mile intervals, at Exeter St Davids, Countess Wear, Turf Locks, Starcross, Dawlish, Bishopsteignton, Newton Abbot, Totnes, and one at Torre to serve a projected branch line to Torbay. The last two were never used, both nonetheless survive along with the one at Starcross.

As Gooch feared, the system had big problems from the start. The vacuum pipe was too small, and so the pumping engines were forced to run faster than their design speed in order to maintain the vacuum.

For whatever reason, they failed to inform the South Devon directors of difficulties which caused the London & Croydon Railway to close after just one year.

This first section of the South Devon Railway opened on 30 May 1846, using steam engines at first, while the vacuum tube and leather and metal valve continued to be laid.

The first two public atmospheric trains ran over the line from Exeter on 13 September 1847, and from 10 January 1848 these services were extended to Newton Abbot, with some freight also being carried.

Isambard had correctly predicted that high speeds could be achieved – 68mph with a 28-ton load and 35mph with 100 tons – but the 20-mile journey from Exeter to Newton Abbot with four stops took a slow 55 minutes due to one train having to wait for the other to pass as the route was still single track.

The biggest tragic flaw was that the raw materials which were needed to make an atmospheric railway successful had not been invented in Brunel's day.

The hinge of the airtight valve and the ring around the piston were both made of leather, an organic material which was totally unsuitable for the purpose. So a large team of men was employed to continually run a sticky sealant on the valve to make it airtight.

This sealant then proved useless after exposure to the air, so a new compound using cod-liver oil and soap was tried without much better success. This compound, along with natural oils in the leather, was sucked into the vacuum pipe, and the leather dried and cracked in the sun, wind and salty air. More famously, the leather was also said to have been gnawed away by rats.

Two miles of the valve had to be completely replaced, while the stationary steam engine pumps kept breaking down.

1850

Experimental introduction of the absolute block system through Box Tunnel.
First goods manager appointed.
The first lavatory on a train was provided for Queen Victoria.
First section of Oxford, Worcester & Wolverhampton Railway opens.
14 March: GWR acquires Wilts, Somerset and Weymouth Railway.
18 June: South Wales Railway opened from Chepstow to Swansea. Twelve Fireflys ferried across the Bristol Channel for use on the line.
2 September: Oxford (Millstream Junction)-Banbury opened.
7 October: Wilts, Somerset and Weymouth's Westbury-Frome section opened.

1851

Season tickets introduced.
11 July: GWR acquired the Kennet & Avon Canal.
9 September: Westbury-Warminster line opened.
19 September: Grange Court-Gloucester opened and leased by GWR.

1852

Monmouth Railway's Newport - Pontypool line opened.
Mixed gauge route to Birmingham completed.
Electric telegraph links London to Bristol.
First eight-wheeled carriages on express services.
South Wales Railway connected to the GWR by Brunel's Chepstow Bridge.
11 March: West Cornwall Railway opened between Redruth and Penzance
21 April: Shrewsbury-Ludlow section of Shrewsbury-Hereford Railway opened.
30 July: Shrewsbury-Hereford Railway opens to Hereford for goods.
25 August: West Cornwall Railway's Redruth-Truro Road section opens.
11 October: South Wales Rail extended to Carmarthen.

1853

Bristol & Exeter opened to Yeovil from Durston.
Ludlow-Hereford line started carrying passenger traffic.
4 June: Evesham-Wolvercot Junction on Oxford, Worcester & Wolverhampton Railway opened.

Nine trains a day ran between Exeter and Teignmouth during spring and summer 1848, reaching average speeds of 64mph. They were popular with passengers, apart from those in third class who were asked to get out and push when they broke down.

However, the South Devon Railway directors were horrified to hear that it cost 37 pence to run an atmospheric train for a mile as opposed to 16 pence for steam.

The directors, along with Charles Russell, the chairman of the GWR, demanded explanations from Isambard, who had absented himself from the line, and visited him at his house in Duke Street in London.

Isambard said the performance and reliability would not improve until the pipes and the pumps were completely replaced.

With shareholders having lost nearly £500,000 on the scheme, the directors voted to convert to locomotive haulage as from 10 September 1848. Thirteen days before, Isambard told angry shareholders in Plymouth he had been wrong about atmospheric propulsion, but waived his fee for overseeing the construction of their railway until it opened throughout to Plymouth on 2 April 1849 – as a steam line.

As such, the route was a major success, and section by section was converted to double track throughout in order to handle increasing volumes of traffic. The South Devon Railway became part of the GWR on 1 February 1876.

Yet what about Brunel's ultimate goal of Penzance?

The tidal River Tamar at Saltash, the historic great physical boundary between Devon and Cornwall, was the massive obstacle that lay between Isambard and his dream. Yet just as he had mastered the Thames crossing, so he set out to cross the Tamar near the point where it is 1100ft wide and 70ft deep..

The official opening of the Royal Albert Bridge at Saltash on 2 May 1859. ILLUSTRATED LONDON NEWS

The Cornwall Railway was promoted in late 1844, just after the Bristol & Exeter was completed by Brunel. Captain William Moorsom, who had been involved with the Bristol & Gloucester Railway eight years before, was asked by local businessmen in 1843 to survey a line and drew up plans for a 66-mile line from the Plymouth terminus of the South Devon Railway to the naval port of Falmouth. Moorsom's plan involved a ferry to cross the Tamar.

His scheme was rejected by the House of Lords and the Cornwall Railway replaced him as engineer with Isambard, whose plan involved a high-level bridge across the Tamar. Parliament approved the scheme on 3 August 1846, and Isambard again chose broad gauge.

The construction of the Cornwall Railway began at Truro in 1847, but money kept running out, leading to regular and lengthy stoppages. The route crossed several deep river valleys, which are a trademark of the landscape of the coastal fringes of Devon and Cornwall, and involved 34 viaducts over the 53 miles between Plymouth and Truro, each built in timber.

In the west of Cornwall, the standard-gauge Hayle Railway had opened in 1837, running from Hayle Foundry to Pool and Portreath, and was extended to Redruth the following year, linking the Redruth-Camborne tin and copper mining areas to the coast, and using steam locomotives from the outset.

The West Cornwall Railway was authorised on 3 August 1846 and took over the Hayle Railway, also bringing in Isambard as engineer. The plan was to convert it to 7ft 0¼in gauge and extend the Hayle Railway to Penzance in one direction and Truro in the other, so it would link up with the future Cornwall Railway.

The West Cornwall was completed between Penzance and a temporary Truro terminus in 1851, and opened on 11 March 1852. Nine more viaducts were to follow on the West Cornwall Railway, which crossed eight river estuaries, and 30 valleys were crossed.

Brunel's distinctive trestle structures, known as fan viaducts because of the shape of

GWR 4-6-0 No 6024 *King Edward I* hea 'Thank you Barry' special charter throu Dawlish station on 7 July 2008. Barry was Britain's longest serving railway general manager, running the Paignton Dartmouth Steam Railway for a third o century until his retirement. DON BISHOP

the supports, involved timber constructions of masonry pillars, and were a cost-effective way of bridging the Cornish terrain. Although they were all replaced from the late 19th century onwards with more expensive and longer-lasting stone alternatives, the old columns can still be seen standing alongside the new viaducts in many places. The last to survive in Cornwall was College Wood Viaduct on the Falmouth branch which stayed in situ until 1934.

Attempting to revive the stalled Cornwall Railway project after it ran out of money, the GWR, Bristol & Exeter and South Devon Railway took on a partial lease of the project from 1855, and continued to bail it out as construction proceeded.

To span the Tamar, Isambard first suggested building a timber bridge with one main span of 255ft and six further spans of 105ft each, but the Royal Navy demanded that it must allow headroom of 100ft to allow tall ships to pass beneath.

A second plan involved a single-span bridge to clear the river in one go, but the Cornwall Railway could not countenance the estimated £500,000 cost.

It would be third time lucky. Isambard came up with an amazing and radical design based around two arched tubular girders, fastened to four cast-iron columns in the middle of the river, and supported by suspension a pair of 450ft spans which would carry a single track railway from one side of the river to another. A double-track version had been slimmed down to save money.

A huge wrought-iron cylinder was sunk in the middle of the estuary to allow to dig down to the rock strata so that a solid granite

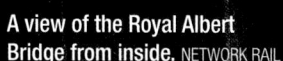
A view of the Royal Albert Bridge from inside. NETWORK RAIL

column could be fixed in it. This column would support the cast-iron pillars supporting the great tubular arches.

The 1060-ton tubular girders were assembled on the east bank and floated across the river into position on pontoons. Hydraulic presses were used to jack them up to the required height, as crowds gathered to watch the operation which began on 1 September 1857.

Attached to each tube were the suspension chains, linked to each other by 11 uprights. Diagonal bracing was added to provide extra rigidity.

The great bridge, which has an overall length of 730 yards, took seven years to build and cost £225,000. Despite the huge expense, the directors of the Cornwall Railway heaped praise on him, knowing that it would outlive their lifetimes and many, many more, and it was nonetheless a truly economic solution.

By the time the bridge was ready, the remainder of the Plymouth-Truro line had been completed, all set for the first trains. The last county in Britain without a link to the national rail network was now connected.

The structure was named the Royal Albert Bridge, as it was officially opened by the Prince Consort on 2 May 1859. Civic dignitaries from Cornwall including the mayors of Truro and Penzance arrived by train and were presented to the prince.

Both banks of the river were packed with onlookers, while others crowded on hills and rooftops overlooking the river desperate for a glimpse of the proceedings. A flotilla of steamers and small boats plied their way up the river estuary for a grandstand view.

One person was glaringly absent from the celebrations, which included a grand civic banquet in Truro Town Hall the following day, a special train leaving Plymouth at 10.30am and arriving just before 1pm. Isambard Kingdom Brunel.

Brunel's blueprint for the bridge over the Tamar at Saltash. NEWWORK RAIL

The great tubular girders of the Tamar bridge being lifted into place. PLYMOUTH MUSEUM

He was suffering from a kidney ailment and his health was rapidly deteriorating while pulling out all the stops to complete his biggest project of all, building his third transatlantic liner, the *Great Eastern*, in London.

On 4 May, the Cornwall Railway was opened to the public. Despite his health, he managed to ride across the bridge a few days later, lying on a couch mounted on a truck pulled by a Gooch engine.

Isambard visited his great ship on 2 September that year, but after two hours he collapsed and had to be taken home. He had suffered a heart attack and was dying. Confined to bed in his Duke Street house, he was unable to see the *Great Eastern* set off on its maiden voyage five days later. However, in typical Isambard fashion, he insisted on receiving news of his ship, which brought out the crowds as it passed every south coast town.

He even wrote to the GWR directors asking them to give all the workers at Swindon the day off along with special passes so they could take the train to Weymouth to see his ship when it arrived

In steam days, the GWR's largest engines, the Kings, were prohibited from crossing the bridge and there is no official confirmation that any exception was ever made in the steam era. However, in 2007 we see the combination of King and Castle doubleheading as No 6024 *King Edward I* and No 5051 *Earl Bathurst* drop down the grade off the bridge and into Devon with the 'Great Britain' railtour, running 10 minutes early on 7 April. BRIAN SHARPE

End of the line – or the start of it? The Railway Touring Company's 'Great Britain' departs from Penzance at 12.54pm on 7 April 2007 behind GWR 4-6-0s No 6024 *King Edward I* and No 5051 *Earl Bathurst* bound for Thurso. BRIAN SHARPE

there. That was the last letter he ever wrote.

On 15 September, he called his family together for the last time, and died a few hours later, aged just 53.

His funeral, attended by a large contingent of GWR workers along with his many friends and admirers, took place at London's Kensal Green Cemetery five days later.

After his death, the Cornwall Railway directors ordered the name I K BRUNEL ENGINEER 1859 to be displayed above the entry arches of the Royal Albert Bridge in perpetuity. Everyone who travelled into Cornwall via Saltash would be left in no doubt as to the name of its designer.

The final part of the original Cornwall Railway route, from Truro to Falmouth, had to wait another four years before it was opened, progress being halted by the failure of the contractor.

It finally opened on 24 August 1863, but by then, Falmouth had declined in importance because the Royal Mail Packet Service fleet had been switched to Southampton. The West Cornwall railway redrew its blueprint and relegated the line from Truro to Falmouth to branch status, with the route to Penzance becoming the main line.

In 1864, the standard gauge West Cornwall Railway was leased to the above-mentioned consortium of the GWR, Bristol & Exeter and South Devon Railway to lay a third rail to allow broad gauge trains to run over it.

Brunel's dream was finally realised on 1 March 1867, when a through service between Paddington and Penzance was begun, with locomotives supplied by the South Devon Railway.

The West Cornwall Railway was taken over by the GWR in 1876.

A branch line nearly five miles long from St Erth on the main line to St Ives was opened on 1 June 1977. Apart from an extension to a freight branch at Plymouth's Sutton Harbour, and the addition of a third rail to a line at Hayle wharf later that year, it was the last new Brunel broad gauge line to be built.

One last truly spectacular Brunel-designed bridge was constructed, but five years after his death, as a memorial to him by the Institute of Civil Engineers.

It was Clifton Suspension Bridge, the plans for which had helped get him the job as GWR engineer.

Around 150,000 people turned out for the grand opening of the bridge on 8 December 1864, when a huge procession from the city centre was accompanied by the army and 16 bands.

The bridge, spanning the Avon Gorge within sight of his Bristol & Exeter Railway, remains a magnificent tribute to an even more magnificent man.

Clifton Suspension Bridge, as portrayed in a modern-day mosaic at Temple Meads station. ROBIN JONES

The River Tamar aside, Brunel had to cross numerous rivers valleys to take the Cornwall Railway on to Truro and beyond. GWR 4-6-0s No 5051 *Earl Bathurst* and No 5029 *Nunney Castle* head Pathfinder Tours' 'Cornubian' railtour across Tresulyan viaduct on 29 May 2004. The original 'Cornubian' was the final Western Region steam special to Penzance in 1964. BRIAN ASTON

1854
2 January: South Wales Railway opens Carmarthen-Haverfordwest section Pontypool (Coedygric)-Hereford on Newport, Abergavenny & Hereford Railway opens.
16 January: Departure side of new Paddington station brought into use.
29 May: Paddington arrival side opens. Gloucester-Standish narrow gauge line opened to allow Midland Railway access to Bristol.
8 June: Great Western Royal Hotel at Paddington opens.
1 September: Amalgamation of the Shrewsbury & Birmingham and Shrewsbury & Chester with the GWR.

1855
GWR built its first standard gauge engines.
Grange Court-Hereford line opened.
Charles Spagnoletti appointed Telegraph Superintendent.
1 February: Postal service between Paddington and Bristol introduced.

1856
Broad gauge reaches Wolverhampton.
Didcot and Reading loops were opened with mixed gauge.
2 February: First GWR goods trains reached Birkenhead.
15 April: The South Wales Railway reached New Milford and a service to Ireland started by using contractors' vessels.
1 May: First GWR passenger trains reached Birkenhead.
30 June: Warminster-Salisbury opened.
1 September: Frome-Yeovil opened.

1857
Bridport and Devizes lines opened.
20 January: Extension from Yeovil to Weymouth where a steamer service to the Channel Islands was introduced.
24 January: Duffryn Junction-Llandilo opened by the Llanelly Railway.
2 February: Trowbridge-Bathampton opened.
1 June: Henley-on-Thames branch opened.

1858
29 November: First slip coaches introduced, between Slough and Banbury.

1859
Reading Signal Works established.
2 May: Formal opening of Royal Albert Bridge by the Prince Consort.
4 May: Cornwall Railway trains run from Plymouth to Truro.
11 May - Cornwall and West Cornwall railways linked at Truro. 18 July: Brentford branch opened for goods.
25 July: Henwick-Malvern Link opened.
2 August: Dartmouth & Torbay Railway's Torre-Paignton section opened
15 September: Death of Isambard Brunel.

This watercolour by Sean Bolan depicts a broad gauge locomotive designed by Sir Daniel Gooch in 1847. NRM

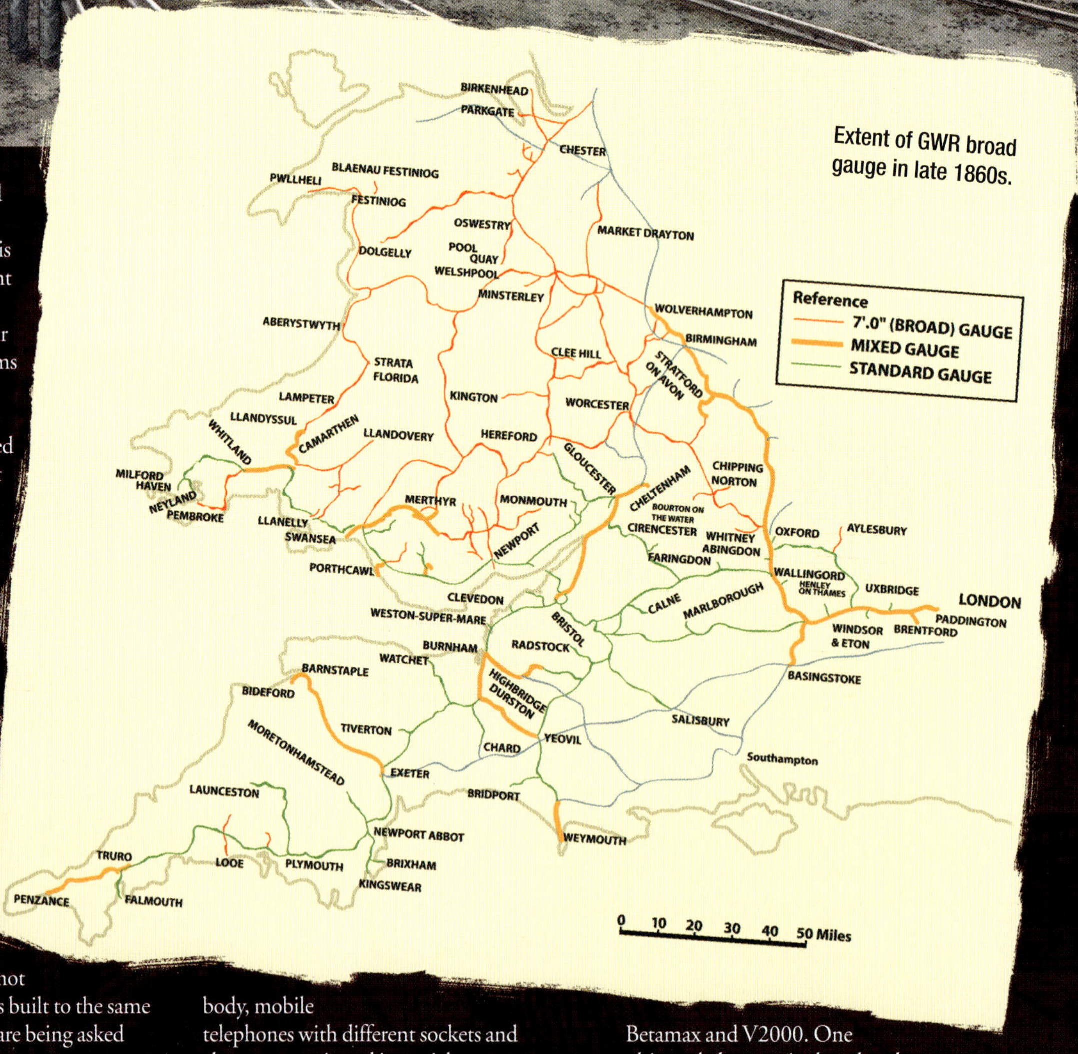

Copper domes & stovepipe chimneys
the broad gauge years

Extent of GWR broad gauge in late 1860s.

Reference
- 7'.0" (BROAD) GAUGE
- MIXED GAUGE
- STANDARD GAUGE

Brunel designed his broad gauge system to beat the world – and it did, with his locomotive superintendent Daniel Gooch building locomotives which in their day were matchless in terms of speed.

Yet today, the only operational steam-powered 7ft 0¼in railway is a short demonstration line at Didcot Railway Centre, where the splendid replica of *Fire Fly* offers rides in an open and a covered early GWR-era coach from a station created inside a typical wood transfer shed. This was a structure where a broad gauge freight train would arrive, and the goods would be transferred manually to a standard gauge train alongside.

It is so easy to ask the basic question – why not have all main line railways built to the same gauge? Similar questions are being asked today, in photography, where one manufacturer's lens will not fit onto another's body, mobile telephones with different sockets and chargers, metric and imperial measurements – and the video market battles between VHS, Betamax and V2000. One ultimately has to win, but that does not guarantee that it is the best. It was a case of the

locomotives like Iron Duke 4-2-2 *Great Britain* were the fastest in the world. GWT COLLECTION

Possibly the smallest broad gauge engine ever built, *Tiny* is displayed inside the South Devon Railway's Buckfastleigh museum. ROBIN JONES

New-build Peppercorn A1 Pacific No 60163 *Tornado* stands alongside the replica *Fire Fly* at Didcot Railway Centre in 2009, highlighting the comparative sizes of top-link express passenger locomotives designed a century apart. FRANK DUMLBETON/GWS

Reading station in broad gauge days. GWT COLLECTION

GWR Iron Duke 4-2-2 *Eupatoria*, photographed between 1878 and 1892. NRM

Bristol Temple Meads station in 1870, showing broad and mixed gauge. ROBIN JONES COLLECTION

Gooch engines, with their ability to haul much wider loads at more efficient speeds, versus a stifling but ultimately necessary one-size-fits-all approach in the rest of the country.

Gooch's steam locomotives were truly colossal engines typical of the early Victorian age of oversized copper domes, stovepipe chimneys, boilers coated with wooden planks, no cab roofs or sides to offer protection to drivers and firemen, and gargantuan central driving wheels, designed on the basis that the bigger they were, the faster the engine would go. It was a world apart from the steam-operated main line of the 20th century and, Didcot apart, all of our standard gauge heritage railways today.

Gooch's Firefly 2-2-2s, of which 62 examples were built by seven different outside manufacturers, set exacting new standards for train travel. He had the honour of driving the first-ever Royal Train, when Queen Victoria travelled on a special from Slough to Paddington on 13 June 1842 behind his locomotive *Phlegethon*.

Not only was Gooch a brilliant engineer, but a hands-on engineman too, and understood the task from all angles.

His Firefly class engines were painted with chocolate-brown frames, green wheels with black tyres, vermillion buffer beams – and a green boiler and firebox – which evolved into the famous Brunswick green which became the trademark of the Swindon empire right up until the end of steam, was even adopted by British Railways for its express passenger locomotives built elsewhere and carried by early main line diesels too.

The powers that be saw the gauge problem coming from afar, and in 1845 trials were held between broad and standard gauge locomotives in a bid to establish which system was best. Firefly *Ixion* exceeded 60mph and ran from London to Didcot with a 71-ton load at nearly 55mph, a far better performance that anything the 4ft 8½in lobby produced. A Royal Commission, which

The replica *Fire Fly* hauls a train comprising a new broad gauge covered carriage unveiled at Easter 2010. FRANK DUMBLETON/GWS

Third class passengers rode in open carriages in the early days of Brunel's GWR, as demonstrated on this train hauled by the replica *Fire Fly* at Didcot. FRANK DUMBLETON/GWS

Mixed gauge track on the Didcot demonstration line. ROBIN JONES

had been set up to adjudicate over the issue, came down in favour of standard gauge despite the facts in its favour. A subsequent Gauge Act ruled that no more broad gauge lines were to be built, although existing broad gauge companies could maintain their track and even expand within set limitations.

As locomotive technology evolved and newer designs with bigger capacity replaced the Fireflys, several were rebuilt to soldier on as saddle tanks.

Averaging around 500,000 miles in service, the last one, *Ixion*, was withdrawn as late as July 1879.

Gooch produced the smaller and less successful Sun class of 21 2-2-2s in 1842, followed by the 18 Leo 2-4-0s, the GWR's first purpose-built goods engines, and the Hercules class 0-6-0s, the company's first of this wheel arrangement. In 1842, the GWR owned 136 engines from 11 different makers, and Gooch clearly saw the need for the company to build its own.

As previously mentioned, the 2-2-2 *Great Western* became in 1846 the first to be built there in its entirety, the average speed of 57mph produced on its famous first trip from Paddington to Exeter, sending shock waves far and wide as far as the railway market and general public were concerned.

The first class of engines to be built entirely at Swindon were the six Prince 2-2-2 passenger locomotives, which entered service between August 1846 and March 1847, later on the Oxford and Birmingham lines, and were withdrawn in 1870 after covering an average of 600,000 miles.

Meanwhile, Gooch produced his star turn, the 29 members of the Iron Duke class of 2-2-2s with 8ft driving wheels, of which 21 were built at Swindon. The first was named *Iron Duke* because its trial run took place on 29 April 1847.

The Iron Dukes were no less than cutting-edge technology and quickly established themselves as the flagship locomotives of Brunel's broad gauge,

In 1848, one of them, *Great Britain*, maintained average speeds of 67mph on its Paddington-Didcot runs, while regular service trains maintained 60mph.

The most famous Iron Duke of all, notched up 800,000 miles in 30 years with its original boiler. *Iron Duke* itself clocked up 607,412 miles before its withdrawal in August 1873, while *Lightning* reached 816,601 in 31 years before it was sidelined in 1878, a resounding endorsement of the quality of Swindon technology.

The Iron Dukes were followed in 1847 by the six-strong Pyracmon 0-6-0 freight locomotives, and in 1851 by the eight Caesar 0-6-0s.

The biggest type of all numerically was the Ariadne or 'Standard Goods' class with 102 built at Swindon between 1852-63.

Gooch also designed many successful broad gauge locomotives for other lines where Brunel had been

No 3028, a 2-2-2 'convertible' built for the broad gauge but which could be adapted to standard gauge. GWR

Broad gauge 4-2-2s *Great Western* and *Swallow* at Didcot in May 1892, the last month of GWR broad gauge steam, with the Down Paddington-Penzance service. GWT COLLECTION

Typical early broad gauge signal replicated at Didcot Railway Centre. ROBIN JONES

appointed engineer – the Bristol & Exeter Railway, the Vale of Neath Railway and the Cornwall Railway.

To tackle the daunting South Devon Railway inclines following the scrapping of the atmospheric system, he designed the Corsair 4-4-0 saddle tanks with a leading bogie axle, a major innovation in design.

Swindon did not have it all its own way on the GWR broad gauge, for in 1855, Robert Stephenson & Co in Newcastle delivered the class of 10 Waverley 4-4-0s, the only tender locomotives with this wheel arrangement to run on 7ft 0¼in gauge. They mainly worked services to South Wales, Gloucester and Bristol.

Gooch eventually faced up to what for him was the very sad fact that with the growing problems caused by breaks of gauge and delays while passengers and goods were transferred from one system to another, the end of the broad gauge era was in sight. Ready to adapt to the changing market, he began designing standard gauge locomotives instead. His last class designed for the GWR was the 22 Metropolitan 2-4-0Ts, built between 1862-64, the company's only GWR broad gauge engines to have outside cylinders. Fitted with condensing apparatus to nullify the discharge of steam in the tunnels, they worked over the underground Metropolitan Railway, extending the Brunel empire eastwards beyond Paddington

Inside the Didcot transfer shed, which highlights the break of gauge that brought down the slow but inevitable downfall of broad gauge. FRANK DUMBLETON/GWS

Nowhere to go: the year is 1892, and 15 miles of siding at Swindon are crammed with broad gauge locomotives and rolling stock which no longer have any track on which to run. GWT COLLECTION

1860
The first official use of the title of stationmaster.

McKenzie & Holland locking frame installed at Paddington.

GWR switched from coke to coal as the fuel for locomotives.

Birkenhead, Chester & Birkenhead and Birkenhead, Lancashire & Cheshire Junction railways absorbed by GWR.

1 July: The West Midlands Railway from merger of the Oxford, Worcester & Wolverhampton, Newport, Abergavenny & Hereford and Worcester & Hereford railways.

10 October: Hatton-Stratford-upon-Avon link opened.

1861
1 July: GWR and West Midland joint working began.

14 August: The first standard gauge train at Paddington.

1862
Several branches opened, including the Severn Valley, Kington and Witney.

1863
10 January: Metropolitan Railway opened and worked by GWR.

30 July: Tenby-Pembroke opened.

1 August: Great Western, West Midland and South Wales Railways amalgamated.

24 August: Cornwall Railway line from Truro to Falmouth opened.

8 September: Bristol-New Passage (for Severn ferry) opened.

1864
Gooch resigned as Locomotive Superintendent and replaced by Joseph Armstrong

The early carriages livery of dark chocolate brown was modified with the upper panels painted white, becoming a pale cream after being varnished and exposed to the weather.

These panels were later painted in cream to give a similar effect, and provided an early 'chocolate and cream' livery.

The post of Superintendent of the Line was created.

8 August: Tenby-Pembroke line extended to Pembroke Dock.

1865
1 February: Vale of Neath Railway amalgamated with GWR.

1 July: West Cornwall Railway acquired.

2 November: Gooch becomes GWR chairman. The same year, he lays the first transatlantic cable and is elected at Conservative MP for Cricklade.

until 15 March 1869 when the mixed gauge running rails were removed from its system.

After a total of 407 broad gauge and 98 standard gauge locomotives were built to his designs, around half of them in Swindon, Gooch stood down in September 1864 after years of arguments with the GWR board. Nevertheless, a year later, he returned to the GWR – as chairman!

His successor as locomotive superintendent, Joseph Armstrong, built another 70 broad gauge engines, beginning with 26 Hawthorn 2-4-0 tender engines with 6ft driving wheels, some of which were later converted to saddle tanks, the 14-strong Swindon class of 14 0-6-0 goods engines, later sold to the Bristol & Exeter, and six Sir Watkin 0-6-0Ts, fitted with condensing gear for use on the Metropolitan Railway, with three later sold to the South Devon Railway and all later rebuilt as saddle tanks.

Saving the best for last, he produced 24 Rover class 4-2-2s, based closely on the Iron Dukes but with vacuum brakes on both the driving and trailing wheels.

Modern-day health and safety experts look away now. Gooch's Iron Dukes had brakes only on the side of the tender, and none at all on the engine!

The highest number of miles closed by a Rover 4-2-2 was 787,174, recorded by *Rover* itself between 1871-92.

By this time, it was not a question of if broad gauge would become extinct, but when. As a stop-gap measure, Armstrong designed 7ft 0¼in locomotives which could be converted to run on 4ft 8½in gauge, starting in late 1878 with 10 Armstrong saddle tanks. No more broad gauge designs would be produced, and when the older engines were withdrawn, they were replaced by 'convertibles'.

Armstong died in June 1877 and was superseded by his assistant Willam Dean, who designed and produced 41 convertibles at Swindon, the final batch being 20 0-4-2STs for passenger use. They proved unsatisfactory and were converted into 4-4-0 tender engines.

One of Dean's biggest immediate improvements was his decision to provide cabs for engine drivers. Although any modern audience would gasp in amazement at the fact that weather protection had not been provided much earlier, as it was not exactly rocket science, Armstrong had stoutly refused because he believed that open footplates prevented drowsiness.

All broad gauge carriages built from 1877 onwards were convertible to standard gauge. Larger carriages emerged under Dean, whose stock featured the first lavatories and electric lights, heralding a new era of passenger comfort.

Surprisingly, broad gauge lasted for a third of a century after its champion Brunel's death.

As the smaller standard gauge railway companies began to merge into or be taken over by bigger ones, more mixed gauge lines were laid over part of the GWR network. Mixed gauge operation finally reached the heart of the 7ft 0¼in system, Paddington, in August 1861. The battle had been lost.

Gooch, as GWR chairman, gave up the fight, and instigated towards large-scale conversion of routes to standard gauge, beginning in 1866, when there were still 1427 miles of broad gauge including 387 miles of mixed gauge.

The first to be converted were the routes north of Oxford in 1869, the South Wales main line in 1872 and around 200 route miles in Berkshire, Wiltshire, Hampshire and Somerset the following year.

The last broad gauge engine to be built for the GWR, Rover class 4-2-2 No 24 *Tornado*, appeared from Swindon in July 1888.

The end came on Saturday 21 May 1892, when, in a massive military-style operation involving more than 4200 tracklayers, all 177 miles of the Paddington-Penzance main line were converted to standard gauge overnight.

That day, the last broad gauge engines, coaches and wagons returned to Swindon for storage on 15 miles of 'death row' sidings where they were to be cut up. A total of 196 engines, 347 coaches and 3544 wagons remained.

The final broad gauge train from Paddington was the 5pm to Plymouth on the Friday, hauled by Rover class locomotives *Bulkeley* to Bristol and *Iron Duke* from there to Newton Abbot. *Bulkeley* also worked the final train to London, the 'Night Mail', which reached Paddington at 5.30m on the Saturday.

The last broad gauge train from Penzance

Adriane or 'Standard Goods' class 0-6-0 *Nemesis* at Trowbridge. GWR

was a 9.10pm empty stock working, hauled by two 'convertibles'. As the final broad gauge train passed through each station, the stationmaster had to confirm to the inspector aboard that there was no broad gauge stock remaining in his sidings. The inspector then gave the stationmaster a certificate, authorising the line engineer to order the platelayers and gangers to begin the conversion.

The mail train from Penzance to Paddington, which left Plymouth at 4.40am on the Monday, was the first to run the length of the new all-standard gauge route.

The final GWR broad gauge engines to steam were South Devon Railway 4-4-0STs *Leopard* and *Stag*, which were used at Swindon for shunting broad gauge stock into the cutting shop. In June 1893, they met the same fate.

Two examples were saved for posterity: *North Star*, which had been preserved after withdrawal in 1871; and Iron Duke class 4-2-2 *Lord of the Isles*, the GWR's exhibit at the Great Exhibition of 1851. The pair appeared at various exhibitions, and Lord of the Isles appeared at Chicago in 1893 and Earls Court in 1897.

With space at Swindon at a premium, the pair were offered to museums as a permanent gift, but there were no takers.

William Stanier, the future legendary Chief Mechanical Engineer of the London Midland & Scottish Railway, cared nothing for history. Then in charge of Swindon Works, he decided to scrap both when GWR Chief Mechanical Engineer George Jackson Churchward was on holiday. It was nothing short of outright heritage vandalism.

Aghast, Churchward salvaged some of the parts of *North Star* when he returned.

Along with the other 'Big Four' railways, the GWR was invited to take part in celebrations to mark the 1925 centenary of the Stockton & Darlington Railway, the world's first public steam-operated line, and the directors realised that they could display no locomotive from their early period,

The surviving parts of *North Star* were tracked down and used to build a static replica at Swindon, which is today exhibited inside STEAM – Museum of the Great Western Railway at Swindon.

When the GWR's own centenary came in 1935, no interest was shown in restoring South Devon Railway 2-4-0ST *Prince*, which dated from 1871, had been converted to standard gauge in 1893 and withdrawn in 1899 before surviving as a stationary boiler in Swindon Works. The GWR scrapped it instead.

However, one broad gauge engine did survive: a little South Devon Railway vertical-boilered 0-4-0 called *Tiny*, built by Swan & Co in Plymouth in 1868 to replace horse traction on the city's Sutton Harbour branch; and which later became a shunter in Newton Abbot yard. Withdrawn in June 1883, it was exhibited at the town's railway works, and is now an exhibit inside the modern-day South Devon Railway's museum at Buckfastleigh.

Delightful as *Tiny* may be, it is as typical or representative of the GWR broad gauge empire as a motorbike is of the British car industry. As the railway preservation movement in Britain gathered pace, there was obviously a glaring hole to be filled.

In 1985, a working replica of *Iron Duke* was built for the National Railway Museum, using the parts from two standard gauge Austerity saddle tanks, as part of the Great Western 150 celebrations.

Before that, retired Royal Navy Commander John Mosse was working as consultant architect to British Rail on the restoration of Temple Meads Old Station in 1981, when he suggested building a replica of *Fire Fly*, and soon won the support of like-minded enthusiasts, including Leslie Lloyd, then general manager of the Western Region, his chief mechanical and electrical engineer John Butt and retired railway engineers including SAS Smith, who as manager of Swindon Works had overseen the construction of Standard 9F No 92220 *Evening Star* in 1960.

The big boost came when Gooch's original Firefly class drawings came to light at Paddington and by 1982 the Firefly Trust was established and fund-raising began.

Gooch would have built it in 13 weeks for £1735, but the trust took 23 years and £200,000.

The project moved from Bristol to Didcot Railway Centre where *Fire Fly*, the first new main line steam locomotive to be built for use in Britain since *Evening Star*, ran under its own power for the first time on 2 March 2005, its public debut following on 30 April that year.

The wheel had turned full circle, and with two replica broad gauge locomotives completed, the public can once again appreciate for themselves the true enormity of Brunel and Gooch's world-beating railway achievements.

Saddle tank *Leopard* flounders with the 'Flying Dutchman' near Camborne during the great blizzard of 10 March 1891. GWT COLLECTION

1866
4 September: Tenby-Whitland opened.
November: Broad gauge rails added between Truro and Penzance.
Forest of Dean Central Railway absorbed.

1867
Steel rails first used, in Paddington yard.
Swindon was made the central workshop for the construction of carriages and wagons, with 13 miles of additional sidings. GWR began building more rolling stock at Worcester.
Wycombe Railway absorbed.
Swansea-Pontardulais line opened.
1 March: Through trains from Paddington to Penzance began.
20 June: Cornwall Railway opens only branch, to Keyham.

1868
Parliamentary orders trains to include smoking carriages.
1 June: Conversion of broad to standard gauge begins, between Whitland and Carmarthen.

1869
1 April: Broad gauge was taken out of use between Oxford and Wolverhampton, and from Reading to Basingstoke.
August: Grange Court-Hereford converted to standard gauge.
Bristol & South Wales Union Railway and Tenbury & Bewdley Railway absorbed.

1870
1 February: Stourbridge Railway absorbed.

1871
Wrexham & Minera Railway absorbed.

1872
The first interlocked signalling frame installed, at Taplow.
1 February: GWR took over steamer services from Milford Haven.
11 May: Last broad gauge train runs in South Wales.
Great Western and Brentford and Wallingford & Watlington railways absorbed.
The Carmarthen-Aberystwyth broad gauge line became the last in Wales to be converted to standard gauge.

1873
Work on the Severn Tunnel begun.
The first bogie wagons for heavy loads appeared.
GWR took over Llanelly, Llynvi & Ogmore, Llynvi Valley and Ogmore Valley railways.

Swindon:
the hub of the empire

Two centuries ago, a small market town whose Anglo Saxon name may have meant 'pigs town' eked out an existence as a trading centre for the Wiltshire agricultural community.

Today, Swindon boasts a population of nearly 160,000, and is a thriving business centre.

Honda has a major car production plant there, while the town is also home to the WHSmith headquarters and distribution centre and the European head office of electronics company Intel. The bases of the UK divisions of North American-based pharmaceutical companies including Patheon and Cardinal Health, insurance and financial companies including Nationwide Building Society and Zurich Financial Services, eCommerce provider Shopatron, energy supplier npower, fleet management company Arval, mobile telephone company Motorola and consumer goods supplier Reckitt Benckiser are among many top names based there today, which do not deal in pigs or any other farming livestock. The head office of the National Trust is also sited in Swindon.

So what transformed a country backwater into a 21st century boom town?

While many brands have a foothold in the town today, just one reigned supreme there for nearly a century and a half, and by itself made Swindon a hallmark of cutting-edge technology as well as social reform for a century and a half.

It was the Great Western Railway.

For it is Swindon's historic position as a transport hub that alone has turned the town into the mini-city of today.

The 'swine town' lay at the junction of two Roman roads, but apart from being mentioned in the Domesday Book when William the Conqueror gave it to Odo, Bishop of Bayeux, in 1066, it remained in obscurity until the Industrial Revolution and the second wave of canal building mania. The Wilts & Berks Canal linking the Thames to the Bristol Avon via the Kennet & Avon Canal arrived in 1810 and the North Wilts Canal, which linked the Wilts & Berks to the Thames & Severn Canal arrived in 1819. The canals brought trade to the area, and the little town's population started to grow, reaching around 1200.

Two decades later, a single letter changed the face of Swindon forever.

It was written to Isambard Kingdom Brunel on 13 September 1840 by Daniel Gooch, the newly appointed GWR locomotive superintendent who had been ordered to select a site for the company's workshops where

A line-up of the mightiest beasts of the GWR, Swindon-built King 4-6-0s Nos 6005 *King George II*, 6008 *King James II*, 6017 *King Edward IV*, 6020 *King Henry IV*, 6022 *King Edward III*, 6023 *King Edward II* and 6024 *King Edward I* at Swindon shed on 3 July 1930. GWS

locomotives, carriages and wagons would be built and maintained.

Gooch, who had earlier considered Didcot as a site for the works, recommended Swindon, which was at the highest point on the London to Bristol line. Also, it lay at the junction of the GWR main line and the branch railway to Cheltenham, and because the canals could supply coal and coke from the Somerset coalfield at a moderate price, as well as water for the locomotives. Building materials for the workshops could also be brought in by barge.

He argued that building a large station at Swindon would house the locomotives necessary for banking the Wootton Bassett incline, and for changing engines on the two 'halves' of the Paddington-Bristol main line, because the gradients on the Swindon to Bristol section were much more arduous than the relatively flat 'Brunel's billiard table' line between Paddington and Swindon.

A somewhat different story claims that while they were surveying a valley to the north of Swindon, Brunel either threw a stone or dropped a sandwich from a picnic lunch and declared that spot to be the new location of the works.

Gooch wrote in his diary: "Mr Brunel and I went to look at the ground, then only green fields, and he agreed with me as to its being the best place."

With the railway passing through town in early 1841, the Goddard Arms public house was used as a railway booking office in the absence of a station. Tickets bought there included the fare for a horse-drawn carriage to the line at the bottom of the hill.

Construction of Swindon Works began in spring that year. Adjacent to the works, houses were built for the workforce, most of whom would be brought in from outside.

London contractor J&C Rigby, which constructed the station in 1842, and operated what was believed to be the world's first railway refreshment rooms there, also built 300 cottages along with a railway hotel, under Gooch's direction. One of the earliest examples of planned industrial housing in Britain, it was designed by Sir Matthew Digby Wyatt, the architect of Paddington station. Much of the stone for the houses came from the excavations of the Box Tunnel. The model estate comprising the cottages was called New Swindon, and is today known as the Railway Village.

The GWR's attitude towards its Swindon workforce was, in terms of social welfare, far ahead of its day. Brunel and Gooch were not only radical in their approach to transport technology and engineering feats, but also in their concern for their workers, in an age in which elsewhere young children still worked in factories and mines and life expectancy among the working classes was comparatively short. To ensure the well being of the workforce, Gooch brought in a works doctor who stayed in free lodgings.

New Swindon had three pubs and a church, St Mark's, and a 10½ acre park for sports and recreation. In 1843, a small group of works employees set up a library.

It predated the first council library in Britain, at Salford, which opened in 1852. Next to the church was a school, built in 1845 for the children of GWR workers.

Meanwhile, machinery in the first building, the locomotive repair shed, was installed by 1842, when Swindon station was also opened. The following January, works manager Archibald Sturrock declared the workshops, sited half a mile to the west of the station, to be fully operational.

The works included an engine depot capable of housing 100 locomotives and built parallel to the main line. At right angles to it lay the engine house, which could accommodate up to 36 engines undergoing repairs and maintenance at once. Smaller workshops housed pattern makers, wheel turners, millwrights, toolmakers and copper smiths. Adjoining the north side of the engine house was the erecting house, where 18 locomotives could be built at the same time.

By the end of 1843, 423 men were employed at the works.

The first new GWR locomotive, *Premier*, an 0-6-0 freight locomotive and one of a class of 12, was outshopped from the works in February 1846. However, as its boiler was purchased from an outside manufacturer, it was not the first locomotive to be built entirely at Swindon.

In 1846, the GWR told Gooch, by then installed as works superintendent, to produce a "colossal locomotive working with all speed."

Within 13 weeks, the first all-Swindon-built engine was ready.

Appropriately named *Great Western* and designed as a 2-2-2, on 1 June 1846 it managed the 194-mile trip from Paddington to Exeter with a train of unrecorded weight in 208 minutes, and returned in 211 minutes, with Brunel and GWR chairman Charles Russell on board.

Gooch modified the design after the leading axle fractured when running through Shrivenham, and so *Great Western* was converted to a 4-2-2.

A rip-roaring success, it set the standard for all subsequent broad gauge express passenger locomotives, and Swindon Works was never the same again.

On 29 April 1847 *Iron Duke*, the first of a

The Engine House at Swindon Works, sketched by JB Bourne in the 1840s. GWT COLLECTION

A sketch of 1847 showing Fire Fly class 4-2-2 Fire Brand *at Swindon, with the New Swindon railway village on the left. The first engine shed is located to the right.* GWT COLLECTION

Daily life inside the works during the GWR era. STEAM

legendary class bearing the same name, made its trial trip from Swindon Works. A total of 22 of these engines were built at Swindon, including *Lord of the Isles*, displayed at the Great Exhibition in Crystal Palace in 1851.

By 1851, the works was employing more 2000 men with a locomotive being finished each week. Between 1846 and 1858, 39 passenger and 109 goods locomotives were built for the GWR broad gauge network, and 24 other engines, the first in 1855, to 4ft 8½in gauge for other companies.

The opening of a rolling mill to transform worn or damaged rails into new ones attracted huge numbers of workers from South Wales, creating a large Welsh community in Swindon.

At the heart of New Swindon lay the Mechanics' Institute, which opened on 1 May 1855. Funded by Gooch and works manager Minard Christian Rea's New Swindon Improvement Company, its aim was to provided evening classes for manual workers and their families. The Institute, which now stands derelict amid longstanding uncertainty over its future, also had a theatre and stage, baths and coffee rooms, and served as a community centre.

A GWR Medical Fund Society was established and financed a cottage hospital, and for a small weekly subscription, GWR workers and their families were given a complete medical service, subsidised by the railway, and included doctors' surgeries, dental and eye clinics and a casualty department.

This fund was a world first, and it is said that a century later it became the model for the cradle-to-grave care ideals of Aneurin

Swindon A shop in June 1932. GWT COLLECTION

Aerial view of Swindon Works in the 1920s. GWR

The A Shop in Swindon Works in the early 1950s. GWT COLLECTION

1874
The first bogie carriages appear.
Quadrupling between Paddington and Taplow begins.
1 June: Cornwall Minerals Railway's Fowey-Newquay line opened.
17 September: New Pontypool-Newport link.
East Somerset Railway absorbed.

1875
Vacuum brake first used for passenger stock.
Mixed gauge laid through Box Tunnel, with broad gauge remaining only for through services beyond Bristol and on some branches.
Monmouthshire and Gloucester & Dean Forest railways absorbed.

1876
1 January: GWR absorbed Bristol & Exeter Railway.
1 February: GWR absorbed South Devon, West Cornwall, Dartmouth & Torbay, Launceston & South Devon, Moretonhampstead & South Devon, South Devon & Tavistock and Hayle railways.
1 March: Mixed gauge completed from Bristol to Exeter.

1877
Joseph Armstrong dies and was replaced as GWR locomotive superintendent by his chief assistant William Dean.
The first sleeper saloon appeared in 1877, a six-wheel, four-berth 29ft vehicle.
1 January: New sidings at Acton linked with Acton Wells Junction.
1 June: The last broad gauge branch, to St Ives, was opened.

1878
GWR acquired Millbay Docks and installed a connection from Plymouth North Road.

1879
Severn Bridge opened by the Severn Bridge Railway, linking Sharpness to Lydney and the Forest of Dean.
Last new GWR broad gauge line laid - a short extension at Sutton Harbour in Plymouth.

1880
Electric lighting installed at Paddington, one of the first places in London to be illuminated.
Culm Valley Light and Malmsbury railways absorbed.

1881
26 September: Severn Tunnel headings joined.

GWR | 37

Bevan when he drew up his blueprint for the National Health Service.

With such groundbreaking social innovations, Swindon Works richly deserved to prosper. In 1865, such was the demand for locomotives from outside buyers that the works turned away 18 orders for new engines so it could handle the 30 that had been accepted. Many orders for the building of extra locomotives and rolling stock rolling stock were switched to newer workshops at Wolverhampton, Worcester and Saltney near Chester. Meanwhile, in 1868, GWR's central workshop for building carriages and wagons was opened at Swindon on land north of the station, and produced its first royal saloon in 1874.

The following year, boiler and tender-making shops were opened, making components for locomotives and spares for marine engines used in the GWR fleet of ships and barges and ships.

The works' main locomotive fabrication workshop, the A Shop, which opened in 1920, covered 11¼ acres and was one of the largest covered areas in the world.

In April 1924, King George V and his wife Queen Mary visited the works.

Prior to nationalisation of Britain's railways on 1 January 1948, Swindon was still producing 60 steam engines a year. That year, Swindon began building diesel locomotives in the form of six diesel-electric 0-6-0 shunters.

On 15 November 1950, HRH Princess Elizabeth visited the works and named the last Castle class 4-6-0 to be built, No 7037 *Swindon*.

The first main line diesel hydraulic locomotive for British Railways was manufactured at Swindon in 1957, and afterwards it turned out the Class 52 Western and

Great Western – Daniel Gooch's Swindon-built broad gauge locomotive that spawned a series of express locomotives for the GWR. GWT COLLECTION

Terraced cottages in Swindon's Railway Village, a pioneering example of social welfare in the mid-19th century. ROBIN JONES

The National Railway Museum's 1985-built working replica of *Iron Duke*, the of the most famous class of GWR broad gauge engines. ROBIN JONES

The refreshment rooms at Swindon station in the 1840s. J&C Rigby built Swindon station at its own expense after the GWR agreed to stop all regular passenger trains there for 10 minutes, so they would use the refreshment facilities, which were divided into classes. Passengers welcomed the delay because the first trains had no toilets, but as timings became faster, the condition in the lease became a nuisance, and the GWR bought it outright for £100,000 on 12 November 1895. ROBIN JONES COLLECTION

Waxworks in the STEAM museum recreate an everyday scene from working life in GWR days. ROBIN JONES

A Swindon product back in the great works: GWR 4-6-0 No 4930 *Hagley Hall*, on loan from the Severn Valley Railway, stands on static display alongside a cafeteria in the McArthur Glen Designer Village which now occupies much of the works buildings. ROBIN JONES

One of the most popular exhibits inside the STEAM museum is GWR 4-6-0 No 4073 *Caerphilly Castle*, part of the Science Museum and still retaining the Brunswick green paint it carried in service. STEAM

Swindon's original GWR Railway Museum in Faringdon Road. STEAM

Class 42 Warship types for the Western Region.

Steam production famously ended at Swindon in 1960 with the outshopping of BR Standard 9F 2-10-0 No 92220 *Evening Star*. It was the last steam locomotive built for service on the UK national network under British Railways, and the last such engine to be built until the A1 Steam Locomotive Trust gave its £3-million Peppercorn Pacific No 60163 *Tornado* its first main line run in January 2009.

A works training school was built in 1962 on the far side of the main line to the works, and accommodated 112 apprentices.

In July 1964, the first of a class of 56 locomotives appeared from Swindon Works, later designated as Class 14. They were 0-6-0 shunter types with a central cab and powered by a Paxman six-cylinder Ventura 6YJXL engine. Like many other early types of diesel, they had a short life in British Railways service. Unlike bigger main line locomotives, many Class 14s were sold for industrial use.

The last of them D9555, in 1965 was the final British Railways locomotive to be built at Swindon. Today, it runs on the Dean Forest Railway, which itself was once part of the GWR empire.

A major reorganisation under the British Transport Commission's National Workshops Plan saw the locomotive section of the works all but entirely rebuilt, leaving the works was left with the job of repairing and modifying the existing locomotive fleet, rather than building new ones. As many lines were closed under the Beeching Axe of 1963, less locomotives and stock were needed.

The newly formed British Rail Engineering Limited took over Swindon Works from 1 January 1970. In the 70s, the works overhauled British Rail's ageing diesel multiple unit fleet and the Southern Region's Class 411/412 CEP/BEP electric multiple units, while scrapping many of the diesel hydraulic types as they were being withdrawn from Western Region service, along with redundant carriages and wagons.

Locomotive building returned to Swindon in

1980 when 20-metre gauge 0-8-0 diesel hydraulic shunters were supplied to Kenya Railways.

It would not last.

The town was understandably shocked by BREL's summer 1985 announcement that Swindon Works would close completely from the middle of the following year.

The reason given was declining order books and the lack of contracts from its main customer, British Rail.

To say it was the end of an era was, and still is, a gross understatement.

The works closed as planned, but refused to lay down and die.

Railway enthusiast and chartered surveyor Bill Parker met up with old friend and Swindon Works employee Ivor Huddy who had earlier helped him buy two steam engines, and they drew up a plan to keep part of the works open for the maintenance of locomotives for heritage railways.

After British Rail sold the works site to Tarmac Properties, Bill reached agreement to open a new Swindon Railway Workshop, owned by Swindon Heritage Trust, a charitable trust, in four acres of buildings.

In 1990 it was used as a temporary home for much of the National Collection while the roof of the National Railway Museum at York was repaired. *Evening Star* returned to its birthplace alongside other Swindon classics like GWR 4-6-0 No 6000 *King George V* and No 3440 *City of Truro*.

Echoing the royal visits of GWR days, Bill's invitation to the late Princess Diana to visit the works was accepted, and princes William and Harry stayed for two hours, displaying great fascination for the locomotives.

Sadly, when the value of commercial property collapsed in the late 80s, Tarmac gave Swindon Railway Workshop notice to quit. The decision was later reversed, but by then Bill Parker had moved out, leaving the trust's former works manager, Bill Jefferies, and Hull businessman Ken Ryder, to take up a tenancy with a replacement operation, Swindon Locomotive Carriage & Wagon Works, later Swindon Railway Engineering.

Bill Parker's Swindon Heritage Trust found a new home in 1994 when he bought the Grade 2 listed semi-derelict engine house at Flour Mill Colliery at Bream in the Forest of Dean and used a grant from the Rural Development Commission to help restore it. Although it lay deep inside the great medieval hunting forest on the far side of the River Severn, it still traded under the name of Swindon Railway Workshop.

It was a small world, for the Bream operation's first job was the overhaul of the National Railway Museum's replica Gooch broad gauge 4-2-2 *Iron Duke*, which had been built in 1980. Many more projects followed there, and the 'new' Swindon established a reputation for Swindon-quality workmanship among many top heritage railway sector customers, and is still dong so to this day.

Swindon had been given its own railway heritage attraction in 1962, when Swindon Railway Museum was set up in a former GWR workers' lodging house built in 1847, later sold for conversion to a Wesleyan chapel, in Faringdon Road. It housed five locomotives, the 1925-rebuilt broad gauge 2-2-2 *North Star*, GWR 4-6-0 No 4003 *Lode Star*, Dean Goods 0-6-0 No 2516, pannier tank No 9400 and *City of Truro*, plus GWR railcar No 4.

However, determined to make the most of its railway legacy as the old works slipped into the past, in 1998 Swindon Borough Council announced plans to convert the works' Grade 2 listed Victorian machine shop into a much bigger and replacement museum at a cost of £13-millon as a major visitor attraction, with substantial Heritage Lottery Fund grant aid.

So was born STEAM – Museum of the Great Western Railway, a must visit for anyone who wants to truly appreciate the heritage of the GWR and its world famous workshops.

BR Standard 9F No 92220 *Evening Star* returned to its Swindon birthplace from custodian the National Railway Museum in York for GWR 175 year, and took pride of place in the STEAM museum. The last of a class first outshopped in 1954 when No 92000 appeared from Crewe, *Evening Star* was the last steam locomotive built for British Railways, and the last steam engine outshopped from Swindon, on 18 March 1960. It carried the GWR's Brunswick green livery.

The 9F 2-10-0s, considered by many as the most successful of all the 12 British Railways Standard types, were designed by Robert Riddles, and built with a life expectancy of up to 40 years, yet British Railways ended steam haulage on the national network in 1968.

When *Evening Star* was unveiled, former Swindon Works apprentice and Western Region chairman Reggie Hanks said: "There had to be a last steam locomotive, and it is a tremendous thing that that last steam locomotive should be built here in these great works at Swindon."

Allocated to the Western Region, Cardiff Canton regularly rostered No 92220 on the Up 'Red Dragon' express to Paddington. On the 'Capitals United' express between Cardiff and London in July 1960, it reached 90mph.

Evening Star was chosen to haul the last of the Somerset & Dorset Joint Railway route's famous named train, the 'Pines Express' from Manchester to Bournemouth on 8 September 1962. No 92220 was withdrawn in March 1965, after just five years' service, because of its historical importance; it became part of the National Collection.

After working several railtours and visiting heritage railways, *Evening Star* returned to its Swindon birthplace in 1990, for static display, as part of the National Railway Museum on tour exhibition.

There are no plans to return *Evening Star* to steam, but two other 9Fs are operational on heritage lines. NRM

First Great Western Class 43 HST No 43021 calls at Swindon in February 2007. ROBIN JONES

Apart from the many railway relics, STEAM outlines the social story of Swindon's railway community, with recorded personal experiences and film archives, while waxwork figures show staff at work in GWR days in a series of reconstructions of areas of work, such as office, stores, workshop, signalbox and foundry. There are many hands-on exhibits and interactive displays, and former railway workers are often available to give a personal insight into many of the exhibits. STEAM also houses a substantial archive of books, magazines, photographs, drawings and plans relating to the GWR.

It had been hoped to integrate the Swindon Railway Engineering repair business in No 9 Shop as an added attraction, but this was not to be, as the premises were needed for expansion of the McArthur Glen Designer Outlet, the giant retail shopping mall which, when opened in March 1997, was Europe's largest covered designer outlet and which occupies much of the old works, which were saved from demolition as a result. Attracting three million shoppers a year, it is now a major player in Swindon's economy, as was the railway works before it.

The last locomotive left No 9 Shop on 2 May 2007. It was not a GWR engine, but a humble Peckett saddle tank built in Bristol, which was restored in the guise of fictional children's book character, Ivor the Engine, and now regularly tours Britain's heritage lines.

STEAM marked GWR 175 year by celebrating its own 10th anniversary, arranging a gala dinner on 21 August with guest speakers pop mogul and lifelong enthusiast Pete Waterman and Professor Andrew McNaughton, chief engineer of the High Speed Two Channel Tunnel Rail Link.

The works engineers' office is now the headquarters of English Heritage, where the archive of the National Monuments Record Office is kept.

Preserved largely intact is the Railway Village, where the cottages now enjoy listed building status for their special architectural or historic interest.

Swindon Borough Council bought most of them in the 60s and modernised them inside.

The cottage at 34 Faringdon Road, however, was restored to its late Victorian condition both internally and externally, and remaining lit by gas and oil lamp, was subsequently opened as a Railway Village Museum in its own right.

Swindon still offers live steam along a section of a line that at the Grouping of 1923 was taken into the GWR empire. The volunteer-operated Swindon & Cricklade Railway was formed in 1978 to reconstruct a section of the Midland & South Western Junction Railway that ran from Andover to Cheltenham, occupying Blunsdon station to the north of Swindon. A second station behind which stands a large locomotive shed and works was developed at Hayes Knoll to the north. Hayes Knoll features a restored signalbox that is operational during special days. The current running length is one-and-a-half miles. The line is being extended northwards towards Cricklade and southwards to the outskirts of Swindon. Nearby, the North Wilts Canal, which was partially responsible for the works being built at Swindon, is being restored to navigation in its own right.

David Murray John, Swindon's town clerk from 1938 until shortly before his death in 1974, had foreseen the eventual decline of the railway works, and with colleagues had worked to attract other employers to the town before the axe fell 12 years after his death. As a result of his vision, Swindon has been able to sidestep the economic slump that hit other UK cities following the demise of their manufacturing bases in modern times: its modern prosperity was underlined in February 2008 when *The Times* named Swindon as one of the 20 best places to buy a property in Britain, with the average household income among the highest in the country.

Twilight of Western Region steam: GWR 4-6-0 No 7023 *Penrice Castle* at Swindon in 1963. JOHN STRETTON COLLECTION

1882
The first on-train public lavatories were brought into service.
Gas began to replace oil lighting.
Third class accommodation made available on all but the fastest expresses.
Carmarthen and Cardigan and Berks & Hants Extension railways absorbed.

1883
First of 260 2301 class Dean Goods 0-6-0s introduced.
Torbay & Brixham, Festiniog & Blaenau and Stratford-on-Avon railways absorbed.

1884
1 January: Watlington & Princes Risborough Railway absorbed.
1 March: Weston-super-Mare loop opened.

1885
The 3501 class broad gauge 2-4-0s appeared, later being rebuilt as the standard gauge 3201 class.

1886
Whitland & Cardigan and Faringdon railways absorbed.
9 January: Experimental coal train runs through the Severn Tunnel.
1 September: Whitland & Cardigan Railway taken over.
1 December: Through Bristol-Cardiff passenger services start.

1887
6 April: GWR took over working of Banbury and Cheltenham Direct Railway Kings Sutton-Chipping Norton line on opening to complete new route to Cheltenham begun in 1881.
27 May: Bodmin General branch opened.

1888
Appearance of the first GWR Magazine.
Worcester, Bromyard & Leominster Railway absorbed.
July: The last broad gauge engine to be built for the GWR, Rover class 4-2-2 No 24 *Tornado*, appeared from Swindon.

1889
Last Dean Goods built.
1 January 1889: Birkenhead Town station opened by the Joint Committee of the Chester & Birkenhead Railway, administered by the London & North Western Railway and the GWR.
1 July: Cornwall Railway absorbed.
August: GWR took over the working of the Channel Islands steamers.
15 October: Sir Daniel Gooch died at his luxurious home at Clewer Park, Windsor.

The empire of the west

The GWR as we know it is, of course, far more than Paddington to Penzance.

The success of the early main line was accompanied by the company first acquiring adjoining broad gauge lines which up to then had been built and owned by small independent companies. Such takeovers or mergers brought many mutual benefits, and allowed the GWR to penetrate the territories occupied by other growing railway companies, such as the standard gauge London & South Western.

In 1843, the Great Western absorbed the line from Swindon to Cheltenham and Gloucester, the following year took over Didcot to Oxford as a first step towards the industrial Birmingham and the Black Country region, and in 1845 acquired the Berks and Hants railways from Reading to Hungerford, and from Reading to Basingstoke.

In 1845, parliamentary powers were obtained to build the Oxford and Rugby (became GWR in 1850), the Wilts, Somerset & Weymouth (Bath and Chippenham to Trowbridge, Yeovil and Weymouth, taken over by the GWR in 1851), the Oxford, Worcester & Wolverhampton and the South Wales (Gloucester to New Milford) Railway (both taken over in 1863) to 7ft 0¼in gauge.

The standard gauge companies were expanding too, and in 1840 the Birmingham & Gloucester Railway reached Gloucester before Brunel's broad gauge. It was there that the first major break of gauge conflict arose.

An independent broad-gauge railway between Bristol and Gloucester was completed in 1844, agreeing with the GWR to run over part of the Swindon-Gloucester route for the nine miles into the latter city.

The Midland Railway was formed in 1844 as a merger between the North Midland, Midland Counties, and Birmingham & Rugby Junction railways, and outbid the GWR to buy the Birmingham-Gloucester-Bristol lines, eventually converting the Bristol-Gloucester route to 4ft 8½in gauge.

The 1846 Gauge Regulation Act allowed the South Wales, Oxford & Rugby and Oxford, Worcester & Wolverhampton railways to be built with broad gauge tracks, with the latter two being mixed gauge to allow standard gauge trains into Oxford.

The GWR acquired the Oxford & Rugby Railway in 1846, and opened a new line from Oxford to Banbury on 2 September 1850, extending it to Fenny Compton on 1 October 1852.

The planned extension from Fenny

An early 20th century view of the hotel which formed the front of Snow Hill station. It was demolished in late 1969. ROBIN JONES COLLECTION

Compton to Rugby was not built. Instead, the GWR built the Birmingham & Oxford Junction Railway to Birmingham, creating a terminus at Snow Hill, which saw its first broad gauge trains on 1 October 1852. The route was extended by the GWR to Wolverhampton on 14 November 1854.

In 1853, the broad gauge Oxford-Worcester-Wolverhampton line, then still owned by an independent company, opened.

In 1854, the GWR acquired the standard gauge Shrewsbury to Birmingham and Shrewsbury to Chester railways, giving it a foothold in the north west. However, the broad gauge never extended beyond Wolverhampton.

In 1844, a bill to obtain powers for building a railway across South Wales from Stonehouse on the Swindon-Gloucester railway, bridging the upper tidal River Severn at Newnham, then following the right bank of the Severn to Chepstow and running to Fishguard via Newport, Cardiff, Swansea, and Carmarthen, was promoted. The prize here was a port which could equal Milford Haven for seaborne trade between England and Ireland.

Objections were raised regarding a Severn bridge and the potential hindrance to navigation, but the authority to build a line from the west of Chepstow to Milford, not Fishguard, was approved.

In 1845, a subsequent Act of Parliament authorised the extension of the line northwards from Chepstow to Grange Court on the Gloucester-Ross-on-Wye-Hereford line, thereby linking south Wales to London by rail for the first time and opening up massive new markets for coal and iron, along with faster travel to southern Ireland.

The GWR leased the South Wales line in 1846, and appointed Brunel to build it.

He needed to build bridges over the Severn at Gloucester, over the Wye at Chepstow and over the Usk near Newport. The other major engineering feats were the third-of-a-mile-long Landore viaduct near Swansea and a tunnel nearby.

The Wye bridge was the most daunting task, of about the same length near the same town. Awkward topography meant that a bridge needed a cutting in the cliffs at one end and a high embankment at the other, while spanning a 600ft gap. Brunel designed a tubular suspension bridge with a 300ft span across the river and three 100ft spans over land, producing a design which would later evolve into his blueprint for the Royal Albert Bridge at Saltash. The bridge was opened for one of the two tracks it carried on 14 July 1852.

Brunel's tubular suspension bridge over the River Wye at Chepstow. ELTON COLLECTION, IRONBRIDGE GORGE MUSEUMS TRUST

GWR 4-6-0 No 6003 *King George II* heads the 4.10pm Paddington, Birmingham and Birkenhead express between Gerrards Cross and Seer Green. GWT COLLECTION

GWR 4-6-0 No 5051 *Drysllwyn Castle* (aka *Earl Bathurst*) in BR-lined Brunswick green livery leaves the Severn Tunnel with Past-Time Rail's St David's Day special from Swansea to Paddington on 1 March 2006. DAVID HOLMAN

GWR 4-6-0 No 5051 *Earl Bathurst* heads away from Birmingham Moor Street to Stratford-upon-Avon with a railtour from Didcot in April 1984. Snow Hill station, which closed to passenger trains in 1972, would reopen in 1987, with trains again running through the tunnel from the south. BRIAN SHARPE

The GWR absorbed the South Wales Railway outright in 1861 following friction over the lease, which required the former to provide motive power.

By this time, there were three trunk routes: from Paddington to the West Country, to the South Wales coast and a third to Chester, from which the GWR gained access to Merseyside.

In 1847, the Chester & Birkenhead Railway merged with the Birkenhead Lancashire & Cheshire Junction Railway and opened a line to near Warrington on 18 December 1850. The GWR almost took control of this railway in 1851-2. Eventually, on 1 August 1859, it was renamed the Birkenhead Railway and on 1 January 1860 transferred jointly to the GWR and LNWR.

To cut the long and winding journey to South Wales via Gloucester, a ferry was opened in 1863 over the two-mile-wide Severn estuary. The short Bristol & South Wales Union Railway was built between Bristol and New Passage on the eastern bank of the estuary and from Severn Junction Portskewett on the Welsh side. Pontoons were installed so that steamers could call at all states of the tide and provide a link between the two. A boon to passengers, it was little use for heavy goods traffic. The GWR took over the railway and ferry in 1868.

Also in 1863, the GWR looked at building a railway bridge across the Severn at New Passage, at an estimated cost of £1-million. However, instead they chose a plan by Charles

GWR | 43

Richardson, who had built the ferry stages, to bore a tunnel beneath the river.

Parliamentary powers for the Severn Tunnel were granted in 1872.

Needless to say, it was one of, if not the most, colossal engineering feats that the GWR had attempted. First of all, to clear a 50ft gulley in the bed of the river, the tunnel had to descend 140 feet below the level of the rails on each side. Accordingly, the tunnel length had to be 4 ½ miles long if gradients steeper than 1-in-100 were to be avoided, and also the approach cuttings had to be three-fifths of a mile and one mile long

It took 14 years to build the tunnel. The biggest problem came in 1879 when the tunnellers struck the Great Spring, leading to an inrush of water from an underground reservoir and flooding the workings.

Despite further inundations, the two ends of the tunnel met on 17 October 1884, and by April 1885, it had been lined with brickwork 27in thick.

The Great Spring was never defeated, and the permanent solution was not to try to block out the water, but to allow it to enter the tunnel and pump it to the surface at the rate of 20,000,000 gallons a day.

Fixed Cornish beam engines pumped out the Great Spring until the 1960s, when they were replaced by electrically powered pumps. In the 1930s, the availability of the reliable freshwater supply from the spring led to the choice of an adjacent site for the Royal Navy Propellant Factory in Caerwent.

A coal train became the first to pass through the tunnel on 9 January 1886. It was opened to passenger trains on 1 December that year, the total cost being £2-million.

There was another diversionary route available from 1879, in the form of the 22-span single-track 4162-feet-long and 70ft-high Severn Bridge. It was built by the Severn Bridge Railway to transport coal from mines in the Forest of Dean on the Severn & Wye Railway, which was purchased jointly by the Midland Railway and GWR when it went bust in 1893. It cut around 30 miles off the journey through Gloucester, and was pressed into service when the tunnel was closed for maintenance.

Within a decade, freight traffic had doubled, as the new shorter route opened up vast new markets for the products of the valleys.

A major steamship service between Milford Haven and Waterford had begun in 1872 as the GWR's equivalent of the London & North Western Railway's Holyhead-Dublin sea route, and it was greatly boosted by the opening of the Severn Tunnel.

In 1860, the Oxford, Worcester & Wolverhampton Railway merged two other standard gauge lines, the Worcester to Hereford and the Newport, Abergavenny and Hereford railways, to form the West Midland Railway. The year before, the OWW had been allowed to remove the broad gauge third rail to avoid the break of gauge, and a 4ft 8 ½in gauge corridor had been created between the West Midlands and the south coast. The GWR leased this new railway in 1861, and laid a third rail into Paddington to bring in the first standard gauge trains. As we have already seen, it was another large nail in the coffin for broad gauge.

In the 1890s, interest in building a second major port for Ireland in Pembrokeshire was revived, and Fishguard, which at 54 miles is the closest point to the Irish mainland, was again considered.

In 1898, the GWR built a massive new harbour at Fishguard with a breakwater eventually extending to 3000ft, while the Great Southern & Western Railway of Ireland constructed one at Rosslare. Both companies built extensions to existing lines to access the new harbours, in the case of the GWR, one from Letterton seven miles away. Before it was completed, the first locomotives had to be hauled overland.

The Fishguard-Rosslare service was launched on 30 August 1906.

The last main line built by the GWR ran from Birmingham Snow Hill to Bristol, via Tyseley, Stratford-upon-Avon, Honeybourne and Cheltenham, while reviving the running powers over the Midland Railway line from Standish to Yate. Before this new 95-mile cross-country route opened, passengers faced either a lengthy detour via the

Two locomotive types that made the Cambrian Coast line their own: Dukedog 4-4-0 No 9018 pilots Manor class 4-6-0 No 7800 *Torquay Manor* through Cemmaes Road in August 1956. PAT DALTON/ GWT COLLECTION

Aberdare class 2-6-0 No 2662 at Frodsham with a Birkenhead-Chester freight in August 1939. GWT COLLECTION

GWR Star class 4-6-0 No 4035 *Queen Charlotte* with a Down Weymouth service passes Thornford Bridge Halt on 4 June 1939. GWT COLLECTION

Recreating the heavy freight on the GWR South Wales network for the GWR 150 celebrations in 1985, Severn Valley Railway-based Churchward heavy freight 2-8-0 No 2857 heads a rake of loaded ballast wagons into Newport. BRIAN SHARPE

With the Afon Tywi estuary in the background, GWR 4-6-0 No 6000 *King George V* passes Ferryside between Burry Port and Carmarthen with a railtour in 1985. BRIAN SHARPE

Severn Tunnel, Hereford, Worcester, Kidderminster, a distance of 133 miles, or travel via Didcot and Banbury, a total of 141 miles.

There was already a branch from Honeybourne to Stratford, opened by the OWW 12 July 1859, and this was doubled. The linking Honeybourne to Cheltenham line opened throughout in the summer of 1906.

The North Warwickshire Line between Tyseley, Bearley West Junction and Stratford opened to goods on 9 December 1907 and passengers on 1 July 1908. A second Birmingham terminus, Moor Street, was built that year to relieve congestion. The end result was a GWR route for through trains from the industrialised West Midlands to the West Country and South Wales.

Like the Severn Tunnel, it was a major short cut.

Shortcuts rather than building new lines became GWR policy in the early 20th century, refining the empire rather than expanding it.

All of the company's main routes had sections which needed to be bypassed; there were many who nicknamed the company the 'Great Way Round' because of them.

The first route tackled was the line to Weymouth: the building of a new short line joining the Hungerford-Devizes-Bath line at Patney and Chirton with the old route via Chippenham and Trowbridge at Westbury; the Weymouth service was diverted via Reading and Hungerford and the journey between London and the Dorset port shortened by 14 miles when the shortcut opened in 1901.

1890
Work on quadrupling between Taplow and Didcot began.
7 March: Britain's first train with corridor connections between all carriages entered service, on the Paddington to Birkenhead route.
1 September: Bristol Port Railway & Pier acquired to complete the line to Avonmouth.

1891
Electric Train Staff system adopted.

1892
The external version of the communication cord appeared.
Newent, Ross & Ledbury and Wellington & Severn Junction railways absorbed.
7 March: First corridor train with full lavatory facilities began running from Paddington to Birkenhead.
20 May: The last broad gauge trains left Paddington and Penzance at 10.15am, conversion of the remaining broad gauge to standard gauge following on 21/22 May.

1893
Steam heating was introduced.
Doubling started on the Plymouth-Penwithers Junction section.
The final broad gauge engines steamed: South Devon Railway 4-4-0STs *Leopard* and *Stag* were used at Swindon for shunting broad gauge stock into the cutting shop.
June: The above pair scrapped.

1894
Doubling from Penwithers Junction to Plymouth began.
The Port Talbot Railway & Docks Company incorporated.
1 July: Severn & Wye and Severn Bridge Railway sold to GWR and Midland Railway.

1895
Duke 4-4-0s appeared.
William Dean introduces a policy in 1895 of giving passenger tender locomotives both numbers and names.
1 October: The first trains not to make a refreshment stop at Swindon ran.

1896
Cornwall Minerals, Calne, Corwen & Bala Railway, Llangollen and Corwen, Lostwithiel & Fowey, Newquay & Cornwall Junction, Newquay, Marlborough, Milford, Pembroke & Tenby, Wenlock, Vale of Llangollen railways and Par Tramway absorbed.
May: First dining cars introduced, on Paddington to Plymouth and Cardiff services, but for first class passengers only.

This shortcut also provided a faster route to the south west, when combined with a second new line built to join the Weymouth route near Castle Cary with Langport on the Yeovil-Durston line. It opened on 9 June 1906, creating a London-Taunton route via Reading and Westbury that is 20 miles shorter than Brunel's original route via Swindon and Bristol. Its availability shaved 20 minutes off the 'Cornish Riviera Express' and relieved congestion on the old main line.

Another shortcut, the South Wales Direct line, opened in July 1903. It ran from Wootton Bassett to the west of Swindon to Patchway, a few miles east of the Severn Tunnel, through a new 2 ½-mile tunnel at Sodbury, cutting the distance to South Wales by 10 miles and speeding up communications with Ireland; Newport could be reached from Paddington in two hours 20 minutes, as opposed to the previous four hours.

The London to Birmingham route was next to be tackled. The GWR joined forces with the Great Central Railway, which in 1899 became the last trunk route in Britain to be built before the modern-day Channel Tunnel Rail Link. The GWR built a new line leaving from the old main line near Old Oak Common and running through Brentham, Perivale and Greenford to Northolt, where it joined the Great Central.

From there, a new GWR/GCVR Joint Railway ran Ruislip, Denham, Gerrards Cross and Beaconsfield and a new section laid from High Wycombe through Risborough, Haddenham, Ashendon and Bicester to Aynho Junction near Banbury on the Oxford-Banbury line. This shortcut was opened from London as far as Wycombe on 2 April 1906 and throughout on 1 July 1910, cutting 20 minutes from the inter-city route and with it 20 minutes off express train journeys, bringing the time down to two hours.

During World War One, Britain's railways were taken over by the Government as an emergency measure, and they were not handed back until 15 August 1921. Many were in a parlous state after seven years of austerity measures, poor financial management and a lack of investment.

Whitehall saw the peacetime urgency to reduce both passenger fares and freight rates, and in 1920 the Minister of Transport drew up a scheme whereby the country's 120 independent railways would be merged together in large groups, the theoretical net result being economies of scale.

Accordingly, a Bill was introduced into Commons on 11 May 1921, and on 19 August that year became law as the Railways Act 1921. Popularly known as the 'Grouping', it gathered virtually all railways in Britain and Northern Ireland into four new companies – the London, Midland & Scottish, the London & North Eastern, the Southern and the Great Western. Major concerns left outside the Grouping were the Cheshire Lines Committee, the Midland &

Star class 4-6-0 No 4022 *Belgian Monarch* heads the Down 'North to West Express' near Tram Inn, Hereford, on 2 June 1937. GWT COLLECTION

Grade 2-listed Cardiff Central station, opened by the South Wales Railway in 1850 and rebuilt by the GWR in 1932, is the biggest station in Wales and the tenth busiest outside London. It is pictured during a royal visit in August 1960. GWT COLLECTION

A trio of pannier tanks in Ebbw Vale shed: left to right are Nos 3705, 4643 and 4627. GWT COLLECTION

Penarth Docks in GWR days. GWR

Great Northern Joint Railway, the Somerset & Dorset Joint Railway and the Metropolitan Railway and other London underground lines.

Overnight, there was a vast expansion of the GWR empire, particularly in Wales, with the acquisitions of the Cambrian, Cardiff, Barry, Rhymney, Taff Vale, and Alexandra (Newport and South Wales) Docks and Railway companies. They came with 26 small companies, nine of which had previously been worked by the GWR, four by the Cambrian, two by the Taff Vale and one by the Barry Railway. A total of 560 route miles were added to the GWR network.

The 'Big Four' companies as they were known began operating on 1 January 1923.

The Cambrian Railways, based on Oswestry, gave the GWR access to the coast of west Wales, its spectacular main line serving Pwllheli, Barmouth and Aberyswyth, with its lucrative holiday traffic; its biggest engineering feature being the 800-yard Barmouth viaduct which crosses the Mawddach estuary in 113 spans. The Grouping also brought two classic narrow gauge lines into the GWR fold, the 2ft 6in gauge Welshpool & Llanfair Light Railway and the 1ft 11 ½ gauge Vale of Rheidol Railway, with a third, the Corris Railway, being bought in 1930.

The GWR already had a presence in Aberystwyth, operating the winding Carmarthen and Cardigan Railway/Manchester & Milford Railway cross-country route from Abergwili Junction near Carmarthen, which in 1872 had been the last in Wales to be converted from broad gauge to standard gauge.

Also, the Cambrian main line somewhat paralleled the GWR's Ruabon-Llangollen-Bala-Dolgellau-Barmouth route, which it had finally taken over from its constituent companies in 1896. The route began with the 5 ¼-mile Vale of Llangollen Railway which opened to freight on 1 December 1861 and to passengers on 2 June 1862, and was extended westwards by several companies until it reached Barmouth in 1869. The GWR had absorbed the Bala & Dolgellau Railway section in 1877, and also had the Bala and Ffestiniog Railway, which opened in 1882, giving it a foothold in North Wales.

While the Cambrian routes offered glorious mountain scenery, goods traffic was comparatively sparse, The same could not be said for another major acquisition, the Taff Vale Railway, which derived enormous income from the South Wales coalfield that it served, and was among the most profitable lines in Britain. For the export of millions of tons of coal each year, it leased the giant Penarth Docks which, opened in 1861, covered 26 acres of enclosed water space with 7580ft of quays equipped with 18 hydraulic coaling tips.

The Group turned the GWR into the largest dock-owning company in the world, with the Port of Cardiff, Swansea, the most extensive at 281½ acres of water space), and Newport, Barry, Penarth and Port Talbot in its portfolio, the total quayside length extending to 37 miles and at their height handling around 50,000,000 tons of freight each year, 75 per cent being coal.

Barry Docks, acquired at the Grouping

A modern-day poster extolling the virtues of the Cambrian Coast Main Line with Barmouth Bridge as its centrepiece. ROBIN JONES

along with the Barry Railway, was the busiest for the export of coal, despite its smaller size of 114 acres of water space, with more than 11 million tons a year being handled.

The Cambrian Railways headquarters in Oswestry in 1921. GWR

GWR | 47

Steaming into the 20th century

A contemporary postcard of Saint No 2902 *Lady of the Lake* at Acton. When it headed the first GWR two-hour train from Birmingham Snow Hill to Paddington in July 1910, a well-wisher threw a horseshoe onto the footplate. This horseshoe was then fitted on the engine until its withdrawal from Leamington in August 1949. GWS

When he suddenly died in 1877 from a heart attack, Joseph Armstrong was replaced as GWR locomotive superintendent by his 37-year-old chief assistant William Dean.

Dean faced the task of adapting Brunel's empire to standard gauge, and producing a new fleet of locomotives that were up to the challenge.

He is best remembered for the class of 280 0-6-0 freight locomotives known as the Dean Goods, which were widely known as the 'workhorse' of the GWR, and which lasted so well that they saw service on the continent in two world wars.

In 1900, answering the call for more powerful engines to work heavy South Wales coal trains, he introduced the Aberdare 2-6-0s, a freight version of his Bulldog passenger 4-4-0s. In 1895, Dean introduced the Duke and Badminton 4-4-0s.

Most of his classes, however, followed on from Armstrong, typified by a large single driving wheel.

His Dean Single or 3031 class of 4-2-2 introduced between 1891-99 was shortlived, as they were found to be unstable at speed, although No 3065 *Duke of Connaught* set a new record with the 'Ocean Mails' on 9 May 1904, running from Plymouth to Paddington in 227 minutes.

Dean's Atbara 4-4-0s, which were akin to the Badmintons but with much larger boilers, marked a turning point in GWR locomotive design, ending the single wheels for express

Edwardian splendour: Saint No 2904 *Lady Godiva* at speed with a rake of Toplight coaches. GWS

Star prototype No 40 *North Star*. GWT COLLECTION

trains and ushering in the beginnings of the age in which the company's locomotives would be readily familiar to a modern audience. His introduction of 6ft 8½in driving wheels became a standard feature of GWR design, and he also went for bigger cylinders, making engines even more powerful.

Dean, in many ways, sowed the seeds that would bear many ripe fruits for his successor in 1902, George Jackson Churchward, considered by many to be the finest of all British locomotive engineers.

Churchward, born on 31 January 1857 in Stoke Gabriel, Devon, left school at 16 to work under the Locomotive Superintendent of the still broad gauge South Devon Railway. Three years later he was transferred to the GWR drawing office at Swindon where he later became manager of the carriage works, then works manager and eventually chief assistant to Dean.

His key was his standardisation plan – having a set number of components which could be interchanged between several locomotive types, generating huge economies in scale in both locomotive building and maintenance. Between 1903 and 1911, he turned out nine standard new types, maximising component standardisation.

He limited his new classes to less than a dozen, using standardised boilers, wheels, cylinders, motion and tenders. He drew on American practice for boiler design and French technology for cylinder and valve configuration.

His first class of locomotives comprises the City 4-4-0s, of which No 3440 *City of Truro* became the most famous example.

They were followed by his 4-4-0 County class, which suffered from rough riding at higher speeds.

Churchward undertook performance tests between his engines and three imported French De Glehn engines.

Three prototype locomotives were built at Swindon in 1902/3, the first numbered 100.

Its visual appearance was a marked contrast to anything that the Swindon empire had turned out before, with a thoroughly 'modern' appearance. No 100 became the prototype for the Saint class of 4-6-0s, and was later numbered No 2900, and was named *William Dean*.

Another prototype, a 4-6-0 No 171 and later

Only one Dean Goods 0-6-0 survives, No 2516, inside the STEAM museum at Swindon. ROBIN JONES

Foreman Ward with the Cardiff crew of Saint 4-6-0 No 2942 *Fawley Court* at Paddington in 1916. GWT COLLECTION

Changing times: One of William Dean's great passions was experimentation, producing a series of 'one-off' locomotives to gain a greater understanding of different boiler designs or the centre-less bogie. GWR No 8 *Gooch* was built in 1886 as a broad gauge 2-4-0 compound, but unsuccessful in its trials, it was never taken into stock. In 1894, it reappeared as a conventional standard gauge 4-4-0. GWT COLLECTION

1897

Badminton 4-4-0s introduced.

Absorbed: Banbury and Cheltenham Direct, Buckfastleigh, Totnes & South Devon, Kington & Eardisley, Minehead and Nantwich & Market Drayton railways absorbed.

1898

North Pembrokeshire and Fishguard, Maenclochog, Helston and Leominster & Kington railways absorbed.

Large four-wheeled coal wagons first appeared.

1899

Non-stop Paddington to Exeter and Birmingham services introduced.

1900

Communication cords taken inside coaches: until then a passenger needing to stop the train in an emergency had to lean out of the window and pull a cord above the door. New Milford Boat Train set introduced electric lights and the first second class buffet car.

1 October: Stert-Westbury opened to passengers linking the Berks and Hants line with Westbury to create a shorter the route to Weymouth for the Channel Islands traffic.

1901

2602 class 2-6-0 and 3600 class 2-4-2T introduced.

Golden Valley (Pontrilas to Hay Junction), Bridport and Devon & Somerset railways absorbed.

1902

Six-coupled 4-6-0 locomotives and 2600 class 2-6-0s introduced.

William Dean retired, and replaced by his assistant, George Jackson Churchward.

named *Albion*, was built specifically to compete with the French compound, and for this purpose was briefly converted to a 4-4-2 with two-cylinder simple steam expansion.

While the trials between No 171 and the De Glehn engines were taking place, 19 locomotives were ordered to a design similar to that of No 171.

Thirteen of the new class, which became the Saints, were built as 4-4-2s while the remaining six were built as 4-6-0s, while a final verdict on the best arrangement was reached.

The Saints were considered to be ideal medium-size express passenger engines and eventually numbered 171 locomotives.

However, the tests with the French engines led to Churchward deciding that having four cylinders meant smoother and better balanced running at higher speeds than with two.

The net result was the prototype of the legendary Star class, No 40 *North Star*, built as a 4-4-2 but converted to a 4-6-0 as this wheel arrangement gave twice the adhesion on gradients.

The design of the Stars blueprint drew heavily on that of the Saints, but incorporated the De Glehn cylinder arrangement with four cylinders for smoother riding at speed and two sets of valve gear, but with simple rather than compound expansion, into an otherwise standard GWR design.

This combination of the two cultures on opposite sides of the English Channel and the integration of US practices such as the method of joining the pair of cylinder castings in the middle of the engine, the long travel valves, the tapered boiler and the generous bearing surfaces, produced, quite literally, a star performer, and a type that would remain the basis of the GWR's larger passenger engines until nationalisation. Performance was even more enhanced when superheating was added in 1910.

A total of 73 Stars were built, and the GWR 4-6-0 from henceforth would only get better. Only one, No 4003 *Lode Star*, survives, in the National Railway Museum at York.

In 1903, Churchward did for freight what the Saints and Stars would do for passenger working and came up with Britain's first 2-8-0 design.

His prototype, No 97, renumbered 2800 in 1906, was fitted with the GWR standard No 1 boiler (common to the Saints and the Stars) and had 18in cylinders. Designed to haul 60 wagons, tests showed it could manage 100.

The 2800s were used for long-distance coal traffic, mainly from South Wales to London.

A total of 84 examples of the 2800 class were built. His successor Charles Collett modified the design into the 2884 class of which 81 were built from 1938, and numbered in the sequence 2884-99 and 3800-66.

Sixteen members of the class have been preserved –
Nos 2807, 2818, 2857, 2859, 2861, 2873, 2874, 2885, 3802, 3803, 3814, 3822, 3845, 3850, 3855 and 3862.

Between 1910-23, 105 more 2-8-0s, but this time tank rather than tender engines, were built to a Churchward design. Again, they were Britain's first 2-8-0Ts.

In 1923, the design was modified to increase the cylinder diameter from 18½in to 19in and raise the tractive effort to 33,170lb, creating the 5205 class. Collett later converted them into the 7200 class 2-8-2s by adding a bolt-on extension at the rear which included a trailing wheel, thereby increasing their capacity.

Five 4200s have been preserved, Nos 4247, 4248, 4253, 4270 and 4277, along with three 7200s, Nos 7200, 7202 and

Raw heavy freight power: Churchward 2-8-0 No 3802 heads through Kings Sutton. GWT COLLECTION

George Jackson Churchward.

Churchward classic tank trio: GWR 2-6-2Ts Nos 5542, No 5553 and No 4160 lined up at Minehead on West Somerset Railway on 9 March 2008. JUSTIN KERR-PETERSON/WSR

In 1897, the GWR introduced the Badminton class express passenger 4-4-0s as a development from the earlier Duke class, taking the name Badminton from the foxhunt. No 3295 *Bessborough* was renumbered 4103 in 1912. GWT COLLECTION

Churchward 2-8-0T No 4247 at Bodmin General on the Bodmin & Wenford Railway. JOHN STRETTON

appeared, and by the time the last emerged from Swindon in 1934, 342 had been built. A true utility engine, they could tackle anything from branch line goods to main line expresses. Eleven of them served in France with the Railway Operating Division of the British Army during World War One.

Two examples survive, No 5322 at Didcot Railway Centre and No 7325 at the Severn Valley Railway.

One of the most familiar types of 'modern' GWR locomotive is the 2-6-2T or 'prairie' tank, the several variations of which were used as general workhorses for nearly six decades and much more besides.

The prototype of the 290 large prairies, No 99 (renumbered 3100, the identity by which the class was known), was outshopped from Swindon in 1903 and followed by a first batch of 39 engines with the standard No 2 boiler. In 1906, 41 were fitted with the No 4 boiler and became the 3150 class.

The prototype and Nos 3111-49 were renumbered 5100 and 5111 to 5149 in 1927 and, joined by 50 new locomotives, became the 5100 class, with enlarged bunkers. Forty other 5100s were numbered as the 4100 series and included the last large prairies to be built, Nos 4140-79.

The 6100 class were designed to produce a higher boiler pressure and tractive effort from 24,30lb to 27,340lb.

The prototype of a smaller version of the large prairie, No 115, appeared in 1904 after

GWR mogul No 5355 at Ross-on-Wye in British Railways days. The type was one of the most successful and durable designed by Churchward. GWT COLLECTION

The Great Bear, Britain's first Pacific, was probably built by the GWR for prestige. GWT COLL

being designed for use on branch lines, and a first batch of 10 was ordered.

The next batch had their driving wheels upgraded to 4ft 7½ins to make them more suitable for fast running, and in December 1912 they were renumbered 4500-29.

Altogether, 175 were built, including those turned out by Collett between 1927-29 with larger tanks.

Eleven of the large prairies have survived: Nos 5164, 5193, 5199, 4110, 4115, 4121, 4144, 4150, 4160 and 6106, while 14 small prairies are still with us: Nos 4555, 4561, 4566, 4588, 5521, 5526, 5532, 5538, 5539, 5541, 5542, 5552, 5553 and 5572.

As was the case with Brunel, not everything that Churchward did was successful. Churchward jumped ahead of his time, by building Britain's first 4-6-2, a type which adopted the name Pacific from the USA where manufacturer Baldwin had supplied them to the Missouri Pacific Railroad.

No 111 *The Great Bear*, outshopped from Swindon Works in February 1908, was all but exclusively restricted to the Paddington to Bristol line because of its high axle loading.

His aim appeared to be to show it was possible to build a four-cylinder locomotive with 15in diameter cylinders which could be adequately fed by a standard GWR boiler.

The Great Bear experienced early problems with clearance on curves and springing of the

GWR 2-8-0 No 4704 was first allocated to Stafford Road shed when built in 1922. Later allocated to Birkenhead and Old Oak Common, it was withdrawn in May 1964. GWS

While no Dean single survives, a static replica of No 3041 *The Queen*, built by Madame Tussauds for its Railways and Royalty exhibition at Windsor & Eton Central station, is still on display there. ROBIN JONES

trailing wheels. Modifications were also made to the superheating of the boiler. However, with Swindon Works diverting his attention to supplying military needs during World War One, and Churchward's advances in the development of the 4-6-0s, improving *The Great Bear* was not considered a priority.

In January 1924, *The Great Bear*, then needing heavy repairs to its boiler after just 527,272 miles, was dismantled and some of the parts used to build Castle class 4-6-0 No 2975 *Viscount Churchill*.

Introduced in 1919-21, the 4700 class of nine 2-8-0s were the final locomotives designed by Churchward, and the most powerful and fastest of his heavy freight engine designs. They also hauled passenger services including heavy holiday expresses on summer Saturdays.

Churchward succeeded superbly in yanking the GWR out of the era of oversize brass domes, stovepipe chimneys, single driving wheels and minimalist cabs, while resisting the temptation of experimenting with electric or other modes of traction, as was the case elsewhere. Not only were his achievements magnificent, if only for their simplicity let alone their power, but he also paved the way for his successor Charles Collett to make the GWR kings of the road once more.

GWR 2-8-2T No 7210 in British Railways days. GWT COLLECTION

Duke class 4-4-0 No 3272 *Amyas*, which was built in 1896. Some of the class were later rebuilt with components from Bulldogs to make Dukedogs. GWT COLLECTION

1903

The prototype of the 290 large prairies, No 99, outshopped from Swindon.

City class 4-4-0 *Albion* 4-6-0 and *La France* 4-4-2 (purchased) also appear.

Vacuum brake began to be used on goods wagons.

Dining facilities become generally available to third class passengers.

Ely Valley Railway absorbed.

10 March: First non-stop Paddington-Bristol-Plymouth run.

3 June: Route opens between Old Oak Common-Park Royal and Hanwell/West Ealing.

1 July: The South Wales & Bristol Direct Railway from Wootton Bassett to Patchway to link up with the Severn Tunnel opened for passengers.

14 July: *City of Bath* hauling a 130-ton royal special ran from Paddington to Plymouth via Bristol at an average of 63.14mph.

17 Aug: First GWR motor bus service, from Helston to Lizard Town, launched.

12 October: GWR steam railmotors first used, between Stonehouse and Chalford; elliptical roofs were fitted to GWR steam railmotors in 1903 and then became standard for all carriages, the first being the Dreadnought stock of 1904.

31 October: Bus service from Penzance to Marazion launched.

December: some ballast hoppers given vacuum brakes.

1904

First 10 County class locomotives were built.

Exminster water troughs brought into use.

Experimental fast freight service from Acton to Bristol.

Cornwall Railway route diverted between Saltash and St Germans, eliminating the last Brunel wooden viaducts on the main line to Penzance.

Dark grey livery was introduced for wagons and continued to be used until 1947

General goods wagons constructed with vacuum brakes.

Bogie coal wagons built.

1 March: Bus route from Slough station to Beaconsfield launched

18 March: Bus routes to Windsor launched

9 May - Record 227-minute 'Ocean Mails Express' Plymouth-Paddington run by *City of Truro* and *Duke of Connaught*, the former unofficially achieving 102.3mph down Wellington Bank.

1 July: The world's longest non-stop run, between Paddington and Plymouth, inaugurated the 'Cornish Riviera Express', known as 'The Limited'.

1 Aug: First section of Honeybourne-Cheltenham line opened; completed 1 August 1906. Steel was used experimentally for a coach roof.

7 November: Steam buses introduced on Wolverhampton to Bridgnorth route, replaced by motor buses the following year.

City of Truro
the 'reluctant' legend

The world at large did not suspect it at the time, but 9 May 1904 was a seminal moment in the history of the GWR.

It was on that day, on Wellington Bank on the Bristol & Exeter main line, the route where Daniel Gooch had shown his broad gauge behemoths to be the fastest in the world, that an example of new locomotive superintendent George Jackson Churchward's first design, City class 4-4-0 No 3440 *City of Truro*, became immortalised in legend, if not in undisputable fact.

Observers claimed that it became the first steam locomotive to break the 100mph, reaching 102.3mph while descending the bank with the 'Ocean Mails Special' from Plymouth to Paddington.

A report of the 100mph appeared in a newspaper the following day, after a mail van worker on board conducted some unofficial timings of his own, but the report by and large went unnoticed by the rest of the world's media.

The GWR did not even acknowledge the fact until nearly four years later, fully conscious of increasing public concern about superfast trains, especially in the aftermath of the derailment of a night tourist train at Preston during the 'race to Aberdeen'. Although the GWR and the rival London & South Western Railway were locked in a race for the ocean mails traffic, neither had any intention of admitting actions which might have been considered reckless. At the time, the GWR allowed only the overall timings for the run to be published.

Charles Rous-Martin, who recorded the speed on board the footplate of the locomotive on the 'Ocean Mails Special' at first restricted his reporting of the speed achieved during the event.

And it was only in the edition of *The Railway Magazine* in December 1907 – nearly four years after the event – that the alleged speed of 102.3mph appeared publicly for the first time – and even then was not attributed to a particular engine. Readers had to wait until the following April's edition for the identity of the locomotive to be revealed by him.

Such reticence on the part of railway companies to unveil such achievements to the public gaze may mean that if *City of Truro* did break the 100mph barrier – some historians have questioned this – it may not have been the first to do so.

Truro's now-legendary feat came nearly five years after a series of high-speed test runs took place on the Lancashire & Yorkshire Railway's Liverpool Exchange-Southport line using locomotives from Aspinall's newly introduced 'High Flyer' 4-4-2 class.

It was reported that on 15 July 1899 one such train was formed of Southport-based No 1392 and five coaches. Timed to leave Liverpool Exchange at 2.51pm, it was recorded as passing milepost 17 in 12.75min.

This gives a start-to-pass speed of 80mph but given the permanent 20mph restriction at Bank Hall and the 65mph restriction at Waterloo, the suggestion has been made that this train attained 100mph.

The L&Y never published details or timings of this test run. It is only because passing times were 'unofficially' noted by local enthusiasts that the 100mph claim is known at all.

In his volume *The Lancashire & Yorkshire Railway* (Ian Allan, 1956), researcher Eric Mason wrote: "It is likely that the event will probably be regarded in the same light as the GW *City of Truro* run, because it is alleged no proper records were kept, and has in recent

City of Truro, which slowly became a legend after its high-speed feat in 1904. GWT COLLECTION

GWR outside-framed 4-4-0s line up at the Bluebell Railway's Sheffield Park headquarters : visiting *City of Truro* stands alongside resident Dukedog No 9017 *Earl of Berkeley* on 15 October 2006 after the two engines had shared duties on service trains. The two engines were rostered to double head for the first time during the 'Giants of Steam' gala the following weekend. DAVE BOWLES

years been taken, rightly or wrongly, with a large pinch of salt."

Another of the 4-4-2 class, No 1417 – the test engine for Hughes' back pressure release valves – became enshrouded in "mythical legends" over its performances. Mason wrote. "While there is no confirmation of an alleged 117mph near Kirkby, there is no doubt whatsoever that the engine did perform some really fast running in the capable hands of driver J Chapman of Newton Heath."

Nonetheless, one indisputable fact is that the legendary status went to *City of Truro*.

At the time, the GWR was engaged in fierce competition with its great rival in the West Country, the London & South Western Railway, to see which could bring ocean mails from Plymouth to London the fastest; and while they had not been given permission to do so, some of the Paddington empire's drivers were determined to demonstrate what they and their Swindon-built engines could achieve.

No 3440 *City of Truro* was one of a class of 20. Ten were rebuilt from Dean's Atbara class engines, the first (No 3405) being converted in September 1902 and the rest following in 1907-9. The new 10 were built at Swindon in 1903, and included No 3440.

Driver Moses Clements was rostered to take the train, total weight 148 tons and comprising a light load of eight-wheeled postal vans with around 1300 large bags of mail on board, to Paddington. The load included bullion as a payment by the Americans to the French for ongoing work on the Panama Canal. By the time the train had reached the South Devon banks, it appeared that Clements had decided to "go for it."

By the time the locomotive was racing down the gradient from Whiteball Tunnel on the far side of

City of Truro, repainted in the colours that it carried in latter-day GWR service as No 3717 at Didcot Railway Centre on 1 May 2010, the open day of the venue's nine-day GWR 175 extravaganza. FRAN DUMBLETON/GWS

1905
24 September: William Dean dies at his retirement home in Folkestone.
20 Nov: GWR & Great Central Joint line opened throughout for goods.
Didcot North signal box (38 levers) opened, with power operation.
Carriage lighting improved by the use of incandescent gas mantles
Dawlish tunnels widening completed.
County 4-4-2T introduced.
Wye Valley Railway absorbed.

1906
Churchward 28XX 2-8-0 No 2808 hauled a 107-wagon train of 2012 tons from Swindon to Acton in 1906, tsetting a new haulage record for a British steam locomotive.
Rhondda & Swansea Bay Railway taken over.
Langport & Castle Cary Railway shortens the London to Penzance route between Reading and Taunton.
First six-coupled, four-cylinder locomotives appear.
Aldermaston-Midgham water troughs brought into use.
First 4500 class 2-6-2Ts appear.
1 January: First automatic train control installation, on the Henley branch.
17 March: Old Oak Common locomotive depot opened.
11 June: Curry Rivel-Cogload cut off first used for goods (for passengers from 2 July).
1 July: Lambourn Valley Railway absorbed.
30 Aug: Opening of Fishguard Harbour and a new link to Ireland.

1907
First four-cylinder Stars appear.
1 July: Manchester & Milford Railway absorbed.
August: Semi-automatic signals linked with track circuits, between Pangbourne and Goring, introduced.

1908
Carriages were painted chocolate brown all over.
North Star, which became No 4000, and No 4003 *Lode Star*, fitted with audible signalling equipment in 1908 as part of the installation of automatic train control between Slough and Reading. The 142-ton 4-6-2 *The Great Bear* appeared.
1 January: Port Talbot Railway lines taken over.
1 July: The Birmingham and North Warwickshire line, combined with the Cheltenham and Honeybourne route of 1906, offered a new route from Birmingham via Stratford-upon-Avon to South Wales. The 'Cornishman' introduced between Wolverhampton and Penzance.

Exeter, it was going faster than any member of the class had gone before.

On the footplate was timer Rous-Marten and around 10.45am he recorded a quarter mile in 8.8 seconds on the descent down Wellington Bank, hence the 102.3mph claim.

Sadly, the driver saw a gang of platelayers standing in their tracks a quarter of a mile away ahead, braked fiercely while they moved aside, and carried on into Taunton at just 80mph, ruining the recorder's chance to confirm the speed.

Furthermore, there was no secondary timer on board to confirm the claimed speed, so it was never taken as an official record.

Rous-Marten at first toed the company line and kept quiet about the 102.3mph claim, and when he wrote an article in *The Railway Magazine* a month later, he merely described the trip as setting "the record of records." He added: "It is not desirable at present to publish the actual maximum rate that was reached on this memorable occasion."

In the same month as full details were finally published, April 1908, Rous-Marten died from a sudden heart attack. Even then, it was to be another 14 years before the GWR made much of the feat.

Several writers have expressed the view that it would have been physically impossible for a 1000hp locomotive like *City of Truro* to exceed 92mph on that section of line.

However, the milepost timings provided by Rous-Marten are fully consistent with a speed of 100mph or just over.

Whether or not *City of Truro* did reach 102.3mph, the general public wanted to believe it at the time, but not because they feared high-speed running after all. The feat showed that steam train could travel safely at speeds of more than 100mph, and that meant that as in the great days of Brunel and Gooch, the GWR again led the pack.

The City class, unlike most other Churchward designs, looked back to the days of William Dean rather than to the future. As trains became heavier, larger locomotives were needed and the City class soon found themselves relegated to secondary duties. All but one member was withdrawn and scrapped between 1927-31.

The last, *City of Truro*, was withdrawn in 1931 and acquired by the London & North Eastern Railway for display at a new railway museum at York.

Churchward's subsequent designs went on to revolutionise the GWR, while leaving the past behind. While the City class had a 4-4-0 arrangement with four smaller wheels at the front and four larger drive wheels behind, the type was rapidly making way for Churchward's pioneering 4-6-0s.

Another of Churchward's innovations was the move to external cylinders, which as well as providing greater power, also allowed for much more flowing and modern outlines.

An official record of a steam locomotive breaking the 100mph barrier would not be claimed until 30 November 1934, when LNER Pacific No 4472 *Flying Scotsman* achieved the feat travelling between Leeds and King's Cross.

Four years later, the LNER established an all-time world record for steam locomotive speed,

Centenary replay: *City of Truro* near Sampford Arundel between Beam Bridge and Whiteball Tunnel with Pathfinder Tours' 10 May 2004 'Ocean Mail 100' special. DAVID HOLMAN

City of Truro in British Railway service at Sutton Scotney on 17 July 1957. GWT COLLECTION

when A4 streamlined Pacific No 4468 *Mallard* reached 126mph down a descent of Stoke Bank in Lincolnshire on 4 July 1938.

In 1957, British Railways decided to return the 'preserved' *City of Truro* to running order and the main line, repainted into its original Victorian livery with red frames

Renumbered 3440, it was used for special excursion trains, but it also hauled some regular timetabled services mainly on the Newbury and Southampton line.

Withdrawn for a second time in 1961, it became part of the National Collection, set up by the British Transport Commission to preserve key locomotives from the United Kingdom's railway history.

City of Truro was restored to running order again in 1984 to take part in the 150th anniversary celebrations of the GWR, and afterwards visited several heritage railways. In 1990, it revisited its birthplace as part of the National Railway Museum on Tour exhibition in Swindon Works.

And following a nationwide public appeal in support of custodian the National Railway Museum, *City of Truro* was overhauled to main line standard again in 2004, at a cost of £130,000, to mark the centenary of its unofficial record-breaking run; and returned to Wellington Bank in May that year to haul a series of main line specials for Pathfinder Tours – but was not allowed to attempt to reach anything like the speed quoted by Rous-Marten.

Opinions will always remain divided about unconfirmed feats like this. However, the legend has had far more impact than the physical evidence of the claim.

In 2010, in readiness for GWR 175 and its starring role in the Gloucestershire Warwickshire Railway's Cotswold Festival of Steam, which ran from 29 May to 6 June, *City of Truro* was repainted into the correct livery for its latter years in GWR service as No 3717.

When built in 1903, as No 3440, it was equipped with slide valves and a non-superheated boiler and carried the fully-lined-out Victorian livery with Indian red frames of the GWR express locomotives of the day.

The locomotive was rebuilt with a new Swindon standard No 4 superheated boiler in 1911. The modification resulted in a longer smokebox, top water feeds either side of the safety valve bonnet and a number of other detail differences.

In the early part of the 20th century, the express passenger locomotive livery was disappearing in favour of a rather more plain green unlined livery with black frames. In 1912, the number series was changed to 37XX and *City of Truro* was numbered 3717. Therefore its 2010 livery is historically accurate.

Currently based at the Gloucestershire Warwickshire Railway, it will return to the National Railway Museum at York for static display once its boiler ticket has expired.

City of Truro rounds the curve at Langston rock approaching Dawlish Warren with Vintage Trains' Plymouth-Bristol excursion on 3 December 2004. BRIAN SHARPE

Trains and boats and planes
...and buses too!

Isambard Kingdom Brunel had engineered a truly magnificent railway. Yet nobody ever told him, or its directors, that they could only run trains.

Within months of work starting on the GWR main line, Isambard was developing plans to extend it beyond Bristol… all the way to New York… by building the world's first steam-powered transatlantic liner.

The use of steam power in boats dates back to William Symington, who on 14 October 1788 conducted partially successful trials of a steam engine fitted inside a pleasure boat at Dalswinton near Dumfries.

The world's first steam-operated commercial ferry, the *Comet*, was launched on the Clyde by Henry Bell in 1812, and two years later the steamboat Regent began sailing between London and Margate… designed by none other than Marc Brunel, father of Isambard.

The first cross-channel steamship was the 112-ton *Hibernia* which sailed from Holyhead to Dublin in seven hours in 1816. The first oceanic crossing by a steamship came in 1819 by the *PS Savannah*, built by Francis Fickett of New York. Originally intended for the sail packet service to Le Havre, it set out from Savannah, Georgia, reaching Liverpool on 20 June after 29 days 11 hours. However, the engines were little used and for most of the journey, the ship relied on sail power.

Up to 1835, steamships were still considered suitable only for such short runs in comparatively shallow waters, as these early examples could not carry and burn sufficient coal for anything like a transatlantic voyage.

Marc Brunel himself believed that the consumption of coal by a steam engine would increase in proportion with the size of a ship, and so if the existing vessels could not manage to cross an ocean, a much larger one would certainly fail.

His son rightly disagreed, because the energy needed to drive a ship, whether by sail or steam, did not depend on the vessel's weight, but on the weight of the water that it must shift. He discovered that contrary to established beliefs, the bigger the ship, the more favourable would be the crucial energy-to-weight equation.

At an early GWR board meeting, Isambard was said to have suggested extending the railway by building a steamboat to be called *The Great Western* after the company, and which could steam all the way to New York.

One GWR director, Thomas Guppy, persuaded three others, Robert Scot, Robert Bright and Thomas Pycroft to set up a committee to investigate the possibility, and recruited naval captain Christopher Claxton, who Brunel had met while working on the improvements to the city docks and who had access to official drawings of new Admiralty vessels.

A prospectus was issued before the new Great Western Steamship Company met for the first time on 3 March 1836, giving further details of two proposed transatlantic ships and the estimated cost of £35,000 each. Five of the directors were also GWR board members.

Isambard enlisted Bristol shipbuilder William Patterson, and it was in his yard at Wapping in the Floating Harbour that the keel of the first ship was laid in June that year without pomp or ceremony. At 205ft, it was the longest ever to have been laid.

Crowds gathered on 28 August 1836 to watch the stern post of the great wooden ship raised and the stern frame positioned. Many doubted that it would ever be brought out of the dock because of its size, let alone set out to sea.

Lambeth marine engines manufacturer

The *St Julien* was one of a pair of vessels built in 1925 by John Brown for the GWR's Weymouth services, When war broke out in 1939 she was commandeered for ferrying troops and aided the evacuation of British troops from Dunkirk and Cherbourg in 1940. She spent the rest of World War Two as a hospital ship, including a period operating in the Mediterranean and supporting the Normandy landings. After hostilities ended, she returned to Weymouth for further railway service which lasted until 1961.

Linking London by GWR steam train and steamship to New York: contemporary artist John Walter's oil painting of *The Great Western* on her maiden transatlantic voyage in 1838. SS GREAT BRITAIN TRUST

Maudslay, Son & Field, was contracted to supply a pair to drive twin paddle wheels 28ft in diameter.

On 19 July 1837, when more than 50,000 onlookers crowded into Bristol's docks and on to adjacent vessels to watch the ship being launched.

The ship was named *The Great Western* by Mrs Miles, the wife of one of the steamship company's directors, before 300 invited guests joined the directors for dinner in the ship's main cabin.

On 18 August, *The Great Western* was towed down the Avon estuary by the steam tug *Lion*, and used a four-masted schooner rig to travel around the south coast to London – as a sailing ship, not by steam power!

London crowds were equally enthusiastic about *The Great Western*, which had its engines fitted by Maudslay in East India Dock at Blackwall. In March 1838, *The Great Western* was moved to a berth in the River Thames for trials, during which she attained an average speed of 11 knots comfortably.

Would-be rivals watched from afar and not wishing to be left out in the cold, began to convert existing ships to compete with *The Great Western*.

SS Great Britain in her dry dock today. ROBIN JONES

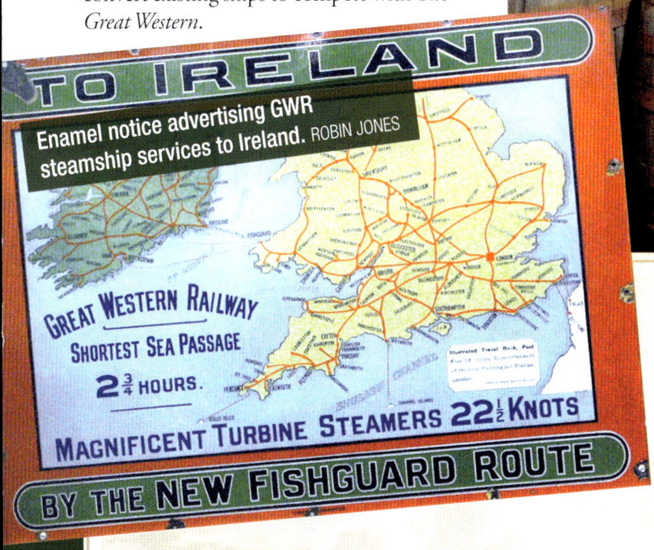

Enamel notice advertising GWR steamship services to Ireland. ROBIN JONES

Bristol's waterfront was packed out on 19 July 1843 as the *SS Great Britain* was floated for the first time, as seen in this John Walter engraving. SS GREAT BRITAIN TRUST

The British & American Steam Navigation Company hired the 703-ton *Sirius* with the intention of making the first scheduled steamship crossing to the United States. The *Sirius* set out with 22 passengers on board in March 1838, while *The Great Western's* engines were still undergoing trials.

At last, on 31 March, *The Great Western* set off for Bristol with Isambard on board to collect her passengers for her maiden trip. Another mishap shortly afterwards saw the boiler lagging catch fire, but it was extinguished, after the ship arrived in Bristol on 2 April, only to find that many passengers had cancelled their bookings after hearing rumours about the ship's 'failings'.

With just seven passengers on board, *The Great Western* set out in pursuit of the *Sirius* on 7 April. She arrived at New York at noon on 23 April, having made the crossing in just 17 days – only to see the *Sirius*, which had run aground there the previous night after exhausting almost all of its coal supply, already moored there.

Nonetheless, the Americans were captivated by the race between the two ships, and crowds boarded *The Great Western* to see Isambard's latest marvel for themselves.

On the homeward journey, *The Great Western* reached Britain in 14 days as compared to the 18 taken by her rival, and proved that unlike her competitor, she could cross the Atlantic with passengers and cargo and still be left with coal to spare. She went on to complete 67 crossings in eight years. Sadly, she could not fit through the lock gates leading into the Floating Harbour, and had to be moored in King's Road in the Bristol Channel at considerable expense, because the harbour authorities refused to widen the lock gates for new bigger ships to pass, a factor which led to the decline Bristol's importance as a port for transatlantic trade.

When *The Great Western* left Bristol for New York on 11 February 1843, it was the last departure of a transatlantic liner from the port for 28 years. Taken out of service at Liverpool in 1846, the ship was bought by the Royal Mail Steam Packet Company and used on voyages to the Gulf of Mexico for ten years, after which she ended her days as a troopship during the Crimean War before being scrapped in 1857.

In 1838, Isambard and his committee began planning their second ship, and the following year chose his design based around 'box girder'-type hull with a two-skinned cellular construction with six water-tight compartment and two longitudinal bulkheads, plus a strong iron deck.

The keel for the new vessel, nicknamed the 'Mammoth', was laid on 19 July 1839, again in Patterson's yard.

Poster advertising the GWR's short-lived air services. The GWR was the first railway company to take to the air. NRM

Meanwhile, Isambard was well impressed by the world's first propeller-driven ship, Francis Pettit Smith's *Archimedes*, when it arrived in Bristol in May 1840, and the steamship company booked the *Archimedes* for six months of tests while ordering all work on the paddle steamers for the second vessel to stop.

Isambard realised that a fully immersed propeller would be far more efficient than paddle wheels, and in December 1840 insisted that the new ship should be driven exclusively by one. Eventually, Isambard designed the 1600 horsepower engines himself, and the company set up the world's first integrated steamship works on land next to the Floating Harbour, building the engines inside.

The cost of the project soared, reaching £125,555, twice that of *The Great Western*, but, boosted by the success of his Great Western Railway, the project managed to attract sufficient investors.

The ship was launched on 19 July 1843, exactly six years after *The Great Western*. Prince Albert, the Royal Consort, arrived from London on a GWR special train driven by Daniel Gooch himself, with Isambard's parents Marc and Sophia Brunel watching proudly as Albert smashed a bottle of champagne on the bows (a first attempt by the same Mrs Miles having missed), naming the ship the *SS Great Britain*.

After the ceremony, the *SS Great Britain* was moved back into the dry dock for fitting out. Trials were undertaken in the Bristol

The Westland Wessex G-AAGW at Cardiff on 11 April 1933. GWS

An early GWR single decker. The GWR broke new ground with the successful running of regular bus services. GWT COLLECTION

out. Trials were undertaken in the Bristol Channel before the ship undertook a 40-hour voyage to London on 23 January 1845.

Queen Victoria and Prince Albert were given a guided tour of the ship, at that time the biggest in the world, on 22 April 1845, and its first Atlantic crossing was made from Liverpool on 26 July, carrying only 45 passengers and arriving in New York just 15 days later at an average speed of more than nine knots.

A four-bladed propeller replaced Isambard's experimental six-bladed version after there were several in incidents of propeller damage on her second voyage, and a third voyage was made to New York on 29 May 1846. On the homeward journey, the *SS Great Britain* made the crossing in just 13 days at an average speed of 13 knots.

However, the ship's fifth trip ended in disaster, as with 180 passengers on board, she ran aground in Ireland's Dundrum Bay on 22 September 1846. After several attempts, she was finally towed off the beach, by *HMS Birkenhead* on 27 August 1847, but Great Western Steamship Company could not afford the repairs and towing charge, and sold her to Liverpool shipping firm Bright, Gibbs & Co for a knockdown £18,000. The company was wound up in February 1852.

After 24 years working the route to Australia, and later being converted to a sailing ship, *SS Great Britain* ended her working days as a humble store ship in the Falkland Islands. In 1970, she was brought back to Bristol, and restored to become a major tourist attraction next to the Floating Harbour.

Isambard's plans for the transatlantic routes from Bristol never materialised, and although these two groundbreaking ships were never owned by the GWR, many railway officials and shareholders also had interests in them.

The GWR began to establish a shipping fleet of its own, for more humble and local voyages, linking with the company's trains to provide services to Ireland, the Channel Islands and France.

An Act of Parliament of 13 July 1871 empowered the GWR to operate ships in 1871. The following year the GWR took over the ships operated by Ford and Jackson on the route between Wales and Ireland. Services were operated between Weymouth, the

GWR bus AF84 on the Helston service.

Channel Islands and France on the former Weymouth and Channel Islands Steam Packet Company routes. The railway also operated tugs at its docks in Wales and the West Country, and tenders to land passengers and cargo from transatlantic liners at Plymouth, while smaller GWR vessels were also used on ferry routes on the River Severn and River Dart. In 1901 the GWR took over the Dartmouth ferry that linked Kingswear station with Dartmouth.

On 30 August 1906 the GWR's Welsh terminal was moved to a new harbour at Fishguard, but hopes of benefiting from passing liners en route to Liverpool failed to materialise.

The GWR built several new branches to shorten its main lines to its ports, notably the Severn Tunnel which opened in 1886 while having the side effect of wiping out the company's ferry service across the River Severn, and the South Wales & Bristol Direct Railway of 1903, which bypassed Bristol Temple Meads and took trains straight from Paddington to Neyland. The completion of the Stert & Westbury Railway in 1900 speeded up services to Weymouth, while the Langport & Castle Cary Railway which opened in 1906 further shortened the distance between the ocean liner port of Plymouth and the capital.

At the Grouping of 1923, the GWR absorbed several smaller railway companies which operated docks and owned small ships. They included the

1909
1 Jan: Operations of Liskeard & Looe Railway taken over.
1 July: New Birmingham Moor Street terminus opened.

1910
Bala & Festiniog Railway absorbed.
4 April: Ashendon Junction-Aynho Junction opened: the Birmingham Direct Linewas built jointly with the Great Central to give a shorter route from London to Aynho and the north.
9 May - Stoke Gifford-Avonmouth opened.
1 Oct: Second Class abolished.

1911
4301 class 2-6-0 introduced.

1912
Red lake livery for carriages introduced.

1913
Work on extending Paddington station begins.
The Swansea District Lines which allowed trains to Fishguard Harbour to avoid Swansea opened. Fishguard had been opened in an attempt to attract transatlantic liner traffic and provided a better facility for the Anglo-Irish ferries than that at Neyland.
Peak year for South Wales exports.

1914
5 Aug: Government took over Britain's railways at the outbreak of World War One. Many GWR staff joined the armed forces.

1915
Title of Locomotive Superintendent changed to Chief Mechanical Engineer.

1917
1 January: Wartime service curtailments.
16 April: Ealing & Shepherds Bush Railway opened for freight.

1919
1 Feb: Introduction of the eight-day week.
26 September: Rail strike, until 5 October.

1920
3 Aug: Ealing & Shepherds Bush Railway opened to passengers.

1921
Most services returned to pre-war specifications.
Aberdeen-Penzance service introduced.
19 Aug: Railways Act passed, paving the way for the Grouping and 'Big Four'.
New general manager Felix Pole oversaw the absorption the South Wales railways

Alexandra (Newport and South Wales) Docks and Railway, Barry Railway, Cardiff Railway, Port Talbot Railway and Docks, Taff Vale Railway and the Swansea Harbour Trust.

The shipping services continued for some years after nationalisation in 1948 in much the same vein as they had done under the GWR.

Just as Brunel was quick to seize the potential of atmospheric propulsion as an early replacement for steam, so the GWR maintained an open mind about expanding their empire using other forms of transport. When the dawn of the 20th century saw that motor road vehicles would shape the future of transport later if not sooner, the GWR looked at providing bus services both as a feeder to its train services, but also as a cheaper alternative to building new branch lines in sparsely populated rural areas which would never pay. They were the first bus services successfully operated by a UK railway.

It all began on the Lizard peninsula in Cornwall. The GWR baulked at the idea of spending £85,000 on extending the Helston branch with a light railway to Britain's southernmost village, Lizard Town, and decided to try motor buses instead. Two vehicles that had been used temporarily by the Lynton & Barnstaple Railway were acquired, the service was launched 17 August 1903, and proved so popular and profitable that other routes were soon established, first locally to Mullion, Ruan Minor and Porthleven, and then further afield at Penzance.

A bus route from Slough station to Beaconsfield was launched on 1 March 1904, followed by routes to Windsor on 18 July that year. Indeed, the first GWR double deckers appeared on the Slough-Windsor service in 1904 onwards. Seen here at Slough station.

A route from Wolverhampton to Bridgnorth was briefly operated from 7 November 1904 using steam buses, motor buses replacing them the following year.

The final bus services operated by the GWR began in the Weymouth area in 1935, jointly run with the LSWR, and were transferred to Southern National on 1 January 1934.

By the end of 1904, 36 buses were in GWR operation, and the Great Western Railway (Road Transport) Act was passed in 1928, the GWR boasted the biggest railway bus fleet. This Act paved the way for the services to be transferred to bus companies, although the railway was to be a shareholder in these operations. On 1 January 1929, the GWR routes in Devon and Cornwall went over to the new Western National Omnibus Company, 50 per cent owned by the railway and the other half by the National Omnibus and Transport Company. That year the GWR acquired 30 per cent of the shares in the Devon General Omnibus and Touring Company.

As with the other major companies the GWR operated an extensive fleet of road vehicles to supplement its rail services. As with the buses, the lorries and vans provided for goods transport and vans and parcels by and large the bodies built at Swindon with the chassis bought in from outside manufacturers such as Mills-Daimler, Thornycroft and AEC.

But why stop with transport on the ground – when it is far quicker to fly by air?

At 2.30pm on 11 April 1933, Captain Gordon Olley took off from Cardiff with the first GWR air service with five of the railway company's officials on board, plus a newspaper reporter. The aircraft was a three-engined Westland Wessex supplied by Imperial Airways and painted in GWR livery. It could carry just six passengers.

They reached Haldon Hill aerodrome near Exeter, in 44 minutes before the passengers attended a reception at Teignmouth Golf Club. The plane took off again with different passengers and landed shortly afterwards at Plymouth's Roborough Airport, where the party was met by the Lord Mayor, the Earl and Countess of Mount Edgcumbe. The earl was a director of the GWR, and the company had become the first to set up an airline.

A regular service began the following day, and offered two flights daily in each direction. The first left Cardiff at 9.15am, Haldon at 10.10am and arrived at Plymouth at 10.35am, Cardiff to Plymouth cost £3 10s single or £6 return.

On 22 May that year, the service was extended from Cardiff to Birmingham's Castle Bromwich Aerodrome, on a one service per weekday basis, the fare being £3 single or £5 10s return. There was a connecting bus to the GWR's Birmingham Snow Hill station, and the company claimed that the air journey from Birmingham to Plymouth would take 170 minutes as compared with 320 minutes behind a steam locomotive.

A local flight from Plymouth to Haldon and on to Torquay might cost as little as 12s 6d single or £1 5s return.

During the first season 714 passengers, 104lb of freight and 454lb of mail had been carried and 62,400 miles were flown.

The service closed for the winter on 30 September 1933 and was taken over by Railway Air Services from 7 May the following year.

RAS was formed by the GWR along with the other 'Big Four' companies, the London Midland & Scottish, London & North Eastern and Southern railways, and Imperial Airways, and had a main operating and maintenance base was at Croydon Airport.

The GWR and SR formed a new company, Great Western & Southern Air Lines, on 5 December 1938. At the outbreak of World War Two on 3 September 1939, all services were discontinued, but on 25 September 1939, the company was given permission to reopen the Lands End-Scilly Islands service and appears to have carried on during the hostilities. In 1946 the company ran the Southampton-Bristol-Cardiff-Weston-super-Mare service while the RAS worked other services, mainly to the north.

In August 1946, the newly elected Labour Government formed state-owned airline British European Airways Corporation which was given a monopoly of scheduled air services within the UK. The state corporation acquired the RAS aircraft, staff and routes from 31 January 1947, ending an era where the GWR had dared to become the first UK railway company to reach for the sky.

The GWR inherited several tank engines when it took over smaller railways in South Wales which had port, harbour and shipping concerns at the Grouping of 1923. One of these was Cardiff Railway 0-4-0ST No 5, now the sole surviving locomotive from that company, the smallest railway absorbed into the GWR. It had been built by Kitson of Leeds in 1898 and renumbered 1338 by the GWR, which in 1943 transferred it to Taunton depot in 1943 for working in Bridgwater Docks. It was switched by the Western Region to Swansea docks in 1960, from which it was finally withdrawn in September 1963, when it was the last of the standard gauge locomotives absorbed into the GWR. It was preserved in 1964, initially at the small and long-gone museum at Bleadon & Uphill station near Weston-super-Mare, and is now part of the Great Western Society collection at Didcot Railway Centre. ROBIN JONES

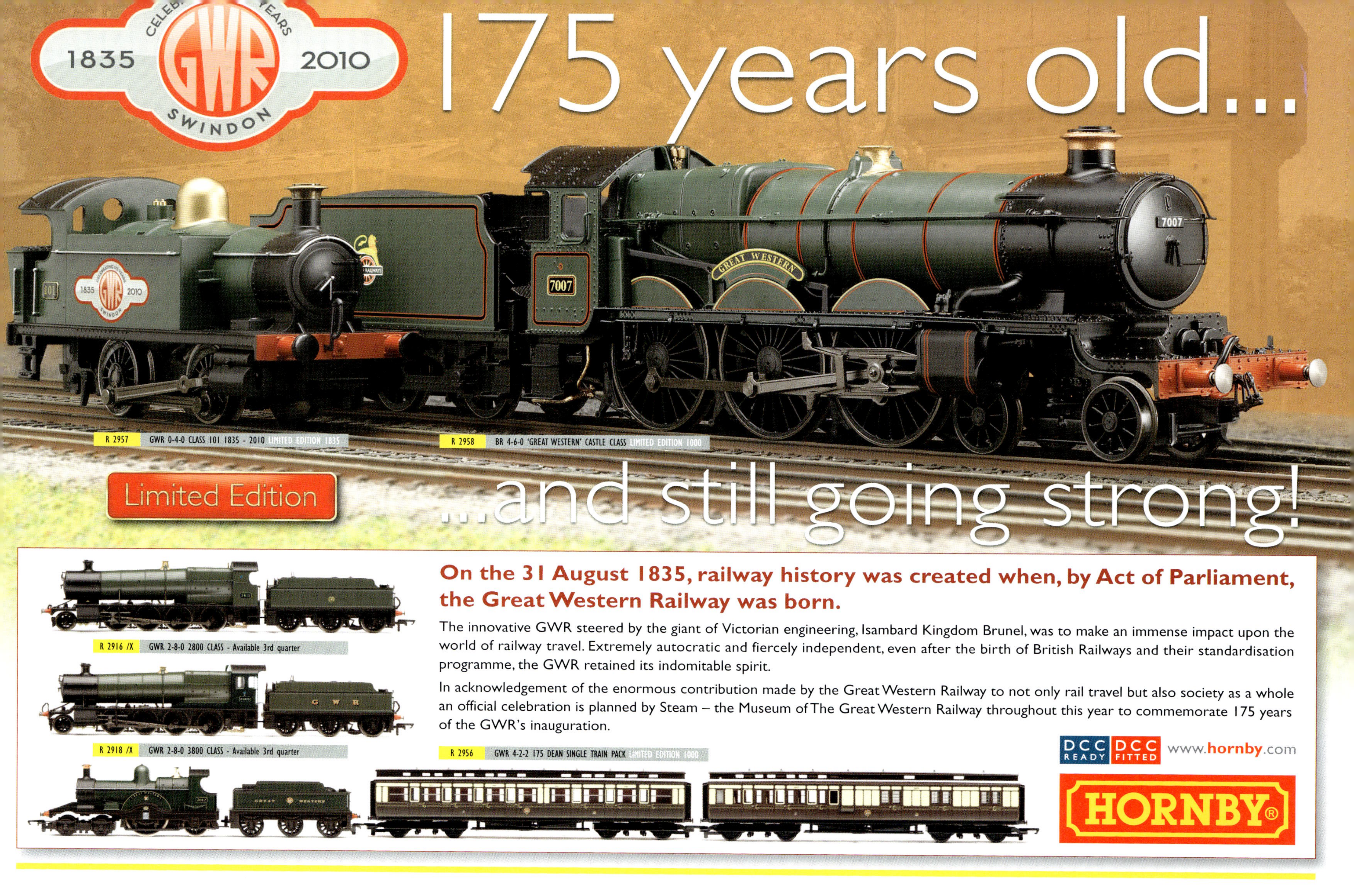

175 years old...
...and still going strong!

On the 31 August 1835, railway history was created when, by Act of Parliament, the Great Western Railway was born.

The innovative GWR steered by the giant of Victorian engineering, Isambard Kingdom Brunel, was to make an immense impact upon the world of rail travel. Extremely autocratic and fiercely independent, even after the birth of British Railways and their standardisation programme, the GWR retained its indomitable spirit.

In acknowledgement of the enormous contribution made by the Great Western Railway to not only rail travel but also society as a whole an official celebration is planned by Steam – the Museum of The Great Western Railway throughout this year to commemorate 175 years of the GWR's inauguration.

Limited Edition

R 2957 GWR 0-4-0 CLASS 101 1835 - 2010 LIMITED EDITION 1835

R 2958 BR 4-6-0 'GREAT WESTERN' CASTLE CLASS LIMITED EDITION 1000

R 2956 GWR 4-2-2 175 DEAN SINGLE TRAIN PACK LIMITED EDITION 1000

R 2916 /X GWR 2-8-0 2800 CLASS - Available 3rd quarter

R 2918 /X GWR 2-8-0 3800 CLASS - Available 3rd quarter

DCC READY · DCC FITTED

www.hornby.com

HORNBY®

Paddington, the great terminus

While the extraordinary engineering feats of Isambard Brunel like Maidenhead Bridge, Box Tunnel and the Dawlish sea wall brought astonishment and admiration from far beyond these shores, the starting point of the GWR empire had been left as a basic and even shabby affair.

Paddington station as built, probably on the cheap to save money for other projects, comprised four platforms and a plain wooden arched truss-roofed trainshed in Bishop's Road in what was a rural village on the city outskirts. It was open to the elements at both sides, a stark contrast to the elegant Georgian station at Bath and the even more impressive original Bristol Temple Meads station.

By the 1840s, it was hopelessly outdated and could not cope with passenger volume, yet it was only in late 1850 that the GWR board agreed to finance a replacement built by Isambard.

Needless to say, he had already been working on the design, and drew much inspiration from Joseph Paxton's 'glasshouse technology' as seen in the Crystal Palace where the Great Exhibition of 1851 was held, although much of the architectural detailing was by Brunel's old friend Matthew Digby Wyatt.

The magnificent new terminus was built in the triangle between Praed Street and Eastbourne Terrace and included a trainshed 700ft long and 238ft wide, comprising the enormous wrought-iron arched roof spans supported by two rows of cylindrical columns cast-iron columns with 10 tracks, five to serve platforms and five to store stock.

The first train departed from the new station on 16 January 1854, while the station was still unfinished. The new arrival side saw its first trains on 29 May that year.

Aware of the need to offer luxury overnight accommodation just as rival the London & North Western Railway was doing with its two hotels at Euston, the GWR board decided to add one of their own at Paddington. The Great Western Royal Hotel, itself a major piece of architecture, with 112 bedrooms and 15 sitting rooms plus lounges, public rooms and restaurants, was opened on 8 June 1854 by Prince Albert and his guest the King of Portugal. In terms of size, comfort and amenities, it showed that the GWR was again setting the pace.

As traffic levels again roared, the capacity at the station was increased by taking out several stock sidings and building extra platforms.

Maurice Earley's photograph of Paddington's sweeping arches and roofs in the 1950s, with GWR 4-6-0 No 5018 *St Mawes Castle* waiting to depart. NRM

The departure of GWR war recruits from Paddington station, led by a Scottish regimental band, in 1915. NRM

Paddington in 1903, clerestory coaches abounding. GWT COLLECTION

The GWR station was linked by a footbridge to Bishop's Road station serving the Metropolitan Railway, which from 1863 conveyed passengers to and from the city centre. Paddington was the original western terminus of the Metropolitan Railway, the world's first underground railway, which was steam worked before it became electrified.

Major alternations to the new Paddington included station offices in 1881, additional departure platforms in 1885, and more arrival platforms in 1893, while the boom in traffic resulting from faster locomotives introduced during the Churchward era from Edwardian times onwards led to a new steel roof span added in 1915, followed by yet more platforms the following year.

On Armistice Day 1922, a memorial to GWR staff who died during World War One was unveiled by Viscount Churchill. Around 50 per cent of the GWR workforce joined the army during the First World War, and many did not return. Between the wars, the GWR was given Government finance to expand the station still further as a job creation scheme during the depression. At this point, Bishop's Road station became absorbed into the main station as the suburban platforms.

Paddington was a Luftwaffe target during World War Two, but there was only one major hit in 1944 when a 500kg bomb broke one of the roof ribs.

In the late 1980s, Isambard's triple-span roof was fully restored in a project lasting several years, greatly improving the station's visual impact and doing justice to both its remarkable design and designer.

Today, Paddington with its 14 platforms is the terminus for commuter trains to destinations such as Slough, Maidenhead, Reading and Swindon and inter-city services to Oxford, Bristol, Bath, Exeter, Plymouth, Cornwall, Worcester, Hereford, Cardiff and Swansea, and occasionally Birmingham services when Marylebone is unavailable, while the Heathrow Express services link it to Heathrow Airport. Paddington is also served by four underground lines, the Bakerloo, Circle, District and Hammersmith & City lines.

Inside the station are statues of Brunel and the children's fictional character Paddington Bear.

1922
Charles Collett succeeded Churchward. Chocolate and cream livery appeared on coaches, while vehicles like parcels vans and horse boxes which ran in passenger trains were often painted just chocolate brown.

Bow-ended coaching stock introduced in both 57 ft and 70 ft lengths.

The Grouping sees the Cardiff Railway, Cleobury, Mortimer & Ditton Priors Railway, Port Talbot Railway, Princetown Railway, Rhondda & Swansea Bay Railway, Rhymney Railway, Taff Vale Railway, West Somerset Railway, Brecon & Merthyr Railway, Burry Port & Gwendraeth Valley Railway and Neath & Brecon Railway taken over.

1923
'Cheltenham Spa Express' named.

Castle 4-6-0 No 4073 *Caerphilly Castle* appears and becomes new GWR flagship.

Beaconsfield West points and signals become operated by electric motors.

January: Alexandra (Newport & South Wales) Docks & Railway, Barry Railway, Vale of Glamorgan Railway, Cambrian Railways, Aberystwyth & Welsh Coast Railway, Llanidloes & Newtown Railway, Mawddwy Light Railway, Mid-Wales Railway Newtown & Machynlleth Railway, Oswestry, Ellesmere & Whitchurch Railway Oswestry & Newtown Railway, Tanat Valley Light Railway, Vale of Rheidol Railway, Van Railway, Welshpool & Llanfair Light Railway, Wrexham & Ellesmere Railway, South Wales Mineral Railway, Penarth Extension Railway, Penarth Harbour, Dock & Railway, Gwendraeth Valley Railways, Llanelly & Mynydd Mawr Railway, Didcot, Newbury & Southampton Railway, Midland & South Western Junction Railway, Swansea Harbour Trust, East Gloucestershire Railway, Exeter Railway, Forest of Dean Central Railway, Lampeter, Aberayron & New Quay Light Railway, Liskeard & Looe Railway, Ross & Monmouth Railway and Teign Valley Railway taken over at Grouping.

1924
Caerphilly Castle displayed alongside *Flying Scotsman* at the British Empire Exhibition at Wembley.

5600 class 0-6-2Ts appear.

Cars carried through Severn Tunnel as an alternative to Aust Ferry.

1 January: Powlesland & Mason (railway shunting contractors at Swansea Docks) taken over.

April: King George V and Queen Mary visit Swindon.

August: 20-ton minneral wagons for South Wales coal introduced.

Collett, Kings, Castles
and much more

GWR icon No 6000 *King George V* celebrated GWR 175 year by taking pride of place in the Great Hall at the National Railway Museum in York. ROBIN JONES

At the Grouping of 1923, the GWR empire was swelled by the addition of 560 miles of track, 18,000 employees and a further 700 locomotives, many of them decidedly non-standard and therefore not wanted.

In the same year, pre-war train speeds were restored, and with 400 ton loads now a regular occurrence, more powerful engines than the Star class were needed.

Taking over from the great Churchward as Chief Mechanical Engineer in January 22 was Charles Benjamin Collett, the son of a journalist, who joined the Swindon drawing office in May 1893 as a junior draughtsman, and by 1900 had worked his way up to become assistant manager of Swindon Locomotive Works. In 1912, he became works manager, a position he held for seven years before becoming Deputy Chief Mechanical Engineer in May 1919, having received an OBE for producing munitions during World War One.

Collett was not a great inventor, but was a magnificent innovator, and took Churchward's revolutionary designs and developed them towards their maximum potential.

Under him, Swindon Works was modernised and expanded to become the finest locomotive manufacturing and repair base in Britain, with vastly improved locomotive building techniques. By 1924, his department employed 45,000 people, with 14,000 of those employed at Swindon Works.

In the post-war years, the GWR experienced soaring demand for holiday traffic to the West Country, and invested heavily in its flagship Paddington-Penzance route.

GWR 4-6-0 No 6000 *King George V* being assembled at Swindon. GWT COLLECTION

Collett designed an updated version of the Stars, one which would conform to the weight limit allowed on the West of England line. An enlarged boiler with a greater evaporative rate, a bigger grate and increased diameter cylinders brought the nominal tractive effort to 31,625lb, making this Castle class the most powerful British express locomotive of its day.

The GWR board was delighted with the end product which emerged from Swindon in August 1923. The first of them, No 4073 *Caerphilly Castle*, was displayed alongside Sir Nigel Gresley's *Flying Scotsman* at the British Empire Exhibition at Wembley in 1924. King George V and Queen Mary visited Swindon Works on 28 April 1924, ascended the footplate of No 4082 *Windsor Castle*, which was heading the Royal Train, and the monarch 'drove' the locomotive to Swindon station.

Sister No 4079 *Pendennis Castle* achieved fame in its own right when it was loaned to the London & North Eastern Railway for trials against that company's new A1 Pacific class, which included No 4472 *Flying Scotsman*, the following year.

Pendennis Castle surprised LNER officials with its sparkling performances, particularly on heavy trains from King's Cross to Doncaster. The GWR then displayed *Pendennis Castle* alongside *Flying Scotsman* at the 1925 British Empire Exhibition, declaring it to be the most powerful passenger express locomotive in Britain.

Between 1923-50, 171 Castles were built, 16 of them rebuilds of Stars and one from the components of Pacific No 111 *The Great Bear*.

The first Castles appeared with a Star-type tender, and did not receive the high-sided 4000-gallon version until 1926. The average coal consumption of the Castles was one of the lowest in the country.

The class was found to be superbly able to haul express trains of more than 400 tons over the South Devon banks and the twisting Berks & Hants route.

Castles hauled the 'Cheltenham Spa Express' which in its day was the fastest train in the world. From 1932, it was timed to cover the 77.3 miles from Swindon to Paddington in 65 minutes, an average speed of 71.4mph.

No 5006 *Tregenna Castle* achieved a record on 6 June 1932, by hauling the up 'Cheltenham Flyer' from Swindon to Paddington in 56 minutes 47 seconds for the 77.3 miles, against a schedule that was normally 65 minutes.

No 4073 *Caerphilly Castle*, in works grey. GWT COLLECTION

Three classic GWR 4-6-0s together at Tyseley Locomotive Works during an open day in June 2009: No 4936 *Kinlet Hall*, No 7029 *Clun Castle* and No 4953 *Pitchford Hall*. ROBIN JONES

The class deservedly gripped the public imagination, particularly those of schoolboy trainspotters.

The design of later Castles was slightly modified by Collett's successor Frederick Hawksworth, giving them a larger straight-sided all-welded tender, while other members of the class were fitted with larger superheaters and double blastpipes and chimneys.

Nine of the class have been preserved: Nos 7029 *Clun Castle*, 4073 *Caerphilly Castle*, 4079 *Pendennis Castle*, 5029 *Nunney Castle*, 5043 *Earl of Mount Edgcumbe*, 5051 *Earl Bathurst*, 5080 *Defiant* and 7027 *Thornbury Castle*.

While the Castles had been designed to the maximum permitted axle loading of 19½ tons, Collett considered such a limit to be a disadvantage, and that the locomotives did not fully address the problems encountered by the heavy, long-distance, non-stop passenger train.

He indicated to company chairman Sir Felix Pole that if the limit was raised to 22½ tons, a more powerful machine could be produced. Pole told him to design a 'Super Castle' capable of hauling heavier passenger expresses at average speeds around 60mph and so Collett came up with the ultimate in GWR motive power…the Kings.

The class of 30 Kings was exactly what the GWR needed after its 1926 rival the Southern Railway introduced its Lord Nelson class of 4-6-0s, which bettered the 31,625lb

Charles Benjamin Collett. GWR

nominal tractive effort of the Castles with 33,510lb. By contrast, the Kings, a larger version of the Castles, had a tractive effort of 40,290 lb.

Collett lengthened the firebox and boiler barrel of the Castle, increasing their diameter by 3in, extended the wheelbase, enlarged the grate and slightly enlarged the cylinders. The Kings' 6ft 6in driving wheel diameter was 2½ins less than the standard for GWR express passenger engines.

The Kings became famous among crews for their surefootedness, their tremendous weight-pulling capability, their excellent adhesion, safe running and the fact that they were nevertheless light on coal. It was the ultimate British 4-6-0 design.

One big difference between the appearance of the Kings and other Swindon engines was in the bogie design, which had outside bearings for the leading axle and inside bearings for trailing to give adequate clearance on curves. They also had a boiler pressure of 250lb per sq in, an increase of 25lb over Swindon standards of the day.

Class members were named after kings of England. The first, No 6000 *King George V*, appeared from Swindon Works in 1927 and was sent by the GWR on a tour of North America. The locomotive was presented with a brass bell by the impressed Americans to mark the great occasion.

LMS Chief Mechanical Engineer William Stanier, a former Swindon Works manager, based his Princess Royal class on the Kings,

The GWR briefly experimented with streamlining in a bid to upstage the LNER. In 1935, 6014 *King Henry VII* and the 4-6-0 *Manorbier Castle* both received air-smoothed casings, but by 1943, they were almost back to normal. The Great Western only ever flirted with streamlining – mainly to upstage the LNER. GWT COLLECTION

Another superb performance on the Bristol & Exeter Railway route in modern times sees Collett Castle 4-6-0 No 5051 *Earl Bathurst* cross the artificial Huntspill River, dug in World War Two to supply water to a secret armaments factory, with Past-Time Rail's 'Torbay Express' on 5 September 2004. DAVID HOLMAN

enlarging the boiler and firebox and turning the 4-6-0 wheel arrangement into a Pacific.

The Kings made the London to Plymouth express the longest non-stop run in the country.

However, the big disadvantage was that while they could indeed haul longer trains, not enough platforms had been lengthened to accommodate them.

With a weight of 22½ tons, the Kings were restricted to the Paddington-Taunton-Plymouth and Paddington-Birmingham-Wolverhampton main lines, which they were given clearance to use only after bridge strengthening had taken place.

When No 6018 King *Henry VI* failed to produce spectacular results on the King's Cross-Leeds route during British Railways' Locomotive Exchanges of 1948, its supporters claimed that the problem lay with the South Yorkshire coal. Subsequently, Swindon stepped up work on four-row superheaters and improvements to the draughting arrangement and successfully tried out these modifications to No 6001 *King Edward VII* in July 1953. Afterwards, double blastpipes and double chimneys were fitted to No 6015 *King Richard III* in September 1955; the whole class was modified.

Raw power unleashed by Collett: GWR 4-6-0s Nos 6849 *Walton Grange* and 5065 *Newport Castle* climb Hemerdon Bank, one of the gradients which caused Brunel to consider atmospheric traction instead of steam, with an Up express on 14 June 1958. TB OWEN/6880 BETTON GRANGE LTD

Friendly rivalry: King No 6011 *King James I* heads an express from Taunton and Castle No 4085 *Berkeley Castle* on a stopping train race through Sonning Cutting in 1930. GWT COLLECTION

Severn Valley Railway-based GWR 4-6-0 No 7802 *Bradley Manor*, a regular main line performer in recent times, recreated the 'Cambrian Coast Express', a named train long associated with the class, at Minehead on the West Somerset Railway on 19 September 1994. ALAN MEADE/WSR

1925
Locomotive exchange trials with the LNER.

1926
Railways affected by the General Strike from midnight on 3 May until 14 May. *Launceston Castle* went to LMS for trials.

1927
July: GWR 4-6-0 No 6000 *King George V* appears and makes maiden trip with the 'Cornish Riviera Express' before being shipped to the USA for the Baltimore & Ohio centenary celebrations.
New station for Newton Abbot.

1928
Hall 4-6-0s appear.
Royal Assent for a GWR Bill for company's involvement in the Western National and South Wales Motors bus companies.
First of 163 'modern' auto coaches appear.

1929
Sir Felix Pole resigned as chairman.
5700 class 0-6-0 pannier tanks appear.

1930
Major extension of automatic train control authorised.
2251 class 0-6-0s appear.

1931
Cogload flyover brought into use after main line between Cogload and Taunton quadrupled.
City of Truro withdrawn and sold to LNER for new York railway museum.
Ocean Saloons built for Plymouth to London 'Ocean Mail' trains.
6100 class 2-6-2Ts appear.
Container wagons introduced.
7 February: Passenger services on Welshpool & Llanfair Light Railway withdrawn.
April: GWR air service inaugurated between Cardiff and Haldon in April.

1932
The 1931 quadrupling was extended from a new station at Taunton to Norton Fitzwarren.
6 June: No 5006 *Tregenna Castle* sets world stop-to-start speed record with the 'Cheltenham Flyer', reaching 81.6mph between Swindon and Paddington).
6400 class 0-6-0PTs, 4800 (later 1400) class 0-4-2Ts and 5400 class 0-6-0PTs appear.
Cardiff General station rebuilt.

The Kings were all withdrawn by 1962, replaced by the less powerful Western Region diesel hydraulics, which they could easily outperform.

Three Kings have been saved from preservation, including *King George V*, No 6023 *King Edward II* and No 6024 *King Edward I*.

The 4-6-0 story did not stop there. Collett was asked to produce an all-round locomotive to replace the Churchward 4300 class 2-6-0s.

He decided to upgrade the Saint 4-6-0s, using No 2925 *Saint Martin* as a guinea pig, and reducing the driving wheel diameter from 6ft 8½in to 6ft. So were born the Halls, hailed as the first true all-purpose mixed-traffic 4-6-0. Popular with locomotive crews because of their versatility – they could tackle anything from slow freight to express trains – they became the most numerous GWR tender locomotive, with 259 built from 1928.

Under Hawksworth, the design was altered to include modifications to the frames, cylinders and saddle, with larger three-row superheaters fitted at first. These examples became known as Modified Halls, and 71 were built between 1944 and 1950.

As a postwar experiment, 11 Halls were briefly converted to oil burning in 1946/7.

Eighteen passed into preservation, 11 Halls and seven Modified Halls, Nos 4920 *Dumbleton Hall*, 4930 *Hagley Hall*, 4936 *Kinlet Hall*, 4942 *Maindy Hall*, 4953 *Pitchford Hall*, 4965 *Rood Ashton Hall*, 4979 *Wootton Hall*, 5900 *Hinderton Hall*, 5952 *Cogan Hall*, 5967 *Bickmarsh Hall*, 5972 *Olton Hall*, 6960 *Ravenglass Hall*, 6984 *Owsden Hall*, 6989 *Wightwick Hall*, 6990 *Witherslack Hall*, 6998 *Burton Agnes Hall*, 7903 *Foremarke Hall* and 7927 *Willington Hall*. Ironically, *Maindy Hall* is being used to undo Collett's innovation under a Great Western Society project to back-convert it into a Saint!

In 1936, Collett developed the Hall design to produce a smaller version, the 6880 class, which had a wider route availability. He oversaw the building of 80 of these successful engines, known as the Granges, until World War Two ended production of them permanently in 1939.

Next off the drawing board was a lighter version, the 7800 Manor class 4-6-0, of which 30 were built between 1930-50.

Preserved are Nos 7802 *Bradley Manor*,

Modified Hall No 7918 *Rhose Wood* Hall powers through Wilmcote on the last GWR main line route to be built, the line from Birmingham to Stratford-upon-Avon, which saw heavy freight until its closure in 1976 and lifting in 1979. MICHAEL MENSING/BIRMINGHAM RAILWAY MUSEUM

WR 4-6-0 No 7827 *Lydham Manor*, long the flagship of the Paignton & Dartmouth Steam Railway, heads past Goodrington Sands en route to Kingswear. DARTMOUTH STEAM RAILWAY & RIVERBOAT COMPANY

Preserved are Nos 7802 *Bradley Manor*, 7808 *Cookham Manor*, 7812 *Erlestoke Manor*, 7819 *Hinton Manor*, 7820 *Dinmore Manor*, 7821 *Ditcheat Manor*, 7822 *Foxcote Manor*, 7827 *Lydham Manor* and 7828 *Odney Manor*.

Collett's 2251 class of 120 0-6-0 tender engines replaced the Armstrong and Dean goods locomotives in use on routes in mid-Wales. Six of the class, Nos 2281-86, were built with tenders from the Aberdare class that they had replaced.

They were primarily used as short-haul main line trains and branch passenger services.

The only example to be preserved is No 3205, at the South Devon Railway.

Collett's fame did not begin and end with the big-glamour express locomotives. He was also responsible for the mass production of one of the most immediately recognisable and mass-produced small British locomotives of all – the six-wheeled pannier tank.

Collett did not invent the pannier tank, named thus because of the way in which the water tanks are carried either side of the boiler, like panniers on a donkey. Its origins lay in Victorian times, when the mixed-gauge era GWR turned out many different sizes of saddle tank. With the introduction of Belpaire fireboxes to the 0-6-0 tank engines of the time, saddle tanks became too difficult to fabricate. The GWR did not particularly favour side tanks, and many saddle tanks built between 1870-1905 were converted to pannier tanks in the years leading up to World War One.

Collett saw only too well that this ageing tank engine fleet needed to be superseded. Using the 2721 of 1897 as a starting point, he added Belpaire fireboxes, closed cabs and large extended bunkers, and in 1929 he unveiled a new type of pannier tank which would become the standard GWR shunter.

It was the 5700 series, of which 863 examples were eventually built, that was the second most produced class of steam British locomotive. Because of the volume, they were numbered in nine different series: 3600-99, 3700-99, 4600-99, 5700-99, 6700-79, 7700-99, 8700-99, 9600-82, 9701-99.

With diesel shunters taking over their duties, the panniers were withdrawn between 1957-65, but 13 were sold to London Transport for use on the Underground, where they operated until 1971, while others found their way into

GWR 4-6-0 No 6024 *King Edward I* celebrated its 75th birthday in July 2005. On 4 June that year, it is seen heading past Froxfield and the Kennet & Avon canal which the GWR owned with Steam Dreams' 'Cathedrals Express' to Weymouth. DAVID HOLMAN

Sole surviving GWR Dukedog 4-4-0 No 9017 *Earl of Berkeley* heads a photo charter goods train over Freshfield Bank on the Bluebell Railway on 4 November 2004. GEOFF SILCOCK

Sixteen of them are preserved: Nos 3650, 3738, 4612, 5764, 5775, 5786, 7714, 7715, 7752, 7754, 7760, 9600, 9629, 9642, 9681 and 9682.

The 5400 class was similar to the 5700s, but with smaller wheels and boiler.

The six-strong 1366 class of pannier tank were built in 1934 for dock working, including the haulage of the 'Channel Islands Boat Express' along the Weymouth harbour branch. No 1369, which in the early 60s replaced the antiquated Beattie well tanks on the Wenford goods branch in Cornwall, is the only one preserved.

Hawksworth built another 210 panniers between 1946-56.

The 9400 series, they were a tank engine version of Collett's 2251 class 0-6-0 tender engine and, designed for heavy shunting and local freight and passenger duties, were the heaviest of all the pannier classes. Two are preserved, No 9400 which is on static display at Swindon's STEAM museum and No 9466, which is privately owned.

In 1949, the 1500 class appeared, differing from the panniers that had gone before because of their outside cylinders, Walschaerts valve gear and lack of running platform. In addition, most of the separate parts were welded instead of riveted together.

Only one survives, No 1501, on the Severn Valley Railway.

Hawksworth's final pannier was the more traditional 1600 class, based on the 2021 class of 1901, of which only one survives, No 1638, on the Kent & East Sussex Railway.

Another Collett tank engine class was the 5600 0-6-2Ts. When the GWR inherited an assorted collection of 0-6-2Ts from the pre-Grouping coal-carrying companies of South Wales, it kept this traditional wheel arrangement for a new breed of heavy freight engines designed to do the same job, but using standard GWR parts. The distinctive feature is the smokebox overhanging the buffer beam.

A total of 200 were built between 1924-8. Nine are still with us, Nos 5619, 5637, 5643, 5668, 6619, 6634, 6686, 6695 and 6697.

Finally, Collett went way back into the history books to come up with a 'new' class of 4-4-0s in 1936/7. He combined parts of the old Duke and Bulldog classes to build the Earls or Dukedogs for use on the Cambrian Coast Line. Because of their ancestry, they were decidedly Victorian in appearance.

Around the same time, certain GWR directors had asked for their names to be carried by a new breed of glamour locomotive. Collett despised pomposity, and accordingly named these revived antiques after them.

When the same directors gathered at Paddington to welcome the arrival of the first Dukedog, they were understandably horrified. The nameplates were subsequently fitted to Castles, but by then Collett had proved his point.

It was not all plain sailing for Collett, for during his years in office, the GWR had to contend with the General Strike of 1926 and the great depression of the 30s, when the slump in South Wales coal production hit the company hard. The rising cost of coal was one reason for the GWR introducing diesel railcars in 1933 (see pages 74-79). At the same time, there was increasing competition from road traffic.

Nonetheless, in 1935, the GWR made history by becoming the first British railway to celebrate 100 years of corporate existence.

World War Two found the GWR at the heart of the action, with Swindon Works building locomotives for the war effort to the designs of other companies, such as William Stanier's LMS 8F 2-8-0. A hundred Dean Goods 0-6-0s were reconditioned for service overseas.

Instead of majoring on coal trains to supply the navy, the GWR provided trains for evacuees into the safer West Country. From London's Ealing Broadway, 163 trains took 112,994 young evacuees over just four days.

Major stations hit by Luftwaffe raids included Bristol, Birmingham, Birkenhead and Plymouth as well as Swindon; but serious damage also occurred at the South Wales docks, especially Swansea.

Collett 0-6-2T No 6695 on the turntable at Minehead on the West Somerset Railway. JUSTIN KERR-PETERSON/WSR

The GWR Exeter Home Guard on parade in 1941. GWR

"Cheer Churchill, vote Labour" was the General Election-winning slogan in 1945 which brought in the Attlee government, with sweeping plans for nationalisation in many sectors of industry, including the railways, which passed into public ownership, for better or worse, on 1 January 1948.

Hawksworth was therefore the last GWR Chief Mechanical Engineer, taking over when Collett retired in 1941. Ironically, he was the only one to be born in Swindon, on 10 February 1884, joining the company on 1 August 1898 as a works apprentice at the age of 15.

The war effort limited his abilities to produce much that was new, with Swindon Works turned over to producing munitions at the rate of 2500 shells a week and other supplies for the military effort, including aircraft components, parts for tanks, armoured cars and midget submarines, naval guns, ambulance trains and landing craft for D-Day, carried out under a shroud of great secrecy.

Because of this, Hawksworth's plan for a second GWR Pacific never left the drawing board.

He is best remembered for his County 4-6-0, basing its boiler on that of the 8F, with a new bigger capacity boiler than the No 1 fitted to the Halls, 6ft 3in driving wheels and 280lb per square inch boiler pressure and a continuous splasher over the driving wheels.

The first of the 30 members of the class, No 1000 *County of Middlesex*, emerged from Swindon in August 1945.

Following modifications over the next decade, they became popular with crews. They excelled on the South Devon banks because of their tractive effort at high speed.

Hawksworth stepped down as Chief Mechanical Engineer at nationalisation, but worked in locomotive design for British Railways until his retirement in 1949. He died in 1976.

At nationalisation, the GWR had 3737 route miles, 6577 miles of running lines, 9244 miles of track including sidings, 3857 steam engines, 37 diesel units, 8368 coaches, 87,403 wagons, 16 harbours, docks or wharves owned or partly owned and a workforce of 113,601.

GWR 4-6-0 No 6028 *King George VI* heads the Down 'Cornish Riviera' through Newbury on 30 July 1949. GWT COLLECTION

Hawksworth 4-6-0 No 1002 *County of Berks* in its Swindon Works birthplace on 26 April 1959. RC RILEY/GWS

1933
Experimental AEC diesel railcar No1 debuts on Paddington-Didcot services.
March: Westbury and Frome avoiding lines opened.
Special motor car vans appear.
11 April-30 September: GWR air service from Plymouth's Roborough Airport to Haldon and Cardiff launched.
22 May: Air service was extended from Cardiff to Birmingham's Castle Bromwich Aerodrome.
December:
19 December: Churchward knocked down by a steam locomotive on a foggy day while crossing tracks close to Swindon Works. He is buried in the churchyard at Christ Church, Swindon.

1934
7200 class 2-8-2Ts and 136 0-6-0PTs introduced.
3 January: Death of Lord Victor Albert Charles Spencer Churchill, born 1864, who joined GWR board in 1905, and had been chairman since 1908.
Express diesel railcar service introduced from Cardiff to Birmingham.

1935
Grange 4-6-0s appear.
9 September: 'The Bristolian' introduced.
New 'Cornish Riviera Express' stock introduced to mark GWR centenary.
Bristol Temple Meads rebuilt.
31 August: Special GWR centenary celebrations in Bristol.
30 October: GWR centenary celebrations in London.

1937
GWR Staff Association formed out of the Great Western Social and Educational Union.

1938
Manor 4-6-0s appear.

1939
Report on Taunton-Penzance electrification published.
1 September: Takeover of railways by the Government and the evacuation of children began as World War Two starts.

1940
GWR orders gas turbine locomotive.
June: GWR ships help in the evacuation of Dunkirk, with *St Helier* making seven round trips.
4 November: Crash at Norton Fitzwarren killing 27 and injuring 56, with No 6007 *King William III* scrapped.

A trickle to a torrent

A GWR steam railmotor waits at Chalford station on the Golden Valley route where such vehicles made a resounding impact. GWT COLLECTION

GWR steam railmotor No 93 at Clevedon. The branch from Yatton may have passed into history, but not so No 93! GWS

Look around Britain's railway network today and where, heritage steam services apart, will you see the equivalent of a King, Castle, Hall, Grange or Manor?

Passenger services today are largely dependent on multiple units, diesel or electric, where the traction unit is incorporated into a coach body to form a driving motor coach or trailer. Locomotive-hauled timetabled services nowadays are few and far between. Indeed, the Class 43 High Speed Train has been part and parcel of the original GWR main line for over a third of a century.

Today's diesel multiple units, both the inter-city and cross-country versions as well as those used on local services, can trace their ancestry back to one of the humblest types of GWR traction that has been largely forgotten since the 1930s, and yet may well be deemed to have had a far bigger impact on the future shape of railways than any illustrious record-breaking express passenger locomotives or named trains.

The steam railmotor was an entity in which the steam locomotive was built into the carriage in the form of a motor bogie, and which could be driven from either end, eradicating the need for running round or turning.

The GWR did not invent the railmotor, the origins of which can be traced back to an experimental broad gauge self-propelled steam carriage designed by William Bridges Adams and which was tested on the West London Railway in 1848. Two years later, it was used on the Bristol & Exeter Railway's Clevedon and Tiverton branches, and was given the number 29. Seating 16 first class and 32 second class passengers, it was recorded as having reached 52mph; however, in 1951, the carriage section was removed and the steam bogie rebuilt as a shunting locomotive.

The idea was taken up at the start of the 20th century with the Taff Vale Railway experimenting with battery-electric and petrol-electric railcars. The GWR itself drew up plans for a petrol railcar in 1903 but took it no further.

The Swindon empire, however, was impressed with the steam railmotor concept, and built 99 between 1904 and 1908 for use both in suburban and rural areas. Economical to run, they were superb for lightly used branch lines with unmanned halts, and could provide additional services

Dawn of the modern age? The bus-like interior of a GWR steam railmotor. GWS

between normal scheduled services along with extra stops. They could also haul one purpose-built trailer or an ordinary coach.

One route famously associated with railmotors was the Golden Valley line in Gloucestershire between Chalford and Stonehouse, where they were held responsible for a 597 per cent increase in passenger numbers.

However, if the locomotive unit had to be repaired, the whole vehicle had to be withdrawn, often needing the whole body to be lifted off, and servicing in engine sheds led to problems with cleanliness of the passenger accommodation.

Also, the GWR steam railmotors were a victim of their own success. As they boosted passenger numbers, it was soon found that they were unable to cope with demand. Accordingly, by the beginning of World War One, some steam railmotors began to be withdrawn, with their coach bodies converted to auto trailers, special coaches with a driver's compartment at one end, so it was possible to control the steam locomotive pushing it from the other, with just the fireman remaining on the engine footplate. The auto train had the advantage that the locomotive could be used separately if required, while retaining the benefits of the steam railmotor, and so won the day. The conversion of the GWR railmotors was carried out over nearly two decades up to 1935.

With the concept by no means new to the company, the most familiar type of GWR autocoach was introduced in 1928, and became a trademark of branch lines, with 163 examples being built. In so many ways, the auto coach is the predecessor of the diesel multiple unit driving trailer.

Charles Collett took out the GWR history book to design a new class of locomotive to haul them, although several types of tank engine were fitted with auto-train apparatus.

He decided to update Armstrong's Wolverhampton-built 517 class 0-4-2Ts, which appeared in 1879, with several still in traffic in the 30s and the last, No 848, being withdrawn in 1945.

Collett's new class of 75 locomotives, built between 1932-36, was first numbered 4800-74, and they were fitted with auto gear. A later batch of 20 were not auto fitted, and became the 5800 class. After several 2800 class 2-8-0s were experimentally converted to oil burning, they were renumbered in the 4800 series, and Collett's original class bearing that number sequence became 1400, with the members renumbered accordingly.

Yet as they were being built, a new form of traction which combined the advantages of both the railmotor and auto train appeared, one which would eventually make the 1400s redundant.

Steam railmotor No 61 and its trailer. GWS

1941
Collett retires and is replaced by FW Hawksworth.
April/May: Severe bombing at Plymouth.

1942
Gloucester-Cheltenham widened to four tracks.

1944
Modified Hall 4-6-0s appear.

1945
Hawksworth County 4-6-0s appear.

1946
New 64ft Hawksworth coaches came into service.
Fluorescent lights tried in new coaches.
First GWR oil-fired steam locomotive appeared

1947
Transport Act is given Royal Assent for the nationalisation of Britain's railways.
Special demonstration of GWR's automatic train control system.
9400 class 0-6-0PTs appear.

1948
1 January: The nationalisation of Britain's railways. Locomotive Exchanges subsequently take place.
Hawksworth stepped down as Chief Mechanical Engineer.
5 March: Final meeting of the Great Western Railway Company.
20 August: Last Corris Railway train runs.

1949
New Western Region took over the former LNWR lines in South and Central Wales.
WR receives gas turbine locomotives No 18000 from Brown Boverie and No 18100 from Metropolitan Vickers.
1500 and 1600 class 0-6-0PTs introduced.
Hawksworth retires from locomotive design.
British Transport Commission created the Branch Lines Committee with a remit to close the least-used branches.
23 December: Great Western Railway Company formally wound up.
December: First 4400 class small prairie to be withdrawn was No 4402.

GWR railcar No 2 in its early days in service. GWT COLLECTION

GWR railcar W22W in the broad gauge transfer shed at Didcot Railway Centre. FRANK DUMBLETON/GW

As stated above, other companies had considered the idea of railmotors powered by internal combustion engines rather than steam. The North Eastern Railway introduced two petrol-electric railcars in 1903.

The diesel railcar took the concept one stage further, and here it was the GWR that in 1933 found itself yet again at the forefront of progress.

CF Cleaver of Hardy Railmotors Limited, a subsidiary of the Associated Equipment Co Ltd (AEC), saw that the 130bhp six-cylinder AEC diesel engine, which had been so successful in London buses and other commercial vehicles, could power a lightweight self-contained railcar. It would be even more effective if the railcar had aerodynamic streamlining.

The body of Cleaver's first prototype was based on the Deutsche Reichsbahn 'Flying Hamburger' diesel unit. However, after undergoing wind tunnel tests at the Chiswick laboratory of the London Passenger Transport Board, it was transformed into an 'art deco' streamlined design.

The 69-seater body was built by Park Royal Coachworks of Willesden, another AEC subsidiary, and the finished vehicle had a maximum speed of 63mph with control shared between the ends of the railcar.

Impressed, the GWR bought the railcar before it was finished, and showed it at the International Commercial Motor Transport Exhibition at Olympia in November 1933, generating immense public interest. Its rounded lines led to it being nicknamed the 'Flying Banana' while officially named Railcar No 1.

Its first official journey, from Paddington to Reading, took place on 1 December 1933. Three days later, it entered public service, running from Slough shed to Windsor and Didcot.

Having completed 60,000 miles and carried 136,000 passengers in its first year alone, the GWR board was so pleased that it ordered six of the railcars from AEC, which made improvements including the instalment of two AEC 8.85-litre diesel engines, thereby raising the maximum speed to 80mph.

Three units were fitted with a buffet bar for use as an express businessman's service between Birmingham and Cardiff and entered service on 16 July 1934.

History was made again: the trio comprised Britain's first regular diesel working run to a fast schedule in Britain with the 117½ miles between the two cities completed in two hours 20 minutes.

Eventually, 38 GWR railcars were built, 20 of them at Swindon, and with several variations including parcels cars and vehicles fitted with drawgear for hauling vans.

The expansion of the fleet was impeded by World War Two, but the success of railcars was noticed way outside the Swindon empire. A committee set up after nationalisation in 1948 to consider British Railways' future motive power requirements recommended in 1952 the diesel railcar should be developed for local and branch line services, as they could cut costs on unprofitable routes.

Whitehall then approved the spending of £1.5-million on the first eight Derby 'lightweight' two-car diesel multiple units, which appeared in 1954. The next year, the BER Modernisation Plan authorised the immediate construction of a huge fleet of both DMUs and railcars from both BR workshops, including Swindon, and outside manufacturers.

Collett 0-4-2T auto tank No 1450 with matching auto coach W178 recreates a timeless GWR branch line scene, in this case on the Dean Forest Railway on 1 June 2004. GEOFF SILCOCK

The replica steam engine for under-reconstruction Railmotor No 93 steams for the first time. GWS

One heritage line where GWR auto trains have become a trademark is the South Devon Railway. In a timeless scene which might well be on any GWR country branch line of the 1930s, Collett 0-4-2T No 1420 heads an auto-train through Staverton station. GEOFF SILCOCK

While the Class 126 Swindon 'Inter-City' three and six-car 70mph DMUs were built in 1956 for Scottish Region use, the first six three-car sets operated until 1959 on the Western Region's Birmingham-South Wales services. The Swindon 'Cross-country' two car Class 120 DMUs appeared in October 1957, and totalled 194 cars comprising 58 sets for the Western Region and seven for the Scottish Region. Swindon also designed and built the Class six-car 124 DMUs for cross-Pennine services.

All of these paved the way for better and more sophisticated designs, including the Blue Pullman (see pages 98-99), with the evolutionary process still very much continuing today, in a world where the multiple unit reigns supreme.

The original GWR railcars were relegated to branch line duties, where they ousted many of the Collett auto trains in the 50s. The first withdrawals of 1400 class 0-4-2Ts came in 1956, and by spring 1961, the 5800 class had gone, none to survive.

The final four 1400s were taken out of traffic in November 1964. Four members of the class have been preserved: Nos 1420, 1442, 1450 and 1466. The last GWR railcars were withdrawn in the 60s, as branch line closure both before and after the Beeching Axe made them redundant.

Three were preserved: Swindon, 1940-built W20W at the Kent & East Sussex Railway (where on 3 February 1974 it worked the newly re-opened heritage line's first revenue-earning public train); W22W at Didcot Railway Centre and Park Royal 1934-built W4W at the STEAM Museum in Swindon.

The impact made by the GWR steam railmotor, the auto train and the early railcars should never be underestimated in historical terms. Britain reshaped the world with the invention of the steam engine, but also produced a series of developments to traction and rolling stock which did not grab headlines with record-breaking speed runs but subtly made an arguably wider and more profound impact in the longer term.

The first of these three forms of traction was rendered extinct in the 30s, but a GWR railmotor and a trailer are being recreated by a ground-breaking Great Western Society project officially launched at Didcot Railway Centre in 1998.

The body of 1908-built Railmotor No 93, converted to auto trailer No 212 at Swindon in May 1935 following withdrawal, is being equipped with a new steam bogie constructed at Tyseley Locomotive Works and an upright boiler manufactured by Israel Newton of Bradford, steamed in January 2007.

First allocated to London's Southall shed, No 93 had several spells working in the West Midlands from Stourbridge shed and around the Bristol area. It also had periods at Pontypool Road, Whitland, Croes Newydd, Gloucester, Reading and Taunton. Auto-trailer No 212 was withdrawn in May 1956, but survived by being converted by BR into a 'Work Study Coach' and being used in an office in Birmingham. The sole surviving example of a railmotor body, it was preserved at Didcot in 1970 after being obtained from Old Oak Common.

Trailer No 92 was built in September 1912 with a seating capacity of 70 persons. Condemned in 1957, it was obtained by the society in 1970 from Guest Keen Iron & Steel Works, East Moors, Cardiff, where it had been used as a mess room.

In June 2007, the Heritage Lottery Fund awarded £768,500 for the restoration of the original timber bodies and steel underframes of both vehicles at the Llangollen Railway.

When the two-car set finally reappears in as-built form, it will fill one of the biggest 'missing links' in British railway history, and provide an unsurpassed insight into the beginnings of modern main line trains.

*Anyone wishing to contribute to the Great Western Society's railmotor project is invited to send donations to: Steam Railmotor Fund, Great Western Society, Didcot Railway Centre, Oxfordshire OX11 7NJ.

A 1957-built Swindon Class 120 Cross-country DMU forms the 12.52pm Taunton-Minehead service, seen passing Leighwood crossing near Crowcombe, on 18 July 1970, the last year of British Rail operation of the GWR branch partially engineered by Isambard Brunel. Such units were the predecessors of today's modern DMU stock, and had an ancestry which could be traced back to the steam railmotor concept. HUGH BALLANTYNE

The Holiday Line

Coupled with improvements in working conditions in the great industrial conurbations towards the end of the 19th century, including the advent of statutory paid weeks holidays, the railways did more than anything to facilitate the development of the UK's holiday resorts.

The GWR found itself at a major advantage in this respect, for its Paddington-Penzance main line gave access to the sunniest and warmest part of England, the south-west peninsula, and a string of branch lines were built to serve burgeoning resorts which were rapidly developing out of harbour towns and rustic fishing villages as a result.

The jewel in the crown was the English Riviera of Torbay, served by a branch from Newton Abbot to Kingswear for Dartmouth – which had the distinction of being the only town with a station not to be served by trains. The station building lay on the south bank of the River Dart, and was accessed by GWR-operated ferry to the terminus at Kingswear on the opposite side of the River Dart.

In Somerset, the GWR served Clevedon, Weston-super-Mare and Minehead, while making an incursion into rival the Southern Railway's 'Sunny South' with the line to Weymouth.

Then there were the Cornish branches to Looe, Fowey, Padstow (a London & South Western Railway terminus also reached by the GWR via Bodmin Road and Bodmin General), Fowey, Newquay, Perranporth and St Agnes, Falmouth, Helston and St Ives.

In Wales, the GWR served major resorts on the west coast, Pwllheli, Criccieth, Barmouth, Tywyn and Aberystwth, and south coast, including Porthcawl, Barry, Tenby and Newquay.

As the Swindon transport brought fast travel to places which would have taken days to reach by stagecoach, it became increasingly clear that summer holiday and

Boy meets girl: this view from the GWR publicity department was posed by models while the train was stationary in a siding at Marazion, with St Michael's Mount in the background. NRM

Speed To The West is arguably the most iconic GWR poster of them all and dates from 1939. It was designed to promote the company's fast services to the West Country and shows a 'King' on a holiday train for the West Country. It was drawn by Charles Mayo, who worked in the GWR publicity department and produced artwork for posters, booklets and other publicity material. It is one of the most popular posters in the National Railway Museum's magnificent collection. NRM

daytrip traffic would be a major new market.

From its early days, the GWR had realised the enormous value of publicity and advertising in this field. In 1903, it began promoting itself as The Holiday Line.

In the still-embryonic days of cinema, the company produced its own film, *The Story of the Holiday Line*, which in 1914 was shown at the London Coliseum.

An annual publication called Holiday Haunts – listing the attractions of each resort covered by GWR lines – became a firm favourite. The GWR also produced several books on specific resorts, local history and folklore.

Perhaps best of all were the posters promoting travel to the tourist destinations both on the coast and inland. In recent times these posters have come to be recognised as works on art in their own right and originals can fetch sizeable four-figure sums at auction.

The train became seen by millions of people as the way to escape everyday life for one or two weeks in the sun, and in turn engendered much affection for the steam locomotive. Resorts all around Britain had miniature railways on the sea front, such was the fascination of steam to children of all ages. Many a lifelong passion for all things steam on steel wheels began with holidays by train at a tender age.

One area that the Great Western managed to attract widespread publicity was in the speed of its services to the far west, like the legendary 'Cornish Riviera Express' which was introduced in 1904.

The name has been applied to the late morning express from Paddington to Penzance continuously through nationalisation under British Railways and privatisation under First Great Western, interrupted only by two world wars. The name is also carried by the late morning express train running in the opposite direction from Penzance to London.

Through both its performance and attendant publicity, particularly during the GW heyday of the 1930s, it has become one of the most famous named trains of all.

Following the completion of the line that year, through trains from Paddington to Penzance began running on 1 March 1867 and included fast services such as the 10.15am 'Cornishman' and 11.45am 'Flying Dutchman' but these still took at least nine hours or more for the journey.

The new 'Cornish Riviera Express' cut down the number of stops, leaving Paddington at 10.10am and reaching Penzance at 5.10pm. It took six carriages including a dining car to Penzance, plus another coach for Falmouth that was detached at Truro. Other stops were made at Plymouth North Road, Gwinear Road for the Helston and St Erth for St Ives. The return train set out at 10am and also called at Devonport.

A public competition was announced in the August 1904 edition of *The Railway Magazine* to choose the name for the new service, attracting 1286 entries. Two entries, 'The Cornish Riviera Limited' and 'The Riviera Express' were amalgamated into the 'Cornish Riviera Express', although railwaymen referred to it as 'The Limited'.

Following the opening of a 20¼ mile shorter route along the Langport and Castle Cary Railway in 1906, the 'CRE' could set out 20 minutes earlier from Paddington.

Extra slip coaches were added to serve resorts such as Weymouth, Minehead, Ilfracombe and Newquay.

By the middle of World War One, the train had grown to 14 coaches, even running in two portions on summer Saturdays, but the train was suspended in January 1917 as a wartime economy measure.

The introduction of the Castles in 1923 greatly improved performances, and four years later the Kings appeared. They had been designed with particular regard to the West Country holiday traffic.

The GWR's Camp-Coach Holidays guide.

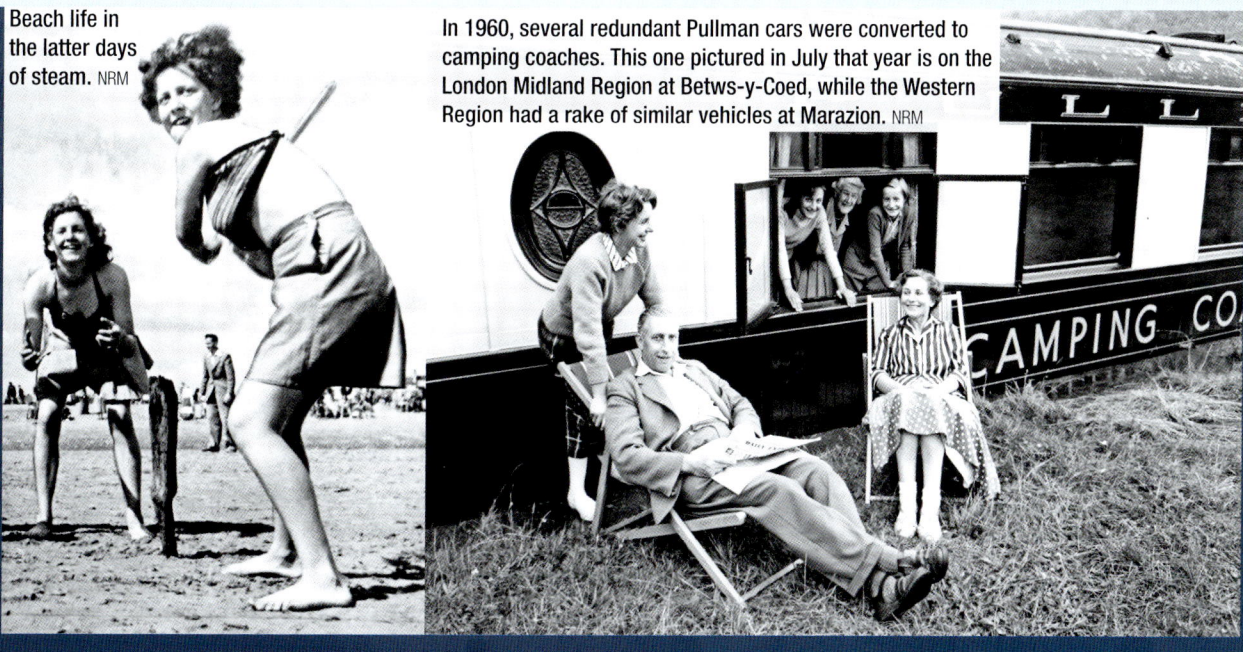

Beach life in the latter days of steam. NRM

In 1960, several redundant Pullman cars were converted to camping coaches. This one pictured in July that year is on the London Midland Region at Betws-y-Coed, while the Western Region had a rake of similar vehicles at Marazion. NRM

Despite World War Two, people still went on holiday, and in summer 1941, the 'CRE' ran in five sections, to Penzance, Paignton, Kingswear and Newton Abbot.

The service was dieselised in the late 50s and the introduction of the Western diesel hydraulics eventually cut the Paddington to Plymouth journey time to 3 hours 35 minutes. The last locomotive-hauled 'Cornish Riviera' ran on 5 August 1979 and was hauled by Class 50 No 50039 *Implacable*. The next day, locomotives were replaced by Class 43 InterCity 125 High Speed Trains.

Another express which became the focal point of the Paddington publicity machine was the 'Cheltenham Flyer' which in 1929 became the fastest train in the world, with a booked average speed of 66.2mph from Swindon to Paddington behind the powerful Castles, taking advantage of the level gradient of 'Brunel's billiard table.'

On 6 June 1932, pulled by No 5006 *Tregenna Castle*, the 'Cheltenham Flyer' covered the 77.25 miles at an average speed of 81.68mph start to stop, setting a new record for steam traction which astonished the world. As an aside, while *Tregenna Castle* the engine sadly no longer survives, its tender is intact and is stored at the Northampton & Lamport Railway.

The GWR publicity department did not stop at posters, but produced a whole range of merchandise to promote its image. There was a series of 44 jigsaws produced from 1924 onwards, priced at 2/6d, barely covering costs, but around a million puzzles were sold. Manufactured by the Chad Valley toy company in Harborne, Birmingham, those in good condition are now highly sought after collectors' items.

In the days when engine drivers and firemen were equivalent to the rock stars and Premier League footballers of today as far as boyhood idols were concerned, GWR produced a series of books for 'boys of all ages'. The mastermind behind these publications was Walter George Chapman, a member of the general manager's staff who joined the GWR in 1896.

His first book, *The 10.30 Limited* describing a non-stop run between Paddington and Plymouth on the

between Paddington and Plymouth on the 'Cornish Riviera Express', was published in August 1923 at five shillings. It was a publisher's dream, selling 71,000 copies in the first six months. Future books included Caerphilly Castle, The 'King' of Railway Locomotives, The Cheltenham Flyer, Track Topics and GWR Engines; names, numbers, types & classes, all of which were best sellers.

The best place to see these magnificent posters and publications is at the National Railway Museum at York, which holds as best a definitive collection as you might wish for. Access to them is through the museum's ground-breaking £4-million Search Engine facility, which, opened in January 2008, allows the public unprecedented access to the vast archives which had for so long remained inaccessible until now.

The Search Engine archives include tens of thousands of hidden treasures such as works of art, posters, film, photography and sound recordings, engineering drawings and documents such as letters and diaries.

The project has been funded by the Heritage Lottery Fund, the Higher Education Funding Council for England, the Department of Culture, Media and Sport and the Friends of the National Railway Museum.

The exhaustive Search Engine archives and small objects form the basis of the museum's Great Western Railway Reflections staged between 28 May and 1 November 2010 to mark GWR 175 year.

Many of the marvellous posters in this chapter are contained in the archives, and some can be bought as postcards of prints from the museum's excellent shop.

The free exhibition was designed to explore the image of the GWR through the technology, advertising and paraphernalia it produced.

All posters: NRM apart from 4 and 88.

GWR 4-6-0 No 6025 *King Henry IV* heads the 'Cornish Riviera Limited' through Reading West on July 1956. JOHN ASMAN/GWT COLLECTION

NRM exhibitions officer Ellen Tait said: "The GWR's changing identities, from the enthusiast's 'God's Wonderful Railway' to the company's own 'The Holiday Line', generated brand images which are still powerful today."

The GWR did much more than encourage people to ride on its trains to holiday destinations. It provided the accommodation too!

One innovation was the use of redundant rolling stock as self-catering accommodation. Old carriages, particularly wooden-bodied examples from the Victorian or Edwardian eras, were converted to provide basic sleeping and living space at country station sidings. The public could hire them for a week or two – provided that they travelled there by train.

Often, these carriages would be removed from their stations in the winter and be overhauled at the GWR's workshops ready to be returned in the spring.

Camping coaches were first introduced by the London & North Eastern Railway in July 1933, with the GWR following a year later, at first referring to them as "camp coaches". The relatively low rent of about £3 per week made them immediately popular.

After the 1940 season, they were taken out of service and used as temporary accommodation for railway staff or others in connection with the war effort. It was not until 1942 that camping coaches returned big time, although their numbers dwindled from the mid-1960s onwards after branch line closures and the reduction in numbers of station staff who would maintain them, while caravan parks became more widespread and better equipped and the public chose other forms of cost-effective holidays made possible by car ownership.

The last were offered to the public by the London Midland Region in 1971, but the Western Region retained several for their own staff at Dawlish Warren and Marazion.

In the past decade, the idea has been revived both on some heritage railways and by private individuals: a GWR broad gauge Travelling Post Office coach built in 1889, later converted to standard gauge and which ran in the 'Ocean Mail Special' behind *City of Truro* when it reportedly broke the 100mph barrier in 1904, stands at St German's station on the Plymouth-Paddington line and is let by Railholiday.co.uk, which also offers a BR Mk1 coach alongside Hayle station.

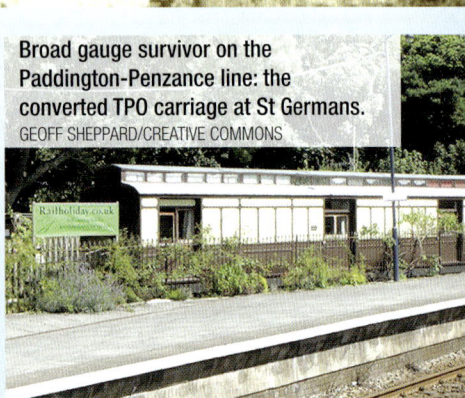

Broad gauge survivor on the Paddington-Penzance line: the converted TPO carriage at St Germans. GEOFF SHEPPARD/CREATIVE COMMONS

Paddington's platforms packed with holidaymakers on a summer Saturday in the late 1930s. ROBIN JONES COLLECTION

STEAM TRAINS FOR ALL SEASONS

Unwind behind a steam engine on the *West Somerset Railway*; let us take you on a leisurely journey between Bishops Lydeard (near Taunton) and Minehead. Take in the sights, the sounds and the unique smells of the golden age of rail travel as you wind your way along the 20 mile journey.

From the *on-board Buffet* available on most of our trains, enjoy hot or cold refreshments, many from the West Country. You can see the Quantock Hills and Exmoor National Park through the windows; notice the constantly changing views of the Glorious Somerset Countryside. Look out across the Bristol Channel with its islands and views of south Wales (you may even see the Brecon Beacons).

2010 SPECIAL EVENTS
Celebrating 175 years since the creation of the Great Western Railway

See the separate leaflets with full details available from our stations, also information on our website - www.West-Somerset-Railway.co.uk

August 1	Toys and Train Collectors Fair, at Minehead Station
August 7-8	Steam Fair & Vintage Vehicle Rally at Norton Fitzwarren
September 4-5	Late Summer Weekend - GWR 175 'The Penultimate Act'
September 11-12	CAMRA Real Ale Festival on the platform at Minehead
September 30 - October 3	Autumn Steam Gala - GWR 175 'The Finale'
December 3-4	Dunster by Candlelight
December 13, 14, 15	Carol Trains
December	Several Santa Trains
December 28-29	Winter Steam Festival

From Spring until early Autumn the Hestercombe Express runs every Wednesday - see our website for details

Advance booking recommended for all the above special events..

TIMETABLE 21 JULY - 3 SEPTEMBER 2010*

		Diesel	Steam	Steam	Steam	Steam	Diesel	Steam	Steam
BISHOPS LYDEARD	d	09.35	10.25	11.05	12.30	14.10	15.05	16.00	16.55
Crowcombe Heathfield	d	09.45	10.40	11.24	12.52	14.24	15.20	16.17	17.14
Stogumber	d	09.52	10.48	11.32	13.00	14.32	15.28	16.26	17.22
Williton	d	10.02	11.00	11.41	13.09	14.52	15.48	16.53	17.45
Doniford Halt (R)	d	10.05	11.04	11.44	13.13	14.55	15.52	16.56	17.48
Watchet	d	10.10	11.12	11.53	13.19	15.00	15.57	17.00	17.52
Washford	d	10.18	11.20	12.01	13.28	15.08	16.05	17.09	18.00
Blue Anchor	d	10.31	11.28	12.08	13.35	15.16	16.21	17.16	18.11
Dunster	d	10.38	11.36	12.15	13.41	15.23	16.28	17.23	18.17
MINEHEAD	a	10.44	11.42	12.21	13.48	15.29	16.34	17.30	18.23

		Steam	Diesel	Steam	Steam	Steam	Steam	Diesel	Steam
MINEHEAD	d	10.15	11.50	12.25	14.05	15.00	16.05	16.55	17.55
Dunster	d	10.21	11.57	12.32	14.12	15.06	16.12	17.02	18.03
Blue Anchor	d	10.30	12.10	12.40	14.19	15.19	16.20	17.18	18.10
Washford	d	10.38	12.17	12.48	14.27	15.27	16.29	17.26	18.18
Watchet	d	10.47	12.25	12.58	14.38	15.37	16.39	17.35	18.28
Doniford Halt (R)	d	10.51	12.29	13.02	14.42	15.40	16.43	17.38	18.32
Williton	d	11.00	12.33	13.11	14.55	15.46	16.50	17.44	18.37
Stogumber	d	11.12	12.41	13.23	15.07	15.58	17.02	17.52	18.48
Crowcombe Heathfield	d	11.21	12.50	13.32	15.20	16.15	17.11	18.01	18.57
BISHOPS LYDEARD	a	11.31	13.00	13.42	15.30	16.25	17.21	18.11	19.07

* A slightly reduced timetable operates on Saturdays, see our website or pick up a leaflet for details.

Steam Engineman Courses

Nurtured childhood dreams now become a reality . . . experience life on the footplate and know what it feels like to be a real fireman or engine driver. Treat somebody special to the thrill of a lifetime, or even yourself!
Contact us at Minehead

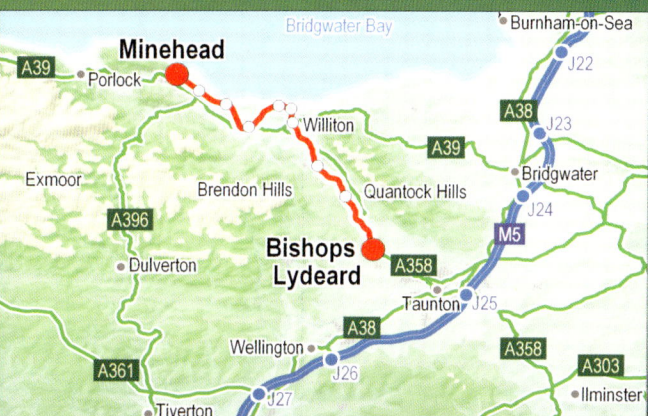

24 hour information & enquiries: 01643 704996
The West Somerset Railway, The Railway Station,
Minehead, Somerset TA24 5BG
E-mail: info@west-somerset-railway.co.uk
Web: www.west-somerset-railway.co.uk

The best value and most relaxing way to travel on the railway is by the
WSR ROVER TICKET
It affords unlimited travel and freedom for the whole family to explore for a whole day. Ask at the Booking Office.

D1010 *Western Campaigner* takes the Up 'Golden Hind' comprising an immaculate rake of British Railways Mk1 coaches over the Dawlish sea wall in May 1964. C WOODHEAD/COLOUR-RAIL DE 1578.

A world without steam

The words Great Western Railway immediately conjure up images of Stars, Castles and Kings, the big powerful glamorous main line express locomotives resplendent in Brunswick green.

Yet as with the rest of the world's major railway lines, it was not a question of whether steam would one day be replaced, but when.

As we have seen, Brunel tried to do exactly that with atmospheric traction in the 1840s.

As countries like the USA moved towards modernisation in the 30s – a process which would almost certainly have followed much sooner in Britain but for the intervention of World War Two and the years of austerity that followed – the GWR set the scene in 1933 with the successful introduction of diesel railcars on cross-country services.

In 1933, the GWR bought its first diesel shunter, appropriately numbered 1. Built by Fowler in 1933, this 0-4-0 with a 70hp engine was used at Swindon Works. It was withdrawn in 1940 and sold to the Ministry of Supply.

Next came No 2, an 0-6-0 350hp diesel electric shunter built by Hawthorn Leslie in 1936 and also allocated to Swindon. It was renumbered 15100 by British Railways in 1948, withdrawn in 1965 and scrapped early the following year.

The GWR wanted to modernise in the 30s, but no diesel locomotive that was powerful enough could be found. The Kings could deliver 2500hp, while the experimental London Midland & Scottish Railway diesels could produce 1300hp in service, so a pair would be needed to equal one 4-6-0.

Undeterred, the board opted for a gas turbine locomotive in 1940, and ordered one from Swiss manufacturer Brown Boveri, with an A1A-A1A wheel arrangement, a 2500hp turbine and a maximum speed of 90mph.

The GWR never saw the locomotive delivered, because it was held up by World War Two, and it was British Railways that finally took delivery of it in 1949, after nationalisation. It duly entered service on the Western Region.

The emphasis was on fuel economy so it had a heat exchanger to recover waste heat from the exhaust and was designed to run on cheap heavy fuel oil, the same fuel as used in steam locomotives that had been converted to oil burning as an experiment.

There was also an auxiliary diesel engine which provided power for starting the gas turbine. The diesel engine was capable of moving the locomotive at a slow speed when the gas turbine was not running. Normally, No 18000 was run from the shed to Paddington station using the diesel engine with the gas turbine started only a few minutes before the train was due to leave, saving fuel and minimising annoyance from noise and exhaust fumes.

No 18000, nicknamed 'Kerosene Castle' by crews, repeatedly suffered from running problems. Ash from the heavy fuel oil damaged the turbine blades, and the complex electrical control systems were extremely complex and gave much trouble to staff who were used only to a steam locomotive environment. While in WR service, one of the traction motors failed and instead of repairing or replacing it, it was taken out, leaving No 18000 with only three traction motors and stopping it from achieving its full power output. No 18000 also used more fuel than had been predicted.

When reliable operation could be achieved, it did live up to expectations. However, overall it fell a long way short of impressing the powers that be sufficiently for it to form a basis of future British Railways motive power.

In 1951, British Railways ordered a prototype main line gas turbine-electric locomotive from Metropolitan Vickers of Manchester. It, too, had been ordered by the GWR in the 40s, and delayed because of the war.

This second gas turbine locomotive, No 18100, spent its working life on the WR, operating express passenger services from Paddington. It had three main generators, each powering two traction motors. Unlike No 18000, there was no

Class 42 D803 *Albion* heads the 'Cornish Riviera Express' towards Teignmouth. PAUL CHANCELLOR COLLECTION

D601 *Ark Royal* arrives at Paddington with an express from Penzance on 2 August 1960. D OVENDEN/P CHANCELLOR COLLECTION

auxiliary diesel engine and the turbine was started by battery power, using the main generators as starter motors. It was used to pave the way for the electrification of the West Coast Main Line, including the testing of overhead line equipment and staff training. This purpose fulfilled, it was again placed into storage at the end of 1961, and not officially withdrawn until April 1968. It was scrapped at J. Cashmore in Great Bridge, West Midlands, in November 1972.

No 18000 was withdrawn at the end of 1960 and stored at Swindon Works before being returned to Europe for use as a testbed. However, in the early 1990s it returned to Britain minus its engines, and was preserved at Crewe Heritage Centre.

By the end of the 60s, other forms of modern traction were ousting steam big time from the GWR network…but the Swindon/Paddington empire was, just as in the days of Brunel's broad gauge, still doing its own thing apart from the rest of the country.

When the GWR became the GWR on 1 January 1948, those in office privately – and occasionally publicly – despite nationalisation refused to concede an inch of the Big Four company's long and proud tradition of independence.

Following the publication of the BR Modernisation Plan in 1955, which called for the eradication of steam and its replacement by diesel and electric traction, the WR, still regarded by many as being a straightforward continuation of the GWR, still carried sufficient clout to get its own way as far as its own territory was concerned, and indeed had already been looking in detail at building diesel hydraulics.

The Modernisation Plan called for the introduction of 2500 locomotives with initial orders for 171 machines, and was seen as taking Britain's railways into a modern age where it would have to compete much harder with road and even air transport.

However, its implementation was little short of a disaster. The estimated £1240-million cost was to be spread over 15 years, but the figure ended up far in excess of that.

Rather than opting for proven standard American designs, British Railways placed the orders for its diesel Pilot Scheme with home-based manufacturers, and then ordered batches of 10 or 20 locomotives without seeing a prototype built first.

While some of the early main line diesel classes were indeed successful, others ended up being withdrawn before the last steam locomotives on the national network.

In 1953/4, several WR executives visited the continent to see the first of a new breed of high-powered main line diesel hydraulics, the V200 series, entering service with the German Federal Railways.

Meanwhile, the North British Locomotive Company of Glasgow separately obtained licences to build German Voith hydraulic transmissions and MAN high-speed diesel engines.

Swindon officials were impressed by German calculations that the reduction in locomotive weight by using diesel hydraulic rather than diesel electric traction meant an increase in haulage weights by an extra coach or two. It was also assumed that a lighter locomotive would also be cheaper to build.

The WR were particularly drawn to hydraulic revolution because of the need to speed up freight

The first Western, desert sand-liveried D1000 *Western Enterprise* passes Dawlish on a Down express in April 1965. BJ SWAIN/COLOUR-RAIL DE575.

1950
Inter-Regional transfer of lines with WR losing its southern extremities and gaining both the SR lines in the South West and the Somerset & Dorset as far as Cole.
Feb: Prairie No 4531 becomes the first of the class to be withdrawn.
Nov: The last Castle to be built, No 7037, was named *Swindon* by HRH Princess Elizabeth during her visit to Swindon Works.

1951
BR Standard Britannias first allocated to Old Oak Common and Laira depots.
WR receives its first BR Standard Mk1 coaches.
The two remaining Corris Railway locomotives and several goods wagons sold by WR to the newly preserved Talyllyn Railway.

1952
5 April: Collett died. His funeral was attended by a small gathering which included Hawksworth, Stanier and Pole.

1953
Ealing comedy *The Titfield Thunderbolt* filmed on the recently-closed Bristol and North Somerset Railway branch.

1954
'The Bristolian' reintroduced.
7 October: Castle No 5069 *Isambard Kingdom Brunel* sets a new record of 3 hours 37 minutes on Plymouth to Paddington.

1955
The year of the ASLEF strike, which many believe began a downturn in British Railways fortunes.
BR Modernisation Plan published.
27 June: 'South Wales Pullman' introduced.
September: Last three 4400 class small prairies withdrawn.

1956
Starting in 1956, 11 5700 0-6-0PTs were bought by London Transport and used on the underground network for works trains.
April: The first 4575 class series locomotive to be withdrawn was No 4586.
5 Nov: Welshpool & Llanfair Light Railway closes.

traffic, which could partially be achieved by fitting automatic continuous brakes to all freight stock. With goods traffic moving at higher speeds, the way would be opened to also accelerating passenger trains, with considerable gains in both line capacity and overall journey times.

British Railways subsequently agreed to allow the WR to concentrate on diesel-hydraulic types, with their design and construction based primarily at Swindon.

The British Transport Commission had already agreed to order two types of diesel hydraulic locomotives from North British, the first being a Type 4 A1A-A1A locomotive with two engines producing a total of 2000hp, which became the D600 Warship series with six built. The second was a Type 2 Bo-Bo locomotive with a single engine producing 1000hp, which became the D6300 'baby Warships' with 58 built.

The advantage of lightweight construction was lost on these, however, as North British had no experience in stressed-skin body construction and changed the chassis design criteria.

Neither of these North British types were wanted by WR bosses, but the British Transport Commission allocated the locomotives to it all the same.

The WR subsequently contacted the manufacturers of the V200, Krauss-Maffei, to begin designing a British version, scaled down to fit the British loading gauge. Swindon designers eventually produced a Bo-Bo 2200hp design using two Maybach engines, Mekydro hydraulic transmission and a lightweight stressed-skin body enabling the desired high power to weight ratio to be achieved..

Prototype gas turbine electric Co-Co No 18100 heads 'The Merchant Venturer' at Bristol Temple Meads station on 31 May 1952. NRM

Carrying a 'Cornish Riviera Express' headboard, maroon-liveried Class 42 Warship D832 *Onslaught* waits at Minehead during a visit in June 2009. ROBIN JONES

Class 14 D9555, a regular on the Lydney-Cinderford line in BR days, waits at Parkend with the last Dean Forest Railway train of the day on 3 December 2005. D9555 was the last British Railways locomotive built at Swindon Works. JOHN STRETTON

North British 'baby Warship' Type 2 D6344 coupled to a GWR 'Toad' brake van at Looe on 25 June 1962. This type, introduced in 1958 and later designated Class 22, is also extinct. Withdrawals began in 1967 finishing with the withdrawal of D6333, D6336, D6338 and D6339 in December 1971. An attempt was made to preserve D6319; but after a purchase price was agreed with BR, it was accidentally cut up by staff at Swindon Works. BR then offered the purchaser a Class 42 at the same price and so D821 *Greyhound* became the first preserved main line diesel locomotive. L ELSEY/COLOUR RAIL

Of the seven Westerns saved for preservation, D1015 *Western Champion* was the least likely to return to the main line, yet so far it is the only one to do so. Withdrawn on 13 December 1976, it had already been partially stripped for spares. Restoration began at Swindon in the summer of 1977 following the locomotive's purchase by the Diesel Traction Group. In 2001, it underwent running-in trials at the Severn Valley Railway and was passed for main line running 18 December, completing a loaded main line test run from Kidderminster to London on 14 January 2002. *Western Champion* heads through the Luxulyan Valley to Goonbarrow with the 1.18pm china clay empties train from Fowey (Carne Point) on 30 August 2002, an event organised as part of an EWS driver familiarisation exercise following its main line comeback.

D1015's biggest claim to fame came when it hauled the empty Pullman stock from Sir Winston Churchill's funeral train from Handborough back to London on 30 January 1965. BRIAN SHARPE

In 1956, production of diesel locomotives in Britain exceeded that of steam for the first time.

The first of the North British class underwent trials between Glasgow and Kilmarnock in November 1957, without either a number or name and also the side stripe was absent. When it was finally named, *Active*, on 15 November that year, it became the first named diesel to operate on the national network. A warship theme was adopted for this class and this was continued for most of Swindon's D800 series.

North British's D600 arrived on the WR in the middle of January 1958 and worked its official launch train from Platform 3 at Paddington at 11am on 17 February that year, to Bristol and back. D601 *Ark Royal* headed the first diesel-worked 'Cornish Riviera Express' out of Paddington on 16 June 1958.

D800 was the first main line diesel locomotive to be built by British Railways at Swindon and, constructed almost entirely by hand in the works, was completed in the following month.

Entering traffic, it was named *Sir Brian Robertson* at a ceremony at Paddington on 14 July that year, working a press trip to Reading and back afterwards.

The next day, D800 headed the down 'Cornish Riviera Express' from Paddington to Plymouth, returning with the 4.10pm from Plymouth.

A total of 38 examples of the class, known as Warships (TOPS Class 42) after being named after naval vessels, were built at Swindon. The British Transport Commission again annoyed the WR by ordering another 33 of them from North British.

Old steam drivers did not readily take to the Swindon Warships at first. They complained about rough riding at speeds in excess of 75mph due to the bogie design, but after tests in 1959/60, modifications solved the problem.

On 27 July 1959, D807 *Caradoc* became the first diesel to haul the Up 'Torbay Express.' Replacing steam on the service led to the Down working times being cut by 10 minutes to 165 minutes between London and Exeter, the fastest time ever recorded between the cities. The D800s proved themselves magnificent performers, capable of exceeding the authorised top speed of 90mph.

Nonetheless, the British Transport Commission still insisted on ordering a variety of diesel-electric types from other manufacturers, leaving British Railways with an assortment of non-standard classes, which proved difficult to service if they strayed from their home region.

Hymek D7017 in BR corporate blue livery with double-arrow logo on the turntable at Minehead on the West Somerset Railway in June 2009. Because of their Mekydro-design hydraulic transmission units, the locomotives became known as Hymeks. ROBIN JONES

Three hydraulics stand at the Swindon turntable on 19 May 1979. D821 *Greyhound*, D818 *Glory* and D7029. Sadly D818 did not survive. BRIAN SHARPE

Finally, the penny dropped, and to end what had been a huge waste of public money, British Railways introduced a rationalisation policy. In 1964, it was decided that because of the relatively expensive costs of maintaining diesel hydraulics, diesel electric traction was to be the norm nationwide.

A rationalisation policy appeared three years later in the form of the National Traction Plan in 1967 and called for all diesel hydraulics to be phased out. Of the 2976 main line diesels in service at that time, only 309 were diesel hydraulics – a proportion somewhat reminiscent of standard and broad gauge miles more than a century before!

The North British Warships were among the first to go. The whole class was condemned on 30 December 1967, less than a decade after their debut into traffic, although D600 and D602 survived long enough to carry BR corporate livery.

All of the North British Warships were scrapped, the last, D601, being cut up at Woodham Brothers scrapyard in 1980 following a failed preservation bid.

A brief renaissance for the D800s came when they were worked in pairs to speed up services to the West Country, but it was not enough to save them and the axe soon started to fall, with D848/63 the first to be condemned in March 1969. All of them had vanished from the main line by 1972 apart from a Swindon-built pair bought privately for preservation. D821 *Greyhound* is now based on the Severn Valley Railway while D832 *Onslaught* is part of the East Lancashire Railway fleet.

A third example survived into preservation. D818 *Glory* was displayed at Swindon as a static exhibit, but because its exterior condition deteriorated, it was cut up in 1985, donating many spares for the other two survivors.

The WR's second Swindon-built diesel hydraulic type, the D1000 Western class (later Class 52), was much more of a British design than the Class 42s had been.

Impressed by the design of Krauss-Maffei's experimental ML3000 3000bhp locomotive, which used the same Maybach MD650 engines and Mekydro K184 transmissions as the D800 class, but uprated to 1500hp, Swindon engineers decided to draw up a blueprint of their own.

It involved Maybach MD655 engines of 1380bhp and Voith L360rV transmissions, with the same stressed-skin method of body construction that had been used so successfully in the Swindon Warships.

The British Transport Commission ordered 74 of what became know as the Westerns in 1959, splitting the order with 35 being built at Swindon and 34 at Crewe, which ended up building five of those allocated for Swindon due to pressure on the works there. The Swindon-built Westerns were numbered D1000-29.

The first member of the class, D1000 *Western Enterprise*, was delivered in December 1961, turned out in a unique desert sand livery with wheels, roof panels, bogies and window frames in black, and the buffer beams and front skirts in carmine red.

By contrast, D1001 *Western Pathfinder* appeared in a maroon livery with white window frames and yellow buffer beams and front skirts. The next three, D1002-4, were painted GWR Brunswick green with small yellow panels applied around the headcodes.

D1015 *Western Champion* was outshopped in golden ochre with the buffer beams painted red. In preservation, it carried this livery when it returned to the main line in late 2001 following a major rebuild, being repainted maroon in 2006.

After D1000 entered traffic, it was sent to Plymouth Laira for tests, while in February 1962, D1001 was chosen to undertake competitive trials in competition against the experimental locomotive D0280 *Falcon*, built by Brush Traction at Loughborough as the prototype of what would become the 512 Class 47s.

Most of the Westerns appeared in 1962-63, the last being D1073 *Western Bulwark* outshopped on 3 December 1963. They were allocated to the West of England main line, Paddington-Swansea and Paddington-Birmingham services.

Unsatisfactory riding led to all but four of the Westerns being restricted to 80mph, but following a programme of bogie modifications, most of the type were restored to working at 90mph by spring 1964. They emerged as a direct replacement for the Kings.

Sadly, the rationalisation policy of 1967 earmarked this splendid class for withdrawal, but they managed to survive for another decade, at first due to the unavailability of sufficient numbers of the West of England main line replacement, the English Electric Class 50 diesel electrics, due to traction motor problems.

The Westerns were not fitted with electric train heating, and therefore could not power BR's new air-conditioned Mk2 coaches, placing them at a serious disadvantage with the completion of the M4 between London and Bristol which presented the WR with even harder competition from road traffic. The Westerns, however, were also top-class freight locomotives, and their duties included the overnight Freightliner from Cardiff to London (Stratford) and milk and cream workings from Devon and Cornwall.

In 1976, the survivors were officially relegated to freight duties, but became enormously popular with enthusiast specials to destinations across the country.

Only 10 remained at the start of 1977, often standing in for worn-out diesel electrics which had been sent to the WR to replace them.

D1013 *Western Ranger* and D1023 *Western Fusilier* hauled the sell-out 628-mile enthusiasts' special, the 'Western Tribute', from London to Swansea and Plymouth on 26 February, departing from Paddington at 9.10am, proudly displaying the GWR coat of arms.

An era ended at 7.40pm when Plymouth saw its last Western departure under BR and the occasion was marked by a firework display as crowds cheered the train off on its return to Paddington.

The last five Westerns were withdrawn two days later, and their passing marked the end not only of diesel hydraulics from the main line, but also Swindon's spirit of independence which had begun with Brunel. The departure marked the final curtain of an era which went west of Paddington was arguably as dramatic as that which finished on 11 August 1968 when the last standard gauge steam locomotive ran in BR service.

The Swindon-built examples still with us are D1010 *Western Campaigner* (West Somerset Railway), D1013 *Western Ranger* (Severn Valley Railway), D1015 *Western Champion* (Old Oak Common, the only one certified for use on Network Rail) and D1023 *Western Fusilier* (National Railway Museum). The Crewe-built survivors are D1041 *Western Prince* (East Lancashire Railway), D1048 *Western Lady* (Midland Railway-Butterley) and D1062 *Western Courier* (Severn Valley Railway).

Also making its debut alongside the Westerns in 1961 were the diesel-hydraulic 1700hp Type 3 Bo-Bo Hymeks (later Class 35), which were built by Beyer Peacock of Manchester, the first being ceremoniously handed over to WR officials at Paddington on 16 May 1961. Fitted with a single Bristol-Siddeley Maybach MD870 engine, the class had a maximum permitted working speed of 90mph and they were designed to operate in multiples of up to three locomotives.

The Hymeks entered revenue-earning traffic on 10 July 1961, firstly in the Bristol area. In October that year, Hymek pair D7023/4 hauled the Royal Train from Paddington to the new steelworks at Llanwern where a short platform and canopy had been erected.

A total of 101 were built before a halt was called to the building of further diesel hydraulics. A

The National Railway Museum's Class 52 D1023 *Western Fusilier* inside the Great Hall at York. D1023 jointly hauled the 'Western Tribute' railtour of 26 February 1977 which many believe was the final end for the Paddington empire founded by Brunel. ROBIN JONES

replacement for the Castles, they ran on many cross-country routes. Many of the class were withdrawn in 1972, although a few remained in traffic until 1975. Four have survived into preservation, D7017 and D7018 on the West Somerset Railway, D7076 on the East Lancashire Railway and D7029 at the Severn Valley Railway.

The last type of diesel hydraulic to be built at Swindon was the Class 14 0-6-0 centre-cab 650hp shunter, 56 of which were constructed between 1964-65, for shunting operations, short main line duties or trip workings, with a speed of up to 40mph.

However, the demand for them fell with the demise of the pick-up freight, and all of the class were withdrawn by 1969, being sold into private industry. Nicknamed 'Teddy Bears', a total of 23 have been preserved.

D1013 *Western Ranger* and D1023 *Western Fusilier* passing Pilning with the 'Western Tribute' railtour of 26 February 1977. BRIAN SHARPE

1957
First pannier 5700 withdrawn.
City of Truro was returned to service by WR both for hauling special excursion trains and for normal services.
October: Swindon 'Cross-country' two-car Class 120 DMUs appear.
November: The first WR North British Warship diesel hydraulic, D600 *Active*, underwent trials between Glasgow and Kilmarnock and named on 15 November.

1958
GWR railcar W4W saved for future Swindon Railway Museum and becomes first diesel railcar to be preserved.
January: D600 arrived on the WR.
1 Feb: Boundary changes give Southern region back lines in Devon, while the northern section of the Somerset & Dorset Joint Railway is transferred to the WR.
17 February: D600 official launch train from Paddington Bristol and back.
16 June: D601 *Ark Royal* headed the first diesel-worked 'Cornish Riviera Express' out of Paddington.
July: D800, the first main line diesel locomotive to be built by British Railways at Swindon completed. Named *Sir Brian Robertson* at a ceremony at Paddington on the 14th, prior to heading the down 'Cornish Riviera Express' the next day.
July: Sleeper service to Milford Haven begins.
December: No 2258 is first 2251 class 0-6-0 to be withdrawn.

1959
Widespread change to diesel traction and scrapping of the first Castle.
Class 21 and 42 diesels appear.
July: First working parties on Welshpool & Llanfair Light Railway, to first part of the Swindon portfolio to be saved by preservationists.

1960
Blue Pullman appears
Gas turbine No 18000 withdrawn
Margam automated hump marshalling yard opens.
Severn Bridge hit by tanker which blew up in fireball: traffic ends.
diesel hydraulics appear.
Major rationalisation at Plymouth.
18 March: BR Standard 9F 2-10-0 No 92220 *Evening Star* unveiled at Swindon Works as the last steam engine built by British Railways for the national network.
May 1960: No 4073 *Caerphilly Castle* withdrawn from Cardiff Canton.
9 September: 5.10pm Paddington to Birmingham left the last WR slip coach at Bicester.

The halcyon twilight years of steam

At first, few noticed the 'join' between the GWR and Western Region. At first, the newly nationalised network was run as four different concerns, as in 'Big Four' days, and continued building tried and tested locomotive designs as before.

Between 1 January 1948 and 1952, the WR built 452 locomotives to GWR designs, including 30 Castles, 49 Modified Halls, 10 Manors, 20 5101 class prairie tanks and 341 pannier tanks.

The last express engine built by the GWR at Swindon, Castle class No 7007 *Ogmore Castle*, was renamed *Great Western* in January 1948 as a tribute to the old company, and the first locomotive built at Swindon in 1846. In February 1948, No 7001 was renamed *Sir James Milne* after the last GWR general manager who had retired at nationalisation.

The last Castle to be built, No 7037, was officially named *Swindon* by Princess Elizabeth, the future Queen, during her visit to the works on 15 November 1950. The borough coat of arms on the splasher below the nameplate honoured more than a century of world-beating steam locomotive technology.

Many saw British Railways as heralding a bright new age for steam, for under Robert Riddles, appointed Mechanical Engineer with the newly formed Railway Executive at nationalisation, having headed the Directorate of Transport Equipment during World War Two, 12 designs of BR Standard locomotives appeared, making a total of 999 locomotives.

Parallels might be drawn somewhat with the Conservative-Liberal Democrat coalition of GWR 175 year, with a mix-and-match 'Big Four' technological input, for their designs were for the large part heavily biased towards London Midland & Scottish practice, Riddles having served as assistant to Chief Mechanical Engineer William Stanier there, although the Swindon influence had a somewhat 'look in' in the boiler design. However, another nod to the GWR empire was given in the adoption of Brunswick green for express passenger locomotives after the early British Railways blue livery was ditched. Therefore we saw classics like Southern railway Bulleid Pacifics, LNER Pacifics and Princess Coronation 4-6-2s carrying the trademark GWR livery with the BR emblem.

Swindon had its fair share of building the new BR Standards, including batches of the 75000 Standard 4MT 4-6-0s, the 77000 Standard 3MT 2-6-0s, the 92000 and the entire class of 82000 Standard 3MT 2-6-2Ts.

Riddles' appointment, however, was a stopgap before the inevitable dieselisation. He retired in 1953, just two years before the BR Modernisation Plan was published.

The 50s were therefore a great time for railway enthusiasts. In the days before pop stars and computer games, schoolboys would gather at each vantage point during the school

WR 4-6-0 No 7029 *Clun Castle* at Putney & Chirton with the Stephenson Locomotive Society's 'Farewell to the Castle Class Tour' from Birmingham Snow Hill to Oxford, Reading, Savenake and back again on 24 January 1965. SLS LIBRARY/STANFORD JACOBS COLLECTION

GWR 4-6-0 No 6971 *Athelhampton Hall* heads into Shirley from the Stratford-upon-Avon direction in 1959. MICHAEL MENSING/BRM

Towards the end of Western Region steam, and everywhere else for that matter, locomotives took on a caked-with-grime appearance as cleaning fell by the wayside. GWR 4-6-0 No 1012 *County of Denbighshire* tackles Hatton Bank on 28 September 1963. BRYAN HICKS

summer holidays, well-worn Ian Allan abc trainspotters' guides in pocket, dodging the unwelcoming stationmaster and occasionally sneaking into sheds to catch a closer glimpse of the giants of steam. The membership of railway clubs boomed as did the sales of railway books and magazines.

The WR was positive towards enthusiast societies, and when they asked to arrange railtours, was very accommodating with requests for rare or elderly motive power, some of which were making final appearances before withdrawal, and to run over goods-only branches.

In 1951, volunteers from the West Midlands took over the independent 2ft 3in gauge Talyllyn Railway, and bought two locomotives from the neighbouring Corris Railway, which in 1948 had become one of the WR's first closures. The Talyllyn Railway Preservation Society began a tradition of running a main line tour from Paddington to Tywyn for its annual general meeting. In September 1955, GWR Star No 4061 *Glastonbury Abbey* headed the special from Paddington to Shrewsbury where LSWR T9 4-4-0 No 30304 took over, being assisted from Welshpool by GWR Dukedog 4-4-0 No 9027.

At Swindon, experiments to hone existing locomotive designs to perfection in the face of a declining quality of coal were carried out.

Such modifications were trialled both on the main line and on the Swindon testing plant. By late 1953, sufficient Kings and Castles had been modified with improved draughting to allow several WR express trains to be accelerated from the summer 1954 timetable onwards, including the 'Bristolian', the 'Pembroke Coast Express' and the 'Cornish Riviera Express'.

The tests highlighted the scope for increasing the efficiency of draughting even more, creating freer running.

Swindon designed a double blastpipe and chimney arrangement for both the Kings and Castles, the

Churchward 2-8-0 No 4703 passes Castle Cary with a relief Plymouth-Paddington service on 19 September 1959. GWT COLLECTION

1961

Midland & South Western Junction Railway closed as a through route.
Western diesel hyraulics took over the Birmingham route.
New diesel maintenance depot built at Bristol.
Four schoolboys who later founded Great Western Society meet and decide to save a 1400 0-4-2T.
Dr Richard Beeching appointed chairman of British Transport commission.
City of Truro withdrawn for second time.
Dec: First Class 52 Western D1000 *Western Enterprise* appears. Class 35 Hymeks appear the same year.

1962

No 6006 *King George I* becomes first King to be scrapped.
Hymeks take over South Wales services.
Last `Ocean Specials' run.
New signal box at Old Oak Common opens.
Swindon Railway Museum in Faringdon Road opened.
15 Feb: Dukedog No 9017 arrived at the Bluebell Railway's Sheffield Park base.
June: No 4702 becomes first 4700 2-8-0 to be withdrawn.
8 September: *Evening Star* hauled the last 'Pines Express' over the Somerset & Dorset line.

1963

LMR takes charge of all WR lines north of Aynho junction while WR takes over Southern lines west of Salisbury including 'Withered Arm.'
Severn Valley line closed between Bridgnorth and Shrewsbury.
1 January: British Railways Board begins operations under Beeching.
April: First Manor withdrawn.
March: Beeching's report *The Reshaping of British Railways* published.
6 April: Western half of Welshpool & Llanfair Light Railway reopens under lease from BR.
June: Great Western Society launched.
17 August: Welshpool town section lost.

modifications being implemented from 1955 onwards, and with several such engines timed at 100mph.

It was too little too late, for by the end of 1958, these magnificent locomotives, finally displaying what they were truly capable of doing, were being replaced by diesel hydraulics.

Prime Minister Harold Macmillan is best remembered by many people for his phrase describing the late 50s: "You've never had it so good."

The worst of the post-war austerity had been passed, unemployment was low, and generally people were seen to have more money in their pocket. The net result was that car ownership rose, and indeed, in many rural areas was seen as a necessity rather than a luxury.

Back in the 50s, branch lines were grossly overstaffed by modern standards, with sparsely used country stations regular engaging several staff to run them. Inevitably, with the increasing transference of passengers from rail to road, losses would soar.

Cost cutting was attempted with the introduction of diesel railcars and multiple units on branch units, but again, the rot had set in and could not be cured. Apart from sentimentality, there appeared to be no economic justification for keeping many of

The end is nigh: once-mighty Kings No 6025 *King Henry III* and No 6026 *King John* await scrapping at Swindon in 1963. GWT COLLECTION

them open, although it may be argued that loss-making branch lines contributed passengers and therefore profitability to the main lines they served.

Another big factor was the decline in the pick-up goods. It had become far easier and cheaper to send goods directly by lorry from the outlet to the end user than to have them taken by road to and from the stations at either end of the journey.

The public at large often talk of the Beeching Axe as if Dr Richard Beeching was

the man who in 1963, with his report 'The Reshaping of British Railways', killed off much of the national network. In reality, he was merely streamlining and speeding up a seemingly inevitable process that was already in full swing.

For example, the WR withdrew passenger services from its Yelverton-Princetown route in 1956, the Princes Risborough to Watlington branch in 1957, the Ashburton branch, and the last timetable passenger trains ran to Moretonhampstead in 1959, the same

Churchward Saint No 2933 *Bibury Court* with a Down stopping train approaches Radley on 15 May 1948. GWT COLLECTION

year as many of the Forest of Dean services, including those on the Wye valley route through Chepstow, Monmouth and Ross-on-Wye were withdrawn, along with Cholsey-Wallingford.

Closures of such routes left not only numerous steam locomotives and stock redundant, but also meant that the days would be numbered for early diesel types that had superseded them.

The Swindon empire also underwent several boundary changes, losing routes in Southern Region territory while gaining that region's lines in the south west and part of the Somerset & Dorset Joint Railway system. The Southern lines were handed back in 1962, only to be taken over again by the WR on New Year's Day 1963. There arose the situation whereas while the pace of dieselisation was fairly rapid on the WR in the early 60s, steam persisted on former Southern Railway routes in WR control…until such time as huge swathes of LSWR territory, such as the 'Withered Arm' west of Exeter, to Padstow and Bude, were closed en masse.

At the same time, the London Midland Region took over all former GWR lines north of Aynho Junction south of Banbury, including the Birmingham and Wolverhampton areas, and all of central and north Wales served by the Cambrian and Ruabon-Dolgellau lines, leaving Worcester as the WR's biggest centre in the north of what had been the GWR empire. This readjustment left many GWR sheds and their engines in the hands of the successor to the rival LMS for the last years of steam.

The Kings were withdrawn in 1962, being replaced by Western diesel hydraulics on the Paddington-Birmingham-Wolverhampton expresses. The LMR was left with two routes to London, and chose its 'own', the Birmingham New Street to Euston line,, for electrification, with the Snow Hill-Paddington station relegated to the status of a cross-country route. Also, the LMR oversaw the closure of many GWR lines in the West Midlands.

WR steam ended sooner than planned. Among 169 locomotives withdrawn at the end of the 1962 timetable were 25 Castles, some of which only the previous year had been overhauled and fitted with double chimneys, while the first of the Manors was taken out of service in April 1963.

Although British Rail imposed a total ban on standard gauge steam in August 1968, with the one exception being No 4472 *Flying Scotsman*, it did honour an agreement with the Great Western Society to run steam shuttles on the Cholsey-Wallingford branch on 21 September that year, with Collett 0-4-2T No 1466 heading auto-coach No 321. Several thousand people were carried. PETER CHATMAN

Pannier L94 heads the last steam train on London Underground on 6 June 1971. Back in its GWR identity of No 7752, it is preserved at Tyseley Locomotive Works. LONDON TRANSPORT MUSEUM/TRANSPORT FOR LONDON

In 1964, market-leading railway publisher Ian Allan marked the 60th anniversary of *City of Truro's* unofficial 102.3mph speed record and the end of WR express steam working with a Plymouth-Paddington 'Ocean Mails Express' behind Castles.

From a shortlist of engines, No 4079 *Pendennis Castle* was chosen to haul the train from Paddington to Plymouth with No 7029 taking over for the journey back to Bristol, and No 5054 *Earl of Ducie*.

The star of the occasion on 9 May was undoubtedly 1950-built *Clun Castle*. On the descent of Wellington Bank in Somerset, scene of *Truro's* legendary feat, the locomotive achieved a top speed of 96mph – the fastest ever recorded timing over the Plymouth-Bristol route.

Clun Castle also hauled the last official steam train out of Paddington, to Banbury, on 11 June 1965.

By autumn 1965, virtually all of the last steam engines on the WR were allocated to sheds in the London Division, including Southall and Oxford, while another last bastion was Gloucester.

All WR steam engines were officially withdrawn from 31 December 1965, but *Clun Castle* was the last Castle in BR service to haul a train, on 1 January 1966, the 5pm from Gloucester to Cheltenham.

Although it had been officially withdrawn, No 6998 *Burton Agnes Hall* was turned out for the final day of WR main line steam two days later, on 3 January 1966, hauling the

Oxford-Banbury section of the Poole-York service, and accordingly was afterwards bought for preservation by the Great Western Society.

Not all GWR engines were taken out of service with the end of WR steam. Several that had passed into LMR control remained on shed in 1966; the last, a handful of 5700 pannier tanks, withdrawn from Oxley and Croes Newydd sheds in late 1966.

On 11 September that year, the Stephenson Locomotive Society ran the 'Farewell to the GWR pannier tanks' tour using Nos 9610 and 9630 on a variety of West Midlands routes, including Birmingham Snow Hill-Handsworth Jn-Old Hill-Halesowen, Halesowen-Old Hill, Old Hill-Dudley-Wolverhampton Low Level, Wolverhampton Low Level-Birmingham Snow Hill-Tyseley-Henley in Arden (1)-Bearley-Stratford-upon-Avon, Stratford-upon-Avon-Bearley-Hatton-Leamington Spa, Leamington Spa-Hatton-Lapworth and finally Lapworth-Knowle & Dorridge-Tyseley-Birmingham Snow Hill. On the ascent of Hatton Bank on the last lap, No 9630 blew the front of one of the cylinders off and was removed at Lapworth. The pannier was towed back to Tyseley by a Brush Type 4 diesel while No 9610 took the train back to Snow Hill.

That was the year in which the Somerset & Dorset system, worked by steam to the last, saw its final passenger services on 5/6 March.

Cross-country expresses still penetrated the WR, including the rerouted 'Pines Express' and the Poole-York train following the closure of the Great Central route in 1966.

Yet *Clun Castle* refused to stop carrying the GWR torch. Having been bought by enthusiast Patrick Whitehouse in 1966 before being passed to current owning group 7029 Clun Castle Ltd, it worked several enthusiast tours in the final days of British Railways steam.

The locomotive remained in the roundhouse at Tyseley until it closed in 1967, and repainted in BR passenger green livery in the new diesel depot, but with the words Great Western on the tender, applied at the request of the workforce at Swindon where it had been built.

Although no longer in BR ownership, *Clun Castle* was used for hauling freight trains to Banbury.

After being withdrawn by the Western Region, several panniers were sold off into industry. Restored to working order at Didcot Railway Centre in 2008, No 3650 temporarily carried the livery of Stephenson Clarke PD Fuels Ltd which bought the engine on 9 October 1963 for use at Gwaun-Cae-Gurwen Colliery in South Wales. It was bought for preservation in October 1969. FRANK DUMBLETON/GWS

GWR 4-6-0 No 6004 *King George III* heads the 3.10pm Paddington-Birmingham Saturdays-only summer service express past Seer Green on 23 August 1952. GWT COLLECTION

In 1967, the GWR main line north of Snow Hill was to be all but closed, and all through Paddington to Birkenhead services would cease.

Two steam specials marked the occasion on 5 March, featuring *Clun Castle* and *Pendennis Castle*. When *Clun Castle* returned to Birmingham at over 70mph, whistling deafening the city centre, it marked the end of BR steam out of Snow Hill.

It was subsequently discovered that on the way back from Birkenhead, one of the valve spindles had been stripped. While the Castle had been saved, it was obvious that workshop facilities would be needed to maintain in it working order. So the owners leased the GWR coaling stage at Tyseley as shed and repair shop.

Clun Castle was repaired in time to head an intensive series of special 'end of BR steam' specials beginning in September 1967, running from King's Cross to Newcastle, over the Settle and Carlisle route and down the West Coast Main Line over the legendary Shap summit.

Back at Tyseley in October 1967, *Clun Castle* could only wait for the final curtain. British Rail steam officially ended on 11 August 1968, when the 'Fifteen Guinea Special' marked the last steam-hauled train on the national network.

GWR panniers remained in main line service after 1968, but on the London Underground, which had bought 11 in 1956 for use on engineers' trains. This move in itself was recreating history, for the first services on the Metropolitan Railway had been operated by the GWR, which built a special type of locomotive, the Metropolitan class, to operate through the tunnels. The last of the London Transport panniers remained in service until 6 June 1971 when a special train was run to mark their demise.

Some panniers also found a new home in industry when their main line days were declared over. No 7754 entered National Coal Board service and remained on shed at Mountain Ash Colliery until 1980, and is now preserved on the Llangollen Railway.

One GWR line, however, remain in steam, with the locomotives uniquely repainted into the BR corporate Rail Blue livery otherwise associated with diesel and electric traction, and carrying the trademark double-arrow logo.

It was the 1ft 11½in gauge Vale of Rheidol Railway, running between Aberystwyth and Devil's Bridge in central Wales, and which ran three 2-6-2 tank engines built by the GWR in 1923/4 after it inherited the line with the Cambrian Railways at the Grouping. The locomotives would return to Swindon for maintenance and overhaul in A Shop. Under the TOPS numbering arrangements for locomotives introduced by British Rail, they were designated Class 98 and were nominally numbered 98007–98009, but they never carried these numbers.

The LMR, by then seeing several narrow gauge preservation schemes elsewhere in Wales be successful, retained the 1901-built line for tourist trains, and so it defied the BR steam ban imposed after August 1968. In the 80s, the Rail Blue livery gave way to more traditional liveries that the locomotives and stock carried in the past, including Brunswick green.

In April 1989, British Rail sold it to Tony Hills and Peter Rampton, owners of the Brecon Mountain Railway near Merthyr Tydfil, and so the final piece of the Swindon empire to remain in steam was privatised.

GWR locomotives, BR diesel livery: Vale of Rheidol Railway 2-6-2T No 7 *Owain Glyndwr* approaches Devil's Bridge on 28 April 1973. JEFF COLLEDGE

1964
Great Western Society buys first locomotive, GWR 0-4-2T No 1466, and auto coach No 231. Its first stock in based on the Totnes Quay branch when it held its first open day on 17 October.
Class 14 diesel hydraulics introduced.
Last GWR Counties, 1400s, 4300s, 4575s and 4700s withdrawn.
BR introduces new Rail Blue livery and double arrow logo.
New freight and coal concentration depot at Taunton opens.
The WR introduces the 'Golden Hind' service.
Pat Whitehouse and Pat Garland bring prairie No 4555 to Tyseley while awaiting move to Buckfastleigh – and it is used on local main line services in the meantime.
2 May: The Brecon & Merthyr Railway's Torpantau Tunnel - also known as Beacons or Beacon Summit Tunnel - the highest tunnel on the UK's standard gauge network at 1313ft above sea level – is closed by BR.
9 May: No 7029 *Clun Castle* timed at 96mph on the descent of Wellington Bank with an Ian Allan special to mark the 60th anniversary of *City of Truro's* unofficial recordbreaking run.

1965
New diesel maintenance depot opens at Old Oak Common.
Last auto-train runs, between Yeovil Junction and Yeovil Town.
Last 2251 0-6-0 and 5600 withdrawn.
Class 14 D9555 is last BR locomotive built at Swindon.
Evening Star withdrawn and preserved.
Barry scrapyard owner Dai Woodham decides to stop cutting up steam engines in favour of the more lucrative wagon and brake van scrapping trade.
First Dart Valley Railway engines arrive on branch.
3 June: D6881/2 with a 360 ton train achieved non-stop records of 3 hours 161 minutes Paddington-Plymouth and 87 minutes Bristol-Paddington.
11 June: *Clun Castle* heads last steam out of Paddington, to Banbury.
6 July: Meeting at Cooper's Arms in Kidderminster decided to set up Severn Valley Railway.

1966
Severn Valley Railway Society and Corris Railway Society founded.
Great Western Society buys No 6106 and moves in to Taplow goods shed.
3 Jan: Last day of WR steam sees No 6998 *Burton Agnes Hall* on final train.
7 Mar: The Somerset & Dorset system finally closed.
November: Last 5700 panniers withdrawn from LMR.

GWR | 97

The Blue Pullman

A Blue Pullman service approaches Tyseley en route to Birmingham Snow Hill in 1963, passing the junction with the North Warwickshire Line to Shirley and Stratford-upon-Avon. MICHAEL MENSING

The writing was on the wall for steam, diesel and electric traction were sweeping the past away, car ownership was becoming the norm rather than the exception and domestic air travel was also becoming more attractive and available.

What was needed was a new state-of-the-art luxury first-class inter-city train for the modern age, a flagship service that would be widely seen as pointing the way ahead.

The answer was the Blue Pullman, a glamorous, sleek and ultra-modern diesel multiple unit that would take British Railways out of the steam age and into the space age, firmly closing the door on the aftermath of wartime austerity.

The Blue Pullmans followed in the wake of British Railways' 1954 Modernisation Plan. Designed by British Railways, a total of five complete Blue Pullman train sets were built by Metropolitan Cammell in Birmingham, and were made up from a total of 36 vehicles. Initially operated by luxury train operator the Pullman Car Company, shortly after their introduction in 1962, the company, already partly acquired by the British Transport Commission, was nationalised and full control of the sets passed to British Railways.

The sets were allocated to the Western and London Midland regions. They were intended to offer a high standard of service never before seen on a British train – meals at every seat, air conditioning, and a staffing level sufficient to ensure that passengers would want for nothing. The maximum service speed was 90mph.

A smoothness of ride was also promised by a new design of bogie – but herein lay one of the sets' biggest failings, because weight difference between a Mk1 coach and a heavy Pullman led to complaints over ride quality which would persist throughout their life.

The Western Region took three eight-car sets and operated them between Birmingham Snow Hill and Paddington, and Bristol and Paddington, at first keeping one set spare.

The Birmingham route proved the most profitable for the sets, while Bristol passengers were critical of the fact that, to travel by Pullman, they were paying a supplement for a service that was slower than the best expresses of the day on Brunel's main line.

Eventually, it was decided to use the spare set to replace steam on the 'South Wales Pullman'.

Negative publicity ensued followed the announcement that the Birmingham Blue Pullman service would cease when the line from Euston to New Street was electrified – effectively downgrading the rival GWR route from Paddington to Snow Hill.

The redundant set was then used to provide more services on the Bristol and South Wales routes, while also taking on board the two London Midland sets.

A 12-car set formed from the two former Midland six-car trains operated out of Bristol on the morning and evening peak service.

The distinctive blue and white livery, which heralded the later British Rail corporate blue livery, was 'modernised' towards the end of the 60s to a far less distinctive white and grey with yellow ends.

By this time, ordinary British Railways Mk2 coaching stock was in regular use, making air-conditioned travel available to the masses, and without the payment of supplementary fares, therefore lessening the advantages of the Blue Pullmans, with their questionable ride quality.

British Railways talked about withdrawing the sets as early as 1969, but they managed to last until 1973, when the new High Speed Train project, which may have been influenced in several aspects by the Blue Pullmans, but which marked a vast leap forward, was progressing at great pace, with the two Class 41 prototype power cars already built.

Although not wholly successful in their own right, the Blue Pullmans demonstrated the possibility of high-speed fixed-formation multiple-unit train services, which today form the backbone of inter-city passenger services on the national network.

Sadly, moves to preserve a set failed and they were scrapped in the mid-70s, although a few relics such as table lamps survive, along with tickets, advertising material and one seat.

An up Pullman working passing Swindon. Its latter-day grey and blue livery with blue front ends was not one of the better post-steam era liveries concocted by British Railways, and severely diluted the impact of the original. COLOUR-RAIL

Luxury table service in what is an apparently well-filled saloon – but in reality was a contrived photo shoot comprising Western Region staff posing as customers. WR

1967
The first WR Freightliner terminal opened at Pengam.
The Reading-Heathrow airport link opens.
Great Western Society moves from Taplow into Didcot shed with three engines.
Severn Valley Railway runs unofficial trains behind Collett 0-6-0 No 3205.
BR's last passenger diesel, the Class 50 diesel electric, introduced.
D600 *Active*, first North British diesel hydraulic, withdrawn.
Express services to Birmingham were diverted from Snow Hill to New Street.
Jan: WR closed most of 'Withered Arm'
5 March: End of through services from Paddington to Shrewsbury, Birkenhead and the Cambrian lines.
5 November 1967: Birkenhead Woodside closed to passengers.

1968
A revised layout for the Paddington approaches including multiple aspect signalling brought into use.
11 August: End of BR main line steam haulage
21 September: Despite the BR steam ban, the Great Western Society runs steam rides over the Cholsey-Wallingford branch.
October: Birmingham Railway Museum holds first open day at Tyseley depot.

1969
Class 14 diesels withdrawn.
March: Mogul No 5322 becomes first GWR engine preserved from Barry scrapyard.
5 April: First Dart Valley Railway train from Buckfastleigh.

1970
Dean Forest Railway Preservation Society founded.
HP Bulmer opens preservation base in Hereford.
Foster Yeoman's Merehead Quarry began forwarding block train loads of aggregates in high capacity wagons.
23 May: Severn Valley Railway runs first public services, from Bridgnorth to Hampton Loade.

1971
Cambrian Railways Society formed.
Teifi Valley Railway Society moves into Henllan station.
5 February: Minehead Railway Preservation Society organises meeting in Taunton about reopening the Minehead branch which close don 2 January.
May: New West Somerset Railway Company was formed to acquire the Minehead branch.
6 June: Last London Underground pannier tanks withdrawn.
2 October: Run by GWR 4-6-0 No 6000 *King George V* marks lifting of BR steam ban.

Preservation:
revival of the country branch line

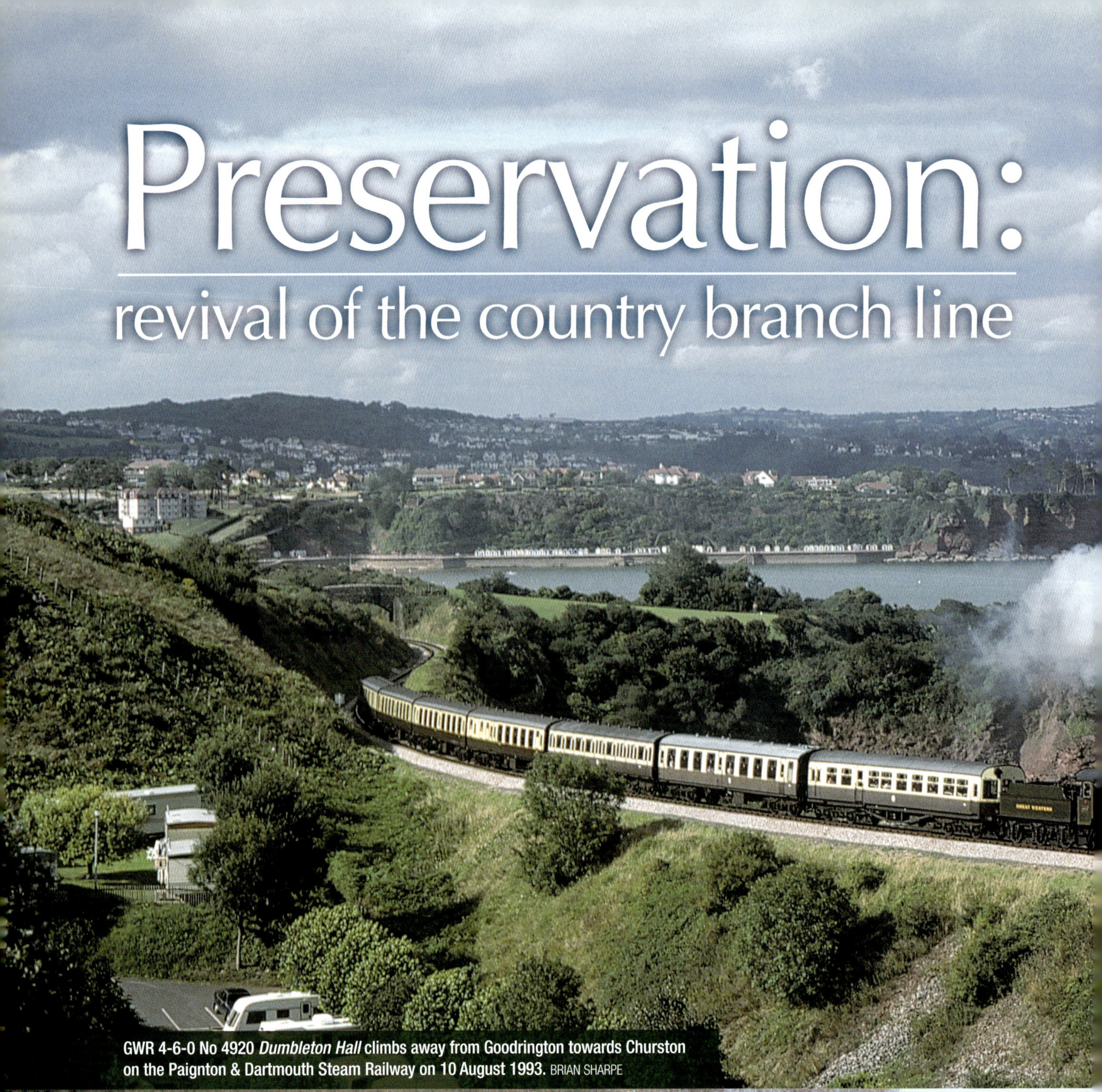

GWR 4-6-0 No 4920 *Dumbleton Hall* climbs away from Goodrington towards Churston on the Paignton & Dartmouth Steam Railway on 10 August 1993. BRIAN SHARPE

The Dart Valley Railway, now the South Devon Railway, was the first GWR standard gauge branch to be reopened. The inaugural service on 5 April 1969 was a 'super auto train' comprising GWR 0-6-0PT No 6412 sandwiched between four auto trailers, and is seen crossing Nursery Pool Bridge. SW LINES

John Hill, who drove the first public Severn Valley Railway train in 1970. ROBIN JONES

Nowhere is the continuing existence of the Great Western Railway to be more immediately appreciated that in the sparkling array of heritage lines that operate in Britain today, including many that were once part of the Swindon empire.

The story of operational railway preservation in Britain dates back to 1951, when volunteers took over the Talyllyn Railway, buying two engines and equipment from the defunct Corris Railway, which had been part of the GWR.

Builder Pat Whitehouse became the first secretary of the Talyllyn Railway Preservation Society, when a group of West Midlands enthusiasts under the leadership of Tom Rolt stepped in to save the 2ft 3in gauge line, which had never been part of a 'Big Four' company. At Tywyn, Pat met Birmingham accountant Pat Garland, and together they struck up a lifelong friends with steam at its heart.

In 1952, hot on the heels of the Talyllyn revival, the Narrow Gauge Railway Society asked the Western Region if it could take over one of the three Welsh narrow gauge lines it had inherited from the GWR, the Welshpool & Llanfair Light Railway, the Corris or the Vale of Rheidol Railway. Society founder secretary Eric G Cope found the Western Region amenable, and an asking price of £6000 for the 9½-mile 2ft 6in gauge Welshpool line was discussed.

The talks petered out because the by-then freight-only WLLR was still running, but that changed when the Western Region announced that services would be withdrawn from 5 November 1956.

Llanfair Parish Council had already invited approaches from enthusiasts who might want to keep the line going. On 15 September 1956, London printer William Morris ran a special over the line in a bid to muster support, and afterwards held a public meeting in the town, inviting people to join a new preservation society.

In early 1959, British Railways offered terms for a 42-year lease, and 4 January 4 1960 saw the incorporation of the Welshpool & Llanfair Light Railway Preservation Company Ltd., with its first meeting taking place at a Paddington pub five days later.

The original two locomotives, Beyer Peacock 0-6-0Ts *The Earl* and *Countess* were overhauled at Oswestry. *The Earl* arrived back on 28 July 1961, steaming in Welshpool yard. Two months later, the first heritage era steam trips in five years were run from Welshpool to Llanfair.

Sixty years to the day after the line's opening ceremony on 6 April 1903, *The Earl* hauled a two-coach special from Welshpool yard to Llanfair, marking the reopening of the line.

Sadly, two days earlier, Welshpool Town Council bought the urban section that ran behind houses through the town to the main line station, and banned the running of trains over it after 17 August 1963.

On 12 March 1974, the freehold of the line was bought from British Rail for just £8,000.

Because of the difficulties in tackling the 1-in-29 Golfa Bank, it was not until 18 July 1981 that public services would be extended from Sylvaen back to the new Welshpool terminus at Raven Square, developed on the western edge of the town, based around the relocated former GWR station building from Eardisley in Herefordshire.

In 1960, the Bluebell Railway became the first standard gauge part of the national network to be revived by volunteers, and although it is located in

1972
Bristol Parkway opened.
Prototype InterCity 125 HST running trials began.
Last Class 42 Warship, D832 *Onslaught*, and Class 22s withdrawn.
First Class 50s on WR appeared.
First Bala Lake Railway trains run on part of GWR Ruabon-Dolgellau branch
1 January: Dart Valley Railway takes over Paignton-Kingswear line.
March: Last WR trains from Birmingham Snow Hill to Wolverhampton Low Level.
22 September: No 6000 *King George V* double heads with *Flying Scotsman* after A3 returns from disastrous US trip.

1973
Class 42 D821 *Greyhound* becomes first BR main line diesel to be preserved
Introduction of a new Speedlink-type Bristol-Glasgow freight service.
Cambrian Railway Society formed at Oswestry.
David Shepherd sets up East Somerset Railway at Cranmore.
Tyseley's No 7752 becomes first pannier on main line since steam ban lifted.
Blue Pullmans withdrawn.
Somerset County Council buys the Minehead branch and leases it back to the West Somerset Railway Company.
Cardiff General renamed Cardiff Central.

1974
BR orders High Speed Train production fleet.
West Somerset Railway granted Light Railway Order.
Lappa Valley Railway built on part of GWR Newquay-Perranporth line.
First BR combined timetable.
12 Mar: Welshpool & Llanfair Light Railway buys lease from BR.
April: Severn Valley Railway extends to Highley.
May: Severn Valley extends to Bewdley.

1975
National Railway Museum opens at York
Last Class 35 Hymeks condemned: No 7017 becomes first main line diesel to be preserved by public subscription:
The line into Gloucester Eastgate closed in favour of Gloucester Central.
Prototype Advanced Passenger Train- averaged 151mph for five miles between Reading and Swindon.
The Gwili Railway formed.
Dean Forest Railway Preservation Society begins developing Norchard as an operating base
Telford Horsehay Steam Trust formed
5 May: Public prototype HST service on the Bristol route starts, and later increased to two per day.
31 August: Stockton & Darlington Railway 150 cavalcade
13 September: Llangollen station reopened by Flint & Deeside Railway Preservation Society with just 60ft of track.

Collett 0-6-0 No 3205 was not only the first locomotive to arrive on the Severn Valley Railway, as pictured at Bridgnorth on 25 March 1967, but also hauled the first train from Bridgnorth to Hampton Loade on 23 May 1970. In May 2010, its latest overhaul was completed on the South Devon Railway. DAVID WILLIAMS/SVR

The right kind of snow: GWR 4-6-0 No 7820 *Dinmore Manor* forges its way north on the 1-in-80 of Churchlands Curve on an icy 28 December 2000 with the 12.25pm Bishops Lydeard to Minehead service. December, with the huge popularity of Santa and Mince Pie specials, is nowadays one of the busiest times of the year for preserved GWR lines. DON BISHOP

deepest Sussex, well away from GWR territory, one of the first locomotives it acquired was a Swindon classic, in the form of Dukedog 4-4-0 No 9017, which was subsequently named *Earl of Berkeley*.

No 9017 was built at Swindon in 1938 using the frames of Bulldog No 3425 of 1906 and the boiler and cab from Duke No 3282 *Chepstow Castle* of 1899. A veteran of the Cambrian Coast line, it was withdrawn from Oswestry in October 1960, and arrived at the Bluebell Railway's Sheffield Park base on 15 February 1962.

A Dukedog has absolutely nothing to do with the London, Brighton & South Coast Railway of which the Bluebell line was one part, yet No 9017 has become a trademark locomotive of the line. It attended Didcot Railway Centre in 1985 for the GWR 150 celebrations, one of its few visits away from Sussex.

Meanwhile, other enthusiasts elsewhere in Britain wondered if they could follow the example set by the Bluebell in standard gauge.

On 28 February 1959, Collett 0-4-2T No 1466, now preserved at Didcot, hauled the last train over the GWR Moretonhampstead branch in south Devon. The closure provoked anger amongst local people, who protested in vain.

Launching a campaign for the restoration of the trains, the Rector of Teigngrace Canon OM Jones and Torquay enthusiast E G Parrott formed the South Devon Railway Society was formed by, and on 6 June 1960, ran a Paignton-Moretonhampstead special charter, 'The Heart of Devon Rambler'. The society leased Teigngrace Halt as its headquarters, but it was not allowed to take over the branch, as part of it was still needed for freight traffic.

The society looked elsewhere for a line to become the Bluebell of the south west. The GWR South Brent-Kingsbridge branch was targeted, but demolition contractors moved in just after a local council voted to back the revival.

On 29 September 1962, the *Western Morning News* carried a report about plans to reopen the Ashburton branch, which had just closed to freight after passenger services ended on November 1 1958.

One of the most stunning vistas in the GWR preservation portfolio is Victoria Bridge near Arley on the Severn Valley Railway. GWR 0-6-0PT No 5764 is seen crossing with a photo charter on 1 November 2006. DON BISHOP

Pat Whitehouse and Pat Garland were among a group of businessmen who saw that steam would soon become a novelty when it was swept away from the national network, and that the branch could be run as a profit-making tourist attraction. So they established the Dart Valley Light Railway Co. Ltd. to buy the line and acquire suitable locomotives.

The two Pats bought their first engine, GWR 2-6-2T No 4555, for £700, which included a spare boiler, an overhaul at Swindon and a load of spare parts.

The pair followed up this initial purchase by acquiring GWR 0-6-0PTs No 6435 (with John Wilkins) and No 1638, and Collett 0-4-2T No 1420, historically appropriate to the Ashburton branch.

In the mid-sixties, the Dart Valley was not ready to house the locomotives, so they had to be stored elsewhere. Pat Whitehouse identified the BR steam depot at Tyseley in Birmingham as a suitable location.

While it was shedded there, No 4555 returned to regular British Railways traffic, even though it was privately owned! Tyseley's shedmaster rostered it for the 5.25pm commuter services from Birmingham Snow Hill to Knowle & Dorridge – and Pat's son Michael fondly remembered: "Pat Garland worked as an accountant in the city, and would catch that train home. He would jump on the footplate and drive his own engine – and get off at Knowle & Dorridge!"

Around the same time, WR 4-6-0 No 7029 *Clun Castle* became available for purchase, and in 1966 Pat Whitehouse provided much of the cash to buy it before transferring it to a new company, 7029 Clun Castle Ltd.

At first intended for static display inside a museum earmarked for Buckfastleigh, being took big to run on the branch, it remained at Tyseley, because still a great demand for it to haul enthusiast railtours.

Tyseley developed as a major preservation centre in its own right, and in terms of overhauling classic GWR express locomotives for main line use, was to become the Swindon of the 21st century. In October 1968, two months after the end of BR steam haulage, Tyseley held its first and very successful open day.

On 5 April 1969, the same year that the Dart Valley Railway bought the line from the WR, the first heritage era trains ran from Buckfastleigh to a point near the main line junction north of Totnes, under the new operator's Light Railway Order, behind GWR 0-6-0PT No 6412. The heritage line was officially opened by none other than Dr Richard Beeching himself.

Sadly, the revivalists could not stop the Ministry of Transport from taking the northernmost two miles for use as part of the new A38 trunk road, and so Ashburton was lost. Buckfastleigh was transformed into a terminus and grew into a major visitor attraction, with a museum, café and shop, otter sanctuary and butterfly farm, while the remaining seven-mile line splendidly rekindled the spirit of the archetypal GWR country branch line of the steam era.

Dart Valley Railway plc soon went on to far bigger fish.

In 1968, the WR proposed the closure of the Paignton-Kingswear line, but the revivalist company stepped in and bought it, taking it over as a going concern on 30 December 1972. It was the first part of the operational WR to be privatised.

A winter service was operated from 1 January 1973 but from the end of that summer it became a purely seasonal operation.

An independent station alongside the main station at Paignton, known as Queens Park, was opened to serve the Kingswear trains on the site of the old Park sidings.

The seven-mile route, better resembling a main line rather than a branch, had always been a major hit with tourists, and is the only heritage line to pay a regular dividend to shareholders. It offers sweeping views of the spectacular Torbay coastline as well as the sylvan Dart estuary.

In 1999 it acquired two riverboat companies, and began offering 'round Robin' trips, with passengers taking the train to Kingswear, a boat upriver to Totnes and a vintage bus back to Paignton. The company also acquired the Kingswear-Dartmouth ferry, bringing it back into railway operation as it has beeen under the GWR, which had a station without tracks at Dartmouth.

For years known as the Paignton & Dartmouth Steam Railway, in 2010 it was rebranded as the Dartmouth Steam Railway & Riverboat Company.

The GWR Severn Valley and Tenbury Wells closed in 1963, and enthusiasts there wondered if they too could have their own Bluebell Railway.

Keith Beddowes, the man credited with the founding of the Severn Valley Railway, said: "I thought that if those down south could do it, why not us?"

Her and a few like-mined enthusiasts organised a meeting at the Cooper's Arms in Habberley near Kidderminster on 6 July 1965, to decide which line to try to save. The 50 people present voted for the Severn Valley, the initial target being the four miles between Bridgnorth and Hampton Loade.

Helped by local Tory MP Sir Gerald Nabarro, the scheme grew from strength to strength, and on 23 May 1970, the first Severn Valley train ran, behind GWR 0-6-0 No 3205, which on 25 March 1967, had become the first engine to arrive on the line.

More of the cross-country was saved, and as the membership numbers swelled to more than 14,000, Bewdley was reached in 1974 and Kidderminster in 1984, making a total of 16 miles. After the North Yorkshire Moors Railway, the Severn Valley is Britain's second most popular heritage line in terms of annual visitor numbers.

Auto fitted pannier No 6430 crossing Dee Bridge Llangollen with a regular service on 13 March 2004. DON BISHOP

Before Swindon so rudely interrupted: Welshpool & Llanfair 0-6-0T No 2 *Countess* in its later guise as GWR No 823 stands at the Llanfair Caereinion terminus with two of the replica Pickering carriages, which replaced the originals scrapped at Swindon after passenger services were withdrawn in 1931. ANDREW CHARMAN/WLLR

The Dean Forest Railway Society was formed in 1970 to preserve the GWR Lydney to Parkend branch line which was still open for goods traffic. Its first steam open day took place in October 1971, with Peckett locomotive *Uskmouth* hauling brake van rides sidings.

Revivalists bought the 4¾-mile line from British Rail in 1986 but it was not until December 2005 that it was able to run trains along the full length of the line.

In 1972, international wildlife artist David Shepherd bought Cranmore station and a section of the closed GWR Cheddar Valley line to accommodate his two locomotives; BR Standard 9F 2-10-0 No 92203 *Black Prince* and BR Standard 4MT 4-6-0 No 75029 *The Green Knight*. Marketed as the East Somerset Railway, the original name of the line, it gave brake van rides in 1973 before extending to Mendip Vale in 1985, with Shepton Mallet the ultimate goal.

Following the closure of the GWR Minehead branch on 2 January 1971, the newly-formed Minehead Railway Preservation Society organised a meeting in Taunton with a view to reopening it privately. Two years later, Somerset County Council bought the line and leased it to the West Somerset Railway Company, which ran its first trains between Minehead to Blue Anchor on 28 March 1976, services reaching the current passenger terminus of Bishops Lydeard on 9 June 1979. Today, the West Somerset Railway is Britain's longest standard gauge heritage line, at 24 miles from the main line connection which now frequently accepts incoming charters.

A turntable has been installed at Minehead while a turning triangle has been built at Norton Fitzwarren, using a short section of the GWR Taunton-Barnstaple line.

After the last freight train ran over the remaining section of the GWR Carmarthen-Aberystwyth cross-country route in September 1973, revivalists stepped in and in April 1975, the Gwili Railway Company was formed to buy eight miles of trackbed between Abergwili Junction and Llanpumpsaint. The first passenger train ran in 1978 and by 2001 services were running 2½ miles from the headquarters at Bronwydd Arms station to a new terminus at Danycoed.

A separate group has revived part of the GWR Newcastle Emlyn branch, which joined the Carmarthen-Aberyswirth troute further north, as the 2ft gauge Teifi Valley Railway, centred on Henllan station, from where trains run to Llandyfriog Riverside.

In 1972, the Flint & Deeside Railway Preservation Society was formed to revive one of the closed lines in North Wales, as first looking at the Dyserth to Prestatyn line. Instead, the Llangollen to Corwen section of the GWR Ruabon to Barmouth line was chosen. A section further west alongside Lake Bala was being revived as a 2ft gauge line, the Bala Lake Railway. After the local council granted a lease, Llangollen station reopened on 13 September 1975, with just 60ft of track. By July 1981, three-quarters-of-a-mile of track ran as far at Pentrefelin.

Progressing in stages, the Llangollen Railway reached Carrog, a distance of 7½ miles in 1996, and is now pushing on to Corwen.

The Telford Steam Railway was formed in 1976 and run over a section of the Wellington & Severn Junction Railway, which was operated by the GWR. Its aim is to extend to Ironbridge. The heritage line based at Horsehay & Dawley first steamed its GWR 0-6-2T No 5619 in 1981 and opened to the public in 1984.

Following the closure of the GWR Stratford-upon-Avon-Cheltenham route after a derailment in 1976 and the lifting of the track three years later, the Gloucestershire Warwickshire Railway was formed the restore the entire route, and in 1981 moved into derelict Toddington station, running its first short trains there in 1984. In 2003, Princess Anne officially opened the line as far the superbly-restored Cheltenham (Racecourse) station, and for the line's GWR 175 celebrations in late May/early June 2010, the first public passenger trains were run over the stupendous Stanway Viaduct towards the next goal of Broadway.

London's GWR Preservation Group, which hopes one day to run steam again on the GWR Brentford branch, was formed in 1981 and operated Southall depot as a working railway centre in the 1990s until it was forced to close it to the public in 1997. The base is now used for restoring and maintaining its locomotives and rolling stock.

With the closure of the LSWR Wenford mineral branch in 1983, the Bodmin Railway Preservation Society was formed to save as much of the surviving GWR system around Bodmin as possible and held its first open day at Bodmin General in 1986, offering brake van rides in the station limits. In 1990, the Bodmin & Wenford Railway ran its first public passenger trips between Bodmin General and Bodmin Parkway, and six years later opened its 'second' line to Boscarne Junction.

Another delightful country branch to be brought back to life is the 3½-mile Chinnor and Princes Risborough Railway. Occupying part of the GWR Watlington branch, which closed to passengers on 1 July 1957 but remained open for freight. The revivalists ran their first passenger train on 20 August 1994.

When freight ended on the GWR Wallingford branch in 1981, the Cholsey & Wallingford Railway Preservation Society was formed to revive the line for tourist services. It first ran train rides for the public in 1985, with regular services over the 2½-mile line starting in 1997.

The surviving complex of GWR lines

Preservation history was made in May 2010 when, prior to the line's GWR 175 celebrations, GWR small prairie No 5542 headed an auto trailer over Stanway Viaduct, marking the first heritage era passenger trains on the line from Toddington north to Broadway. JACK BOSKETT

A modern-day GWR engine shed: Toddington on the Gloucestershire Warwickshire Railway with No 3717 *City of Truro*, Collett auto tank No 1450, Hawksworth 0-6-0PT No 9466 and prairie No 5542, with the Severn Valley Railway's No 7802 *Bradley Manor* in the shed. The engines were gathered for the 29 May-6 June 2010 Cotswold Festival of Steam marking GWR 175. IAN CROWDER/GWR

around Oswestry has been the focus of revival attempts since the Cambrian Railways Society was formed in 1971. The separate Cambrian Railways Trust restored a section of the Oswestry-Welshpool line between its new Llynclys South station and Penygarreg Lane, starting diesel multiple unit trips in 2006, while the society revived the freight-only Nantmawr branch and ran the first trains over the third of a mile line in November 2009. The two groups have now merged under the banner of the Cambrian Heritage Railways with the aim of reopening the mothballed Oswestry branch from Gobowen Junction to Llanyblodwel Quarry as well.

Another revived line is the 1½-mile Barry Island Railway, which runs alongside the Network Rail branch from Barry to Barry Island, ironically a stone's throw from the site of Dai Woodham's scrapyard. It has its origins in the formation of Butetown Historic Railway Society in Cardiff in 1979.

In December 1966 a group of enthusiasts formed the Corris Railway Society with the aim of preserving what was left of the line, opening a dedicated museum, and to perhaps revive part of the route. On 20 April 1985, Corris Railway No 5, a Simplex Motor Rail four-wheeled diesel named *Alan Meaden* in honour of the society's founder hauling a rake of wagons, formed the official "first train" back to Corris in 1985, witnessed by former Corris Railway workers.

In autumn 1996, former Corris locomotive No 4 visited from the Talyllyn to celebrate its 75th anniversary, and passenger trains returned after a 72-year gap, at 11am on 3 June 2002.

The railway has also had a £120,000 replica Kerr Stuart Tattoo 0-4-2ST built as a substitute for the original No 4, which was sold to the Talyllyn by the Western Region. It therefore counts as a replica "GWR inherited" engine.

The Swindon & Cricklade Railway was formed in 1978 to relay a section of the Midland & South Western Junction Railway that ran from Andover to Cheltenham, and which became part of the GWR at the Grouping of 1923. It is hoped to eventually reconnect both towns by rail.

The Plym Valley Raiway currently occupies three quarters of a mile of the GWR Plymouth-Tavistock line at Marsh Mills. It ran its first public trains on 14 October 2001, and hopes to extend to Plym Bridge Halt, a distance of 1½ miles.

Devon Railway Centre is based at Cadeleigh station near Tiverton and includes a 2ft gauge running line on part of the GWR exe Valley trackbed.

In the far west of Cornwall, part of the Helston branch has been relaid at Trevarno Gardens.

A 'secret' revived GWR branch has Herefordshire's Titley Junction station as its headquarters. Not open to the public, it is the property of Robert and Lesley Hunt who bought the station in October 2001 and have since relaid a mile of the New Radnor branch towards Bullocks Mill, with the first steam trip running on 27 August 2005. The couple have named their operation the Kingfisher Line.

Finally, mention must be made of the superb Pendon Museum, in Long Wittenham near Didcot, which has several model layouts based on typical GWR scenes of the 1920s and a large collection of artefacts.

1976

28 March: First West Somerset Railway trains run from Minehead to Blue Anchor.
13 July: Death in Swindon of Frederick Hawksworth, last GWR CME 28 August: West Somerset services extended to Williton.
4 Oct: Full HST service introduced between London and Bristol and South Wales.

1977

Class 40 No 40106 is the last main line locomotive in Brunswick green.
Air-conditioned stock introduced on the West of England services.
Bugle Steam Railway begins operating on a freight spur off the GWR Newquay branch
28 Feb: Last Class 52 Western withdrawn, two days after D1013 *Western Ranger* and D1023 *Western Fusilier* headed the 'Western Tribute' tour.
May: Full complement of 27 HST sets completely replace locomotive-hauled trains on the Bristol and South Wales routes, with 98.2mph reached on Paddington-Reading and 95.8mph Paddington-Parkway. Prototype HST withdrawn: driving car No 41001 is now in the National Railway Museum at York.
29 May: Bill McAlpine sells No 4079 *Pendennis Castle* to Australian firm Hammersley Iron for its Pilbara Historic Railway Society, and is duly exported on this date.

1978

First trains run on Gwili Railway.
Light Railway Order for East Somerset Railway granted.
May: West Somerset services extended to Stogumber.

1979

1 March: *King George V* returns steam to Paddington.
GWR 2-6-2T No 4110 is the 100th locomotive to leave Barry scrapward and moved to GWR Preservation Group's Southall Railway Centre.
BR lifts Stratford-upon-Avon-Cheltenham route.
10 April: A HST sets a new record, 111.7mph start-to-stop between Paddington and Chippenham.
9 June: West Somerset services extended to Bishops Lydeard.
October: HSTs appeared on the West of England line and take over the 'Cornish Riviera Express' in its 75th year.

GWR | 105

Scrapman saves the GWR!

Brunel, Gooch, Dean, Churchward, Collett… all of these were men who made the Great Western great by what they built.

By contrast, the late Dai Woodham inadvertently worked a miracle to help the GWR live on into a third century and hopefully way beyond – by not destroying things.

Dai was a scrapman through and through. His Woodham Brothers scrapyard at Barry was one of many around Britain that took delivery of the thousands of classic main line steam locomotives made redundant by the BR Modernisation Plan of 1955. Many of them perfectly serviceable and some only a few years old, or with relatively new boilers, they were bought for scrap value and at virtually all places, they were cut up within days.

Although the British Transport Commission had drawn up a list of selected locomotives for preservation as part of a National Collection, it was not enough to stop many types being rendered extinct.

One day in 1965, Dai made a fateful business decision which changed the course of British railway heritage. He worked out that it was more profitable to cut up scrap wagons and leave the locomotives in his yard until last.

Accordingly, his scrapyard famously became home to rows of rusting hulks, a real steam graveyard.

At the same time, the volunteer-led railway preservation movement, which had begun in 1951 with the saving of the narrow gauge Talyllyn Railway, was gathering pace. At that time, it was still possible to buy locomotives straight out of British Railways service, but with the end of steam in sight, that option was rapidly diminishing.

Rail revivalists then looked to Barry scrapyard, where many of the engines had been in service in recent years and would require comparatively little restoration to return them to steam.

The first Barry scrapyard locomotive believed to be the subject of a rescue appeal was GWR 2-6-0 No 5322, now at Didcot Railway Centre (repainted in 2008 into its World War One khaki livery of the Royal Ordnance Corps). However, the first to be bought and moved from the yard was Midland Railway 4F 0-6-0 No 43924, which was in September 1968 given a second life at the Keighley & Worth Valley Railway. Buyers were able to obtain spare parts from other locomotives in the yard.

As the years went by and more heritage railways started up, demand for Barry wrecks as medium and long-term restoration projects increased. As the number of locomotives fell below 100 and the amount of wagons arriving also diminished, The Barry Steam Locomotive Action Group was formed 10 February 1979 with the aim of facilitating the preservation of the remaining steam engines on site. That did not prevent

Rows of scrap locomotives, notably GWR pannier tanks, await the cutter's torch at Woodham Brothers scrapyard. Thankfully, for 213 locomotives, it did not come.

Old soldiers never die! Forsaking Brunswick green livery, GWR 2-6-0 No 5322 celebrated GWR 175 in the khaki livery it carried when built at Swindon as a batch of 20 for Royal Ordnance Corps service in France in World War One. Demobbed in 1919 at Chester, it entered 'civvy street' with the GWR; it was withdrawn from Pontypool Road depot in April 1964. In 1969 it became the first GWR locomotive to leave Barry scrapyard for preservation, and at first moved to Caerphilly, where local members of the Great Western Society restored it to working order. It moved to Didcot Railway Centre in 1973, ran for two years; and following a major overhaul, returned to steam again in November 2008. FRANK DUMBLETON/GWS

two locomotives being cut up the following summer in the form of BR Standard 9F 2-10-0 No 92085 and GWR 5101 class 2-6-2T No 4156; however, these were the last to be scrapped. When Dai Woodham announced his retirement, 10 locomotives, known as the 'Barry Ten', were acquired by the Vale of Glamorgan Council for future restoration or museum purposes.

The last engine out of the scrapyard was GWR 4575 2-6-2T No 5553, which left in January 1990 for the West Somerset Railway, and is now owned by pop mogul Pete Waterman, having been restored to running order at Tyseley Locomotive Works.

A total of 213 locomotives were bought or preserved from the scrapyard. They included 95 GWR or WR examples – a generous slice of the 381 British Railways standard gauge steam engines that exist today.

Because Barry lay in Western Region territory and dealt directly with it, most of the engines it bought were GWR or Southern types. By comparison, only one LNER engine, B1 No 61264, was saved from Barry. Hence there is a great imbalance today in the heritage railway portfolio towards the GWR and Southern Railway, as other regions did not have the benefit of an inadvertently benevolent Dai Woodham.

There are many, many success stories of restorations of Barry hulks.

The 50th locomotive to be saved from the yard was 1946-built GWR 2-6-2T No 4144, a veteran of the Severn Tunnel car ferry service now at Didcot Railway Centre, following its 'rescue' in April 1974. The 100th was GWR 2-6-2T No 4110, owned by the Southall-based GWR Preservation Group, and which has yet to be restored.

A scene of desolation masked volumes of heritage hope at Barry scrapyard in the 1970s – but for GWR 2-6-2T No 4561, a new life and full restoration awaited on the West Somerset Railway. BRIAN SHARPE

1980
Last North British Warship, D601 *Ark Royal*, scrapped at Barry.
First Class 14 diesel, D9526, preserved.
HST services on the West of England route extended.
Brecon Mountain Railway runs first train over part of Brecon & Merthyr Railway.
Pannier No 7754 is last in private industrial service, with NCB at Mountain Ash Colliery.
15 Jan: New-1¼-mile line serves the Ford factory at Bridgend.

1981
New timing of 3 hours 4 minutes from Paddington to Plymouth introduced.
Gloucestershire Warwickshire Railway revivalists move into Toddington station.
Swindon & Cricklade Railway occupies Blunsdon station.
Plym Valley Railway founded and moves on to Marsh Mills site on GWR Plymouth-Tavistock trackbed.
Llangollen Railway laid to Pentrefelin, three-quarters of a mile from Llangollen.
22 May: Honeybourne station reopened.
18 July: Welshpool & Llanfair passenger trains return to Welshpool (Raven Square)

1982
John Doubleday's statue of Isambard Brunel unveiled on Paddington concourse.
HSTs debut on North East/South West route.
New 57-tonne Clay Tiger wagons introduced along with a new terminus opened at Stoke-on-Trent for the bulk movement of ECC china clay from Cornwall.

1983
Final railtour over Wenfordbridge freight branch.
Pinhoe and Templecombe reopened along with a new station at Cathays.
11 June: Gala evening at the Brunel Engineering Centre Trust's original Brunel station at Bristol to celebrate the formation of the Bristol Committee of the nascent GWR and the appointment of Isambard Kingdom Brunel.
18 June: Death of Robert Riddles, aged 91.

One for the future: GWR 2-8-0 No 3862 heads a line-up of rusting hulks at Barry in the 70s. Now at the Northampton & Lamport Railway, it is still unrestored in 2010. BRIAN SHARPE

WR 0-6-0PT No 9682, pictured at Hayes Knoll on the Swindon & Cricklade Railway on 17 January 2000, where it became the 100th Barry scrapyard locomotive restored to working order, following the end of its overhaul at Swindon Locomotive Carriage & Wagon Works, which operated in part of Swindon Works where it was built in 1949. No 9682 earned further fame when it became what is believed to be the first restored main line steam locomotive to haul a train carrying the Queen and the Duke of Edinburgh, from Bodmin Parkway to Bodmin General station over the Bodmin & Wenford Railway on 8 June that year. JOHN STRETTON

Ex-Barry scrapyard 2-6-2T No 5526 stands at Carrog on the Llangollen Railway in April 2009. ROBIN JONES

The 10th locomotive to be saved from Barry subsequently went out of existence! When in October 1971, Birmingham Railway Museum took delivery of GWR 4-6-0 No 4983 *Albert Hall*, little did their officials realise that the locomotive was really No 4965 *Rood Ashton Hall*. A latter-day decision in Swindon Works to 'make one good one out of two bad ones' as the steam era drew to a close became apparent only during the final stages of restoration in 1997, when stampings on the locomotive's components revealed that the frames were those of No 4965, despite it running for the final 19 months of WR service as *Albert Hall*.

The 100th Barry scrapyard locomotive to be restored to running order was WR pannier tank No 9682, owned by the Southall group, and which steamed again early in 2000.

GWR 4-6-0 No 4936 *Kinlet Hall* may be considered to be the greatest of all Barry survivors, for it narrowly escaped being blown to pieces by a Luftwaffe bomb dropped on Plymouth in 1941. Withdrawn in 1964, it was bought in May 1981 by airline pilot Pete Weaver and a consortium, and also returned to running order in 2000.

Among the regular performers on the main line today is 1930-built GWR 4-6-0 No 6024 *King Edward I*, which broke new territory in 1998 by becoming the first King to officially cross the Tamar Bridge at Saltash and enter Cornwall, despite the prohibitive weight restrictions in GWR and BR days. And just look at the feat of GWR 4-6-0 No 5043 *Earl of Mount Edgcumbe*, bought by Tyseley initially only as a source of spares for other restored locomotives, in hauling 'The Bristolian' in 2010, as highlighted on pages 124-127.

God bless Dai Woodham.

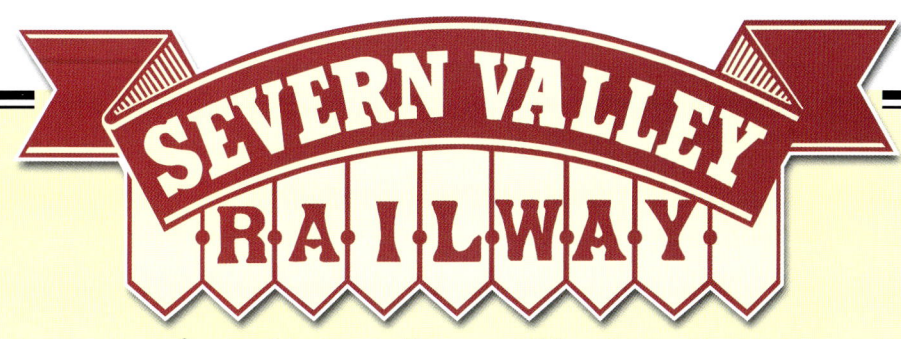

the line for all seasons

AUTUMN STEAM GALA

Fri 24th September - Sun 26th September 2010

**Visiting steam locomotives including:
The iconic GWR 4-4-0 No. 3717
'City of Truro', courtesy of NRM**

SAVE MONEY by booking on-line - click "Ticket Office" at www.svr.co.uk

All events subject to availability

'Heroic' SVR engines produced as 00 Gauge boxed set for GWR 175

Two Severn Valley Railway steam locomotives which helped rescue the 'GWR 150' main line steam programme in 1985 following some unfortunate locomotive failures, have been produced as a limited edition boxed set in 00 gauge by Bachmann, to celebrate 'GWR 175' 25 years later.

The two SVR engines – **4930 Hagley Hall** in GWR green and **7819 Hinton Manor** in lined black just as in 1985 – are presented in a polished wooden box as a limited edition of 500, with certificate of authenticity, selling for £200 inc P&P.

LTD Edition just £200 inc P&P

This giftset can be ordered online from the Severn Valley Railway giftshop at:
www.svr.co.uk/giftshop.aspx

SEVERN VALLEY RAILWAY
**The Railway Station, Bewdley, Worcs DY12 1BG
Tel: 01299 403816 www.svr.co.uk**

Every schoolboy's dream

THE GWR publicity machine made much of the appeal of steam locomotives to youngsters, publishing a series of books to inspire every boy who was enchanted by the sight of a Brunswick green express passenger locomotive roaring past or who wanted to be an engine driver.

Such marketing paid huge dividends, including some that never occurred to the Paddington public relations department of the 20s and 30s.

In the August 1961 edition of *The Railway Magazine*, schoolboy linesider Jon Barlow had a letter published, inviting donations for the preservation of a GWR 1400 class 0-4-2T. He and his friends Mike Peart, Angus Davis and Graham Perry, trainspotting from the footbridge at Southall after classes one day in 1961, expressed their disappointment at the omission of the type from the British Transport Commission's National Collection list and wanted to preserve a complete GWR auto train.

Their initiative led to the formation of the 48XX Preservation Society which held its inaugural meeting on 4 May 1962. It quickly evolved into the Great Western Preservation Society, eventually becoming the Great Western Society in June 1963.

Fund-raising continued during 1962 and 1963, until a shortlist of locomotives that had included Nos 1442, 1444, 1450 and 1466 was reduced to just Nos 1450 and 1466.

No 1450 was perhaps considered favourite but as it was unlikely to be withdrawn for about another year, it was decided at the society's annual general meeting in February 1964 to go for No 1466, which ended its days on the Exe Valley and Tiverton branches as the £750 funding was available.

It was delivered in steam to its temporary home on the Totnes Quay branch from Taunton on 18 March 1964, and first steamed under society ownership the following month. Auto coach No 231 was bought for £300 that November. The first society open day was held at Totnes on 17 October 1964, with No 1466 and 0-6-0ST No 1363 giving rides in Dreadnought coach No 3299. In January 1966, No 1466 moved to Buckfastleigh, where the Dart Valley Railway was being established. It had been intended to run the society's stock on the new heritage line, but members felt that they would be giving up too much control.

As the society quickly grew, branch depots developed at other boltholes like Bodmin General, Hereford and Caerphilly, each having their own small collection of locomotives and rolling stock.

The society then bought GWR 4-6-0 No 6998 *Burton Agnes Hall* and several coaches, leaving no space at Totnes Quay, so another depot was set up at Taplow for the next arrival, GWR 2-6-2T No 6106.

Events were overtaking the founder members as the society's support mushroomed, and it was clear that with the impending closure of Taplow goods yard and the decision not to go in with the Dart Valley on a closer basis, a permanent headquarters was needed.

It came in the form of the BR locomotive depot at Didcot, which had been made redundant by dieselisation. It had been built

A dozen of the GWR locomotives now housed at Didcot Railway Centre, seen on 1 May 2010 from the top of the adjacent water tower, at the start of the venue's nine-day GWR 175 extravaganza. Front row: Nos 5322, 5900, 6998, 7827, 5051, 5029. Second row: Nos 5572, 6697, 4144, 6106, 7808, 3822. FRANK DUMLETON/GWS

Not carrying Brunswick green is the Great Western Society's latest success, the rebuild of Barry wreck GWR 4-6-0 No 6023 *King Edward II*, which was completed in summer 2010 and will appear in the early and short-lived British Railways express passenger locomotive blue livery. The rebuild of the 1930-built single-chimneyed King is particularly remarkable in that its driving wheels were cut in half at Barry, and other restorationists considered it 'mission impossible'. In 1984 it became the 159th engine to leave Barry, having been there 22 years.

in 1932 by the GWR, using loans provided by the government to relieve unemployment, to replace an earlier and smaller structure serving the Didcot, Newbury and Southampton Railway. The site lay in a triangle where Brunel's GWR main line met the line to Oxford and Birmingham, and the big disadvantage that persists to this day is that it has no road access, all stock having to be moved in and out by rail, and visitors accessing what became Didcot Railway Centre only through a subway from the main station.

Nos 1466 and 6998, together with coaches Nos 231, 3299, 5952 and a BR BG carrying stores and spares, moved under their own steam from Totnes to Didcot on 2 December 1967. One of the first tasks after arrival was to letter No 1466's tanks Great Western.

Twice in 1968, on 15 April and 21 September, No 1466 and auto-coach No 231 operated on the Cholsey-Wallingford branch, itself a later target for preservation, but the BR ban on steam running that became effective later in 1968 meant that steamings would from then on have to be concentrated at Didcot, although No 1466 still visited Wallingford in steam for carnival day on 21 June 1969.

No 1466 was steamed for the first public open day held at Didcot on 10 May 1969 giving rides in No 231. It also starred in a 1971 film about Winston Churchill's early life, to be called *Young Winston*, being mocked up with plywood, a cow catcher and a large oil lamp to resemble a 'freelance' British Army armoured train during the Boer War.

In the mid-70s, all the branch group collections were brought to the Didcot site.

Didcot, which has three short demonstration lines where passenger rides are offered, has been a resounding success. Its locomotive collection has grown to 22 standard gauge steam locomotives, GWR diesel railcar No 22, the replica broad gauge *Fire Fly*, the GWR steam railmotor No 93 rebuilding project plus the advanced retro-conversion of GWR 4-6-0 No 4942 *Maindy Hall* into Saint No 2999 *Lady of Legend*, with more new-build projects on their way (see separate chapter).

When the Australian owners of GWR 4-6-0 No 4079 *Pendennis Castle*, who had acquired it in 1976, decided to donate it back to Britain in 2000, they chose Didcot as the perfect home.

Nowhere else today have so many Brunswick green locomotives gathered together in one spot, along with a multitude of GWR relics big and small on display. The Great Western Society in 2010 has been with us 47 years, nearly twice as long as the 25 years that the 'Big Four' GWR lasted. The GWR placed Didcot on the map, and is continuing to do so!

1984
GWR 4-6-0 No 4953 *Pitchford Hall* becomes 150th Barry engine saved, moving to Dean Forest Railway.
Llangollen Railway granted Light Railway Order.
13 Feb: WR headquarters moved to Swindon from Paddington.
14 May: New Westbury panel box brought into operation.
30 July: Severn Valley Railway opens Bewdley to Kidderminster Town section.
30 Aug: HST named *Top of the Pops* after record Paddington-Bristol run of 62 minutes 33 seconds, averaging 112.8mph.
22 April: Transport Secretary Nicholas Ridley officially opens first quarter mile of the Gloucestershire Warwickshire Railway.

1985
GWR 150 anniversary celebrations held across company's former territory.
Steam returns to South Devon banks and mothballed Portishead branch.
Birmingham Railway Museum runs first 'Shakespeare Express'.
Formation of Bodmin & Wenford Railway: merges with Bugle Steam Railway which moves to Bodmin General.
The 2ft gauge North Gloucestershire Railway built alongside the Gloucestershire Warwickshire Railway at Toddington.
Broad gauge *Iron Duke* replica built for NRM.
20 Apr: Goods train marks first working over reborn Corris Railway.

1986
Swindon Works closes.
Replica *Iron Duke* runs first broad gauge train at Didcot since 1982.
First Llangollen railway trains to Berwyn.

1987
Steam returns to Cambrian Coast line with 'Cardigan Bay Express'.
Rebuilt Birmingham Snow Hill opened for services to the south. Services to London were restarted, but to Marylebone, not Paddington.
HST sets new 148mph world speed record for diesels.
Second class becomes Standard class.
27 June: West Somerset Railway opened Doniford Halt to serve a holiday camp at Helwell Bay.

1988
BR decides to sell Vale of Rheidol Railway.

GWR steam
back on the main line

Today's portfolio of heritage railways can only be described as magnificent, especially in view of the fact that most were the product of volunteer labour. However, preserved lines, light all light railways, have a maximum speed of 25mph for passenger services.

To experience the majesty of a King or Castle in full flight, there can be only one place – the main line.

After steam on British Rail's standard gauge officially ended on 11 August 1968, apart from the pre-arranged trip to Wallingford of No 1466 six weeks later, only LNER A3 Pacific No 4472 *Flying Scotsman* was permitted to run over the national network. Steam infrastructure such as water columns and troughs was ripped out, sidings were lifted with the demise of the pick-up goods while much of the classic station architecture was 'rationalised' as a wave of utilitarianism rather than style swept through the system.

For the dismayed enthusiasts, a chink in the iron curtain presented by the ban came in July 1969, when BR allowed Tyseley's GWR 4-6-0 No 7029 *Clun Castle* and LMS Jubilee 4-6-0 No 5593 *Kolhapur*, plus 'Black Five' No 5428 to steam at the Cricklewood Depot open day.

They were permitted to haul short passenger trains up a designated length of track.

Meanwhile, all hope was not lost, Behind the scenes, the Association of Railway Preservation Societies, the forerunner of today's Heritage Railway Association, had been gingerly holding talks with the somewhat obstinate BR board about allowing steam specials back on the main line.

The breakthrough came with the appointment of Richard Marsh as BR chairman in 1971.

Finally, some ground was given, and a trial run in October 1971 was given the green light.

At that time, cider maker Bulmers had opened a steam centre at its Hereford headquarters, and acquired a rake of Pullman coaches on which the umber livery was changed to green.

It was Bulmers managing director Peter Prior who persuaded the BR board to make a 180 degree U-turn was, Having sponsored the overhaul of National Collection GWR icon 4-6-0 No 6000 *King George V*, he wanted to see the engine haul the five-coach Bulmers Pullman exhibition train on a promotional tour of the country

A few extra coaches were added for fare-paying

GWR 4-6-0 No 6000 *King George V* arrives at Tyseley with the Bulmers Cider train in October 1971, marking the end of the British Rail ban on standard gauge steam haulage. CM WHITEHOUSE

passengers and No 6000 made a four-day tour of the Western Region, taking in Kensington Olympia and Birmingham in early October 1971.

It was a huge success, with people of all ages crowding the linesides to glimpse the Brunswick green ambassador from the great days of yore pass by.

The trip was an experiment to see if steam could be run on the modernised system which was geared up only for diesels and electric locomotives. Despite earlier fears by BR, sufficient steam crews were available and solutions were found for coaling and watering the locomotives.

Most importantly, steam locomotives would have to show that while they may be obsolete, they were by no means useless, and must prove that they were reliable working machines and not just antiques. Any breakdown would have immediate consequences on the scheduled timetable, and must be avoided.

A consortium to facilitate main line running was formed jointly by the ARPS and the main preserved steam depots of the day - Didcot, Hereford, Carnforth, and Tyseley.

Following the success of No 6000's trip, BR offered to allow 300 route miles to be reopened for steam haulage. Among five routes chosen for the 'Return to Steam' were Tyseley-Didcot (steam centre at both ends) and Newport-Shrewsbury (No 6000 based at Hereford in the middle).

A total of 23 steam locomotives were listed as being suitable for main line operation. The GWR ones were *Clun Castle*, *King George V*, No 6998 *Burton Agnes Hall* No 4079 *Pendennis Castle*, panniers Nos 7752 and 7760, 2-6-2T No 6106, 0-6-2T No 6697, 0-4-2T No 1466, 2-6-0 No 5322 and BR 9F No 92203 *Black Prince*, which was built at Swindon in January 1959.

The first of the 'Return to Steam' trips took place during 10/11 June 1972. Appropriately, *Clun Castle*, which had hauled main line specials in the sixties after running at the end of WR steam, hauled the first special from Tyseley to Didcot on the Saturday, and back on the Sunday.

Meanwhile, the engine that escaped the ban, *Flying Scotsman*, had been stranded in sunny California, after a promotional tour of North America led to the bankruptcy of its owner Alan Pegler. Multi-millionaire enthusiast Sir William McAlpine bought it and brought it back and its comeback was double-heading the 'Atlantic Venturers Express' on the North & West route with No 6000 on 22 September 1972.

Burton Agnes Hall headed a return trip from Didcot to Tyseley on 1 October,

Early days at Tyseley shed: before the GWR roundhouse was demolished, privately-preserved prairie No 4555 was not only stabled there, but ended up being rostered on Birmingham Snow Hill-Knowle & Dorridge suburban services! These humble beginnings paved the way for Tyseley to develop into today's Swindon equivalent in terms of locomotive rebuilding and maintenance. MICHAEL WHITEHOUSE COLLECTION

while LMS Jubilee 4-6-0 No 5596 *Bahamas* and *King George V* each operated one leg of a Shrewsbury to Hereford return tour on 14 October.

On 11 November 1972, *King George V* hauled the Bulmers cider train from Hereford to Newport for a filming assignment. That year, a total of 12 main line steam trips were run, BR admitting that no real problems were encountered and that a small profit had been made.

The following year, Oxford-Worcester-Hereford, Hatton-Lapworth-Stratford-upon-Avon and Tyseley-Stratford via the north Warwickshire Line were approved for steam. The latter, one of the last routes to be built by the GWR, is a heritage line by the back door, for Earlswood station apart, most of the original station buildings remain intact, along with the original double track, and as well as the busy commuter line from Shirley into Birmingham, it still serves sparsely-used stops like Wood End, Danzey for Tanworth and Wootton Wawen – a real steam age survivor.

On 13 May 1973, a tank engine returned to the main line in the form of Tyseley's GWR pannier No 7752, which ran a shuttle service from Birmingham Moor Street to Stratford, and on 15 July, *Burton Agnes Hall* was joined by No 6106 on the Marlow branch which was celebrating its centenary.

June 24 that year saw the Great Western Society run the 'Great Western Returns' tour with *Burton Agnes Hall* hauling a Didcot-Hereford and back trip, and *King George V* running from Hereford to Shrewsbury and back. Sadly, the Hall failed at Worcester and needed diesel assistant to return to Didcot. Nonetheless, it was back in time to haul 'The William Shakespeare' from Didcot to Stratford and back on 29 September.

More was to follow in 1974, and on 19 October, the Great Western Society's 'Vintage Train' was double headed by No 7808 *Cookham Manor* and *Burton Agnes Hall*, and comprised eight restored GWR coaches.

Evening Star returned to the national network on 31 May 1975 when it headed a special from Leeds to Carnforth, before returning to Keighley.

The preservation movement was shell shocked in February 1977 when Sir Wiliam McAlpine announced that he had sold regular main line performer *Pendennis Castle* to Australian firm Hammersley Iron for its Pilbara Railway Society. It would not return until 2000.

The 'other' Severn Valley railway is Network Rail's branch to Buildwas power station. On 14 November 2009, pannier tanks No 9600 and 9466 climb past Coalbrookdale with Vintage Trains' 'Stephenson Locomotive Society Special'. ALAN CASTLE

Despite the success of the early tours, it was not all plain sailing, for at times there were serious fears that BR would cut the permitted route mileage, rather than continuing to increase it as had been the case. However, in 1978 BR announced it would itself market steam-hauled trains on the main line for the first time since 1968.

One such BR trip on 1 March 1979, to Didcot, marked the 125th anniversary of Paddington station, and marked the return of steam to the GWR terminus in the form of *King George V*, which sadly failed at its destination and did not make it back.

The Great Western Society's 'Vintage Train' made its last-ever appearance on the national network on 26 January 1980, behind the latest main line comeback locomotive, No 5051 *Drysllwyn Castle/Earl Bathurst*.

On 11 June 1983, *King George V* hauled a Bristol-bath private charter to mark the 150th anniversary of the appointment of Brunel to the GWR.

The year 1985 marked GWR 150, with a steam-hauled service running from Swindon to Gloucester, special trains from Bristol to Plymouth, and after it had been replaced by *Clun Castle* on earlier advertised trips, *City of Truro* running from Gloucester to Newport on 20 October. No 6960 *Raveningham Hall* hauled a special between Swansea and Carmarthen while No 7819 *Hinton Manor* and LMS 2-6-2T No 46443 ran over the mothballed Bristol-Portishead line. Something truly different for the heritage era was Churchward 2-8-0 No 2857 taking a heritage goods train to Newport for a 'Rail Freight Spectacular' on 10 September. *Clun Castle* became the first steam engine back on the Cornish main line when it crossed the Royal Albert Bridge with a special from Plymouth to Truro on 5 September.

On 8/9 June, Birmingham Railway Museum ran four return trips between Tyseley and Stratford, featuring *Clun Castle* and *Kolhapur*, which failed after its first trip. These were its first 'Shakespeare Express' trips, and the specials were repeated in 1986 and 1990.

Many milestones in main line running have since been achieved, and the open access policy of 1992 which accompanied privatisation facilitated the availability of previously-banned route mileage which few would have dreamed possible in 1971, including the West of England Main Line via Bristol and to South Wales through the Severn Tunnel. Today, steam over the Dawlish sea wall and south Devon banks is by no means a rare occurrence.

One stalwart in rwecent years has been No 6024 *King Edward I*. The 36th locomotive to be rescued from Barry

GWR 4-6-0 No 7029 *Clun Castle* passing Saltash, making the first preserved steam run into Cornwall, on 5 September 1985, during GWR 150 year. BRIAN SHARPE

King George V, the first member of the GWR's greatest class, had the honour of returning steam to Paddington on 1 March 1979. With GWR No 6024 *King Edward I* available and No 6023 *King Edward II* returning to steam in 2010, it is unlikely to be restored to running order again, especially as the latter two had been modified to fit today's lower network loading gauge. No 6000 spent GWR 175 year on static display at the National Railway Museum in York. BRIAN SHARPE

1989
Brecon Mountain Railway buys Vale of Rheidol Railway from BR.
Bodmin & Wenford Railway opens from Bodmin General to Bodmin Parkway.
Fitzgerald Lighting freight trains run from Bodmin's Walker Lines industrial estate on to main line.
Chinnor & Princes Risborough Railway Association formed to revive part of Watlington branch.

1990
First heritage era main line through train to Minehead.
National Railway Museum on Tour at Swindon Works for the year.
Dart Valley Railway Association leases Buckfastleigh line from Dart Valley Railway plc (which threatened to close its original line) and rebrands it as the South Devon Railway.
Llangollen Railway extends to Deeside Halt.
Jan: Last locomotive, prairie No 5553, leaves Barry scrapyard, making a total of 213 bought for preservation purposes.

1991
No 50035 *Ark Royal* becomes first Class 50 in preservation.

1992
Class 165 Turbo trains appear.
WR ceased to be an operating unit in its own right in the 1980s and was wound up at the end of 1992.
Maesteg line and new stations officially reopened to passengers by Duke of Gloucester after 22 years.
Polish Tkh becomes first engine at attempted North Somerset Railway revival scheme on GWR line at Radstock.

1993
First steam on central Wales line in three decades.
Llangollen Railway extends to Glyndyfrdwy.

1994
BR split into components for sale including 25 passenger franchises, including Great Western, consisting of the express services out of Paddington to the West of England (Bristol, Exeter, Penzance) and South Wales (Cardiff, Swansea).
25 kV 50 Hz AC overhead electrification between Paddington and Heathrow Airport, a joint venture between British Rail and the British Airports Authority.
Engineless Brown Boveri gas turbine locomotive No 18000 reimported from Austria where it had been displayed in Vienna.
Stratford & Broadway Railway Society formed: leases shed at Long Marston MoD depot.
20 August 1994: first Chinnor & Princes Risborough Railway trains.

A restored GWR Barry scrapyard wreck broke new ground by taking the European main line by storm.

Although it is not registered to run on the British national network, 1927-built small prairie No 5521, restored by Bill Parker's Flour Mill colliery at Bream in the Forest of Dean, appeared at the annual spring steam festival at Wolsztyn in Poland in May 2007, 2008 and 2009, occasional hauling regular service trains. It steamed through Poland and Slovakia to Hungary in 2007, and back again in 2008.

No 5521 appeared at the Steam Engine Grand Prix in Zvolen, Slovakia and in Budapest, Hungary, in September, 2007.

On 11 Sept 2007 it piloted nothing less than the Venice Simplon-Orient-Express on its way back from Istanbul to Venice from Budapest's Nyugati station to Kelenfold.

During 2008 it was regularly rostered to operate three daily round-trip suburban passenger trains (36 stops and starts to electric multiple-unit timings) from Wroclaw to Jelcz Laskowice in Poland, under the auspices of the Wolsztyn Experience.

No 5521 experienced no failures during its time in Europe and more than once when double-heading had to haul the whole train due to failure of the other larger locomotives.

GWR 4-6-0 No 4936 *Kinlet Hall* takes on water at Stamford with Vintage Trains' Tyseley-Ely 'Ely Explorer' on 19 July 2008. It was believed to be the first time that a Hall has run over the Midland Railway line from Leicester to Peterborough. ROBIN JONES

scrapyard, in 1973 it was moved to the Buckinghamshire Railway Centre where, on 2 February 1989, it moved again under its own power, and on 26 April that year it was recommissioned by HRH the Duke of Gloucester. Moved to Birmingham Railway Museum, since renamed Tyseley Locomotive Works, it undertook trial runs over the local network and from 15 April 1990 was hauling passenger trains on the main line again. In July that year, it appeared at the National Railway Museum Exhibition On Tour at Swindon Works, where it stood alongside sister *King George V*.

By 1992, No. 6024 was fitted with BR's standard Automatic Warning System, allowing speeds up to 75 mph, and reintroduced steam-hauled express passenger trains to a Cardiff, Bristol Temple Meads, Gloucester, Exeter, Swansea, Worcester, Newton Abbot and Paignton for the first time for many years.

No 6024 has travelled further across the national network than any other member of the class – visiting destinations as far flung as Penzance Fishguard, Crewe, Holyhead, Preston, Carlisle, Blackburn, York, Leeds, Doncaster, Norwich, Cambridge, Salisbury, Bournemouth, Weymouth, and the rival London termini of King's Cross and Victoria.

In 1998, it became the first King to be allowed to cross the Tamar bridge into Cornwall, and in August 2002, it established a new record for steam with the fastest modern-day time for the 52 miles from Plymouth to Exeter, achieved in 58 minutes 6 seconds.

It may have travelled far and wide, but its

For youngsters around the globe, No 5972 *Olton Hall*, pictured at York station 2002, is probably the most famous GWR locomotive of them all, because of its Hogwarts Castle appearances in the seven Harry Potter blockbusters. ROBIN JONES

On the route of the 'Shakespeare Express', Tyseley's GWR 4-6-0 No 4965 *Rood Ashton Hall* heads through Wilmcote on 3 July 2008. ANDREW BELL

fame has been eclipsed on a global scale by a GWR Hall – one that no longer appears in Brunswick green. Also an ex-Barry wreck, No 5972 *Olton Hall* was restored to main line condition by owner David Smith, who runs Carnforth-based train operating company West Coast Railways, and in 1997 made a trial run over Shap at the beginning of its comeback.

In 2001 it was painted bright red after being hired by Warner Brothers to star in the first Harry Potter movies, *Harry Potter and the Philosopher's Stone* as Hogwarts Castle, hauling the 'Hogwarts Express' from Platform 9¾ at King's Cross.. That alone brought it fame and fortune, and model maker Hornby did very well out of its 00 scale version, and it went on to star in another six films. In 2010, a full-size and amazingly-accurate wooden mock-up appeared at the new Wizarding World of Harry Potter theme park in Orlando, Florida.

Sister locomotive No 4953 *Pitchford Hall*, owned by Dr John Kennedy and based at Tyseley Locomotive Works, has cost around £1-million to restore to main line running order from scrapyard condition, perhaps making it the most expensive Hall in history.

It is now one of many locomotives not only to be restored at Tyseley, which as mentioned earlier, had its heritage era origins merely as a place to store prairie No 4555 while the Dart Valley Railway as Buckfastleigh was 'getting ready' in the mid 1960s.

Nowadays, Tyseley is far more than that. With its own main line tour arm, 'Vintage Trains', as a main line steam maintenance and restoration base it is the nearest we have today to Swindon Works. Chief Mechanical Engineer Bob Meanley has overseen the provision and maintenance of a sizeable number of GWR locomotives for the main line - No 4965 *Rood Ashton Hall*, No 4936 *Kinlet Hall*, No 5029 *Nunney Castle*, No 5080 *Defiant*, panniers Nos 7752, 7760 and 9600, and the latest Barry restoration, No 5043 *Earl of Mount Edgcumbe*.

On 20 December 1998, after two years of planning, a new 'Shakespeare Express' was launched, between Birmingham and Stratford, using both the abovementioned North Warwickshire Line and the alternative way back via Lapworth. The first locomotive to haul the new timetabled service was No 4965 *Rood Ashton Hall* – which Tyseley had bought from Barry as No 4983 *Albert Hall* and onlhy in the latter stages of restoration found the correct number stamped on the frames; as its last overhaul at Swindon, it seemed that the WR had decided to 'make one good locomotive out of two bad ones.'

Today, the 'Shakespeare Express' runs two round trips on summer Sundays, and is living proof that GWR is still very much alive, never mind the many other tours that Vintage Trains and other operators run, including the summer 'Torbay Express' from Bristol to Kingswear.

Yet what of the most famous locomotive of all in Tyseley's ranks, the one that was there are the end of WR steam and the start of the 1972 'Return to Steam' series – the one that hauled the last steam out of Paddington…*Clun Castle*?

Clun Castle, one of the standout locomotives of GWR 150, missed out on GWR 175. After hauling many memorable special trains during the 1970s and 80s, during the early 90s it became part of Tyseley's fundraising "Drive a Loco" courses where hundreds of eager customers were given the chance to take the controls of a GWR Castle.

The boiler became due for overhaul in 2002 when it was taken out of service and its wheels need retyring. Meanwhile, Tyseley pressed on with the rebuild of *Earl of Mount Edgcumbe*, which had originally been bought as a source of spares.

With No 5043 restored to working order, Tyseley has begun the overhaul of No 7029, tackling the tender and the renewal of old copper pipes first of all.

Tyseley's target during GWR 175 year is raise sufficient funds to complete the overhaul, with new tyres, boiler tubes, stays etc., and has launched a national appeal.

Bob Meanley said: "No 5043 has already proved what a properly repaired double chimney Castle is capable of. Just imagine what we could do with two of them!"

*Anyone wishing to contribute to the *Clun Castle* restoration appeal – and therefore help continue the GWR story towards its second century - is asked to send donations to 7029 Clun Castle Limited, a registered charity, at the Clun Castle Appeal Fund, 670 Warwick Road, Tyseley, Birmingham, B11 2HL. Cheques should be made payable to 7029 Clun Castle Ltd, and Gift Aid forms are available.

The return of Great Western

The Conservative Government's Railways Act 1993 in many ways turned the clock back to 1947, by privatising the national network.

The big difference was that this time round, Britain's track and infrastructure would be owned by a single body, Railtrack plc, while the train services would be redivided up into regions and franchises, with the operations of the British Railways Board split up and sold off.

Great Western Trains was formed as one such division of British Rail prior to the franchise being let. The illustrious name itself heightened optimism for a future in which train services would, in theory, depend less on subsidy from the taxpayer and more on competition.

The new Great Western sector comprised of the express services out of Paddington to the West of England – Bristol, Exeter, Penzance and South Wales – Cardiff and Swansea.

A holding company, Great Western Holdings, partially owned by the Badgerline bus group, won this new franchise. Badgerline subsequently merged with the GRT Group to become FirstGroup and in 1998 bought Great Western Trains outright. It was then rebranded as First Great Western.

First Great Western consisted of the express services out of London Paddington to the West of England (Bristol, Exeter, Plymouth, Penzance) and South Wales (Cardiff, Swansea).

The 'new' Paddington/Swindon empire 'reclaimed' GWR territory on 1 April 2006 when First Great Western, First Great Western Link and Wessex Trains combined into a new Greater Western franchise, after

Often dubbed the most beautiful stretch of railway in Britain, the section which runs over Brunel's sea wall between Dawlish and Teignmouth is also the most costly to maintain, because of cliff falls, high tides and the fear of more frequent storm surges because of global warming. FGW

First Group beat off rival bids from National Express and Stagecoach to win it.

First Great Western Link, which operated from 2004-6, ran the Thames Trains franchise, which included services from Paddington Station to destinations such as Slough, Reading, Didcot, Oxford, Goring and Streatley, Henley-on-Thames, Newbury, Bedwyn, Hereford, Worcester, Banbury, Reading and Basingstoke.

The Thames Valley routes were privatised in the mid-90s and partly sold to the managers who had run the services under British Rail and partly to private operator Go-Ahead

1995

First privatisation franchise awarded: Stagecoach takes over South West Trains.
Holding company Great Western Holdings, part owned by the Badgerline bus group, later won the new Great Western franchise. Badgerline later became FirstGroup after a merger with the GRT Group.
No 70000 *Britannia* returns steam to Penzance after 30 years.
First Chinnor & Princes Risborough Railway trains run.
Revived Cholsey & Wallingford Railway opens throughout.
24 Sept: Services from Birmingham Snow Hill north to Smethwick and onwards to Worcester resumed. The first day saw steam-hauled special trains to Stourbridge Junction.

1996

Bodmin & Wenford reopens Bodmin General to Boscarne Junction.
Dean Forest opens through from Norchard to Lydney Junction.
Llangollen Railway extends to Carrog.
Phyllis Rampton Trust takes over Vale of Rheidol Railway.
Llangollen Railway extends to Carrog.
Cambrian Railways Trust starts DMU trips over part of Oswestry-Welshpool line.

1997

Railtrack floated on stock exchange.
March: The McArthur Glen Swindon Designer Outlet, the largest of its type in Europe, opened iniside former Swindon Works building, with 105 stores.

1998

GWR 4-6-0 No 6024 *King Edward I* becomes first King to officially cross Royal Albert Bridge at Saltash.
FirstGroup purchased Great Western Trains outright, rebranding it First Great Western.

1999

In recognition of the railway's historical importance, parts of Brunel's original Great Western Main Line were added to UNESCO's tentative World Heritage Sites list.
The Birmingham Snow Hill-Wolverhampton line was reopened as the Midland Metro light rail system.
Dart Valley Railway plc buys riverboat company to run alongside Paignton & Dartmouth Steam Railway.

Group, which later took sole control and ran them as Thames Trains. Wessex Trains was founded on 14 October 2001 when the Wales and West and Valley Lines franchises were reorganised. Wales and West Passenger Trains Ltd, which was owned by the National Express Group, adopted the trading name of Wessex Trains along with most local services in south-west England.

The new combined franchise operator decided to keep the name First Great Western, with all services carrying the brand name and livery.

The early years of the franchise operation did not live up to the reputation that the GWR had earned time and time again in the steam era, and First Great Western was repeatedly beset by negative publicity.

Passengers were repeatedly left frustrated and angry by a high volume of cancellations, and public dissatisfaction was loudly expressed with a new timetable introduced in December 2006, with the company denying rail campaigners' claims that evening commuter services were being cut.

In December that year and the following month, a higher than normal incidence of cancellations and delays were reported, many put down to shortages in train crew or a lack of serviceable trains, leaving some branch lines with just bus services.

Around the same time, figures released by the Office of Rail Regulation said that one in four First Great Western inter-city trains had run late the previous year, with the company blaming extreme weather conditions in the early part of the summer. Infrastructure provider Network Rail was also criticised by the rail regulator regarding the Great Western routes, its performance there being described as 'exceptionally disappointing'.

On 22 January 2007, Bath to Bristol

A Class 43 HST unit exits Box Tunnel en route to Bath and Bristol on 30 April 2010. ROBIN JONES

A First Great Western power car carrying the company's original green livery at Reading station.

commuters on the service staged a protest about overcrowding, issuing imitation tickets printed with 'Ticket type: standing only', 'Class: cattle truck', 'Destination: to hell and back', 'Price: up 15 per cent'.

Two days later, the company's managing director Alison Forster, apologised to its customers about the recent problems, on the same day that Wantage Conservative MP Ed Vaizey raised the matter of the timetable changes in the House of Commons.

Changes to the First Group management structure on 6 September 2007, apparently aimed at boosting the First Great Western commuter services, were welcomed by Anthony Smith, head of the rail users council, Passenger Focus.

However, passengers held another fare strike in January 2008, and the following month, Secretary of State for Transport Ruth Kelly stated that First Great Western had 'fallen persistently short of customers' expectations and been unacceptable to both passengers and government'.

The Government issued the company with a fresh set of demands for improvements, estimated to cost around £29-million. It was ordered to hire new drivers, guards and engineers, pay passengers more compensation and cut fares as part of an emergency remedial plan to tackle overcrowding, cancellations, late-running trains and rising fares.

FirstGroup responded by saying: "Following discussions with the DfT we have agreed to make additional investments to provide an enhanced service for passengers and agreed a plan to improve operational performance."

This time, the promises held true and the measure taken worked.

From being labelled as the worst operator in the country, by May 2009, the company

On a branch line where GWR prairie tanks once reigned supreme, a First Great Western Class 150 two-car DMU crosses Carnon Viaduct with a 5.30pm Falmouth Docks-Truro working. The pillars of Brunel's earlier wooden trestle viaducts, typical of the Cornish valleys, can be seen below. FGW

First Great Western HST No 43004 passes the old Swindon Works buildings in February 2007. ROBIN JONES

Classic traction in service today

Just as the GWR was renowned for its express passenger steam locomotives, a modern traction classic of equal magnitude is regularly seen in First Great Western colours today.

Some of the Class 43 InterCity 125 High Speed Train diesel multiple units have been as long in service on the GWR system as were the legendary Kings and Castles, and the youngest has been running for 28 years.

Built by British Rail Engineering Ltd from 1976-82, the class is the fastest diesel unit in the world, with an absolute maximum of 140mph, and 125mph regular service speed

The prototype Class 41 High Speed Diesel Train set was developed at the Railway Technical Centre, Derby, with the power cars, Nos 41001 and 41002, being constructed at Crewe in June and August 1972 and the Mk3 carriages by BREL at Derby's Litchurch Lane works.

Following proving trials on the Eastern Region, the set was transferred to the Western Region for use on Paddington-Bristol/Weston-super-Mare services. From 5 May 1975 there was one public prototype HST daily service on the Bristol route, later increased to two per day.

The trials were successful and orders were placed for more HSTs for the Western Region as well as the Eastern, Scottish and London Midland regions.

Before the introduction of HSTs, the maximum speed of British trains was limited to 100mph. however, the HSTs' increased speed, rapid acceleration and deceleration allowed journey times to be cut.

Indeed, the prototype power cars (renumbered 43000 and 43001) set a world record for diesel traction at 143mph on 12 June 1973, while on 27 September 1985, a special press run for the launch of a new Tees-Tyne Pullman service from Newcastle to King's Cross, formed of a shortened HST set, hit 144mph north of York, setting a world record for the fastest diesel train carrying passengers.

While they have now long given sterling service, there have been repeated calls for them to be upgraded. They are earmarked for replacement by the Hitachi Super Express Train or SET under the Government's Intercity Express Programme, but the last HSTs may not be withdrawn until 2015 because insufficient replacement stock will be available.

In 2005, First Great Western Class 43 power cars Nos 43004 and 43009 were fitted with new German MTU (Motor [Engine] and Turbine Union)16V 4000 engines before being tested in passenger operation. In December that year, First announced that all of its power cars would be fitted with the MTU engine, which gives the benefits of reduced noise, smoke and exhaust emissions, improved reliability and fuel efficiency over the existing Paxman 12RP200 Valenta engines.

What will happen when the final Class 43s are withdrawn? Will one or more be saved for preservation, to be used by a private operator for main line charters, or on a heritage line like the West Somerset Railway? Or will the type suffer the ignoble fate of the Blue Pullman, the last set being scrapped in the mid-70s?

One of the two power cars, No 43000, is preserved inside the Great Hall at the National Railway Museum in York, a fitting place for one of the world's most successful and enduring examples of motive power, the other, sadly, having been scrapped in 1990.

---

had seen an eight-point rise in its performance. The following month, figures showed that First Great Western had turned around its performance to being heralded as one of Britain's most punctual operators, with 94.6 per cent of trains arriving on time.

There was also been a 10 per cent increase in passenger satisfaction, with 82 per cent of customers saying they were now happy with First Great Western.

In February 2010, First Great Western was named Train Operator of the Year at the national Rail Business awards. The judges said: "The joint efforts of colleagues across the company have seen First Great Western move from bottom of the industry performance league table to seventh place out of more than 19 train operators."

First Great Western managing director Mark Hopwood said: "This is a really fantastic achievement – we have come a long way in providing a good service for our customers. There is still more to do, but I'm really proud of everyone and what we have achieved so far."

In March 2010, the Department for Transport approved a new First Great Western service to strengthen business links between the West Country and London. The new early morning train leaves Paddington at 7.06am and arrives in Paignton at 10.17am, allowing people travelling from London to do a fuller day's business in the region.

Torbay Mayor Nick Bye enthused: "This a real boost for tourism. Torbay, Dawlish and Teignmouth need more trains to London and this is a step in the right direction."

In April 2010, the company also claimed a world first in new passenger facilities.

The company teamed up with Volo TV to install touch-screen television screens on the back of every seat in one coach onboard a HST to bring a choice of high quality TV programmes to customers. With an initial launch of 16 carriages, all of its 54 HST units were set to include a coach with screens by end of the year.

Passengers can choose from comedy, drama, documentaries, children's programmes and sport and will be able to pause, fast-forward and rewind at their leisure. Other features include the latest news as well as a moving map.

Every customer can try the entertainment system completely free of charge on their first journey, after which it will cost just £3.95 each time they use the televisions.

Such innovations, the icing on the cake of the company's vastly improved performance, have, in the eyes of many, finally justified First Great Western's use of the name of Brunel's legendary world-beating railway. At last Isambard and Daniel Gooch would certainly approve!

First Great Western HST No 43037 at Totnes prepares to pass the Brunel atmospheric pumping station, which was never brought into service to haul trains before the revolutionary system was abandoned in favour of steam. Next to the town's main line station, in recent times it served as part of a dairy, which has since closed. The building has been listed by English Heritage as the future of the site remained under discussion with potential developers. ROBIN JONES

International status bid for Brunel's line

The bid for international recognition on the same level as the Taj Mahal, the Great Wall of China and Stonehenge talks about its engineering works having 'achieved a grandeur at that time unmatched elsewhere in the country and, as they were suited to high speed running, most of these structures have survived and are in daily use'.

The survival of the magnificent termini at Paddington and Bristol Temple Meads, the portals of Box and Middle Hill tunnels, the bridges over the River Avon and over the Thames at Maidenhead, Swindon Railway Works and Village, the cutting in Sydney Gardens, Bath and Hanwell Viaduct, Bath, combine to make the Great Western Railway the most complete railway of its date in the world, the submission argued.

In this respect, the early GWR is better preserved than other important early lines from the primary phase of world railway development, including the Stockton & Darlington, Liverpool & Manchester and the London & Birmingham Railway.

At a conference in Bristol in 2006, English Heritage deemed the line and its array of tunnels, cuttings, bridges and stations, a 'breathtaking' monument to British endeavour and one that should achieve worldwide recognition, and 'a string of pearls, with precious beads nestled between the jewels'.

However, since the bid was submitted, the goalposts appeared to have been moved.

UNESCO said that it wanted more sites from developing countries and a slowdown on European bids.

In 2009, the Labour Government launched a consultation that could lead to sites like the railway that feature on the 'tentative' list being blocked from the next stage of the process.

The apparent change of heart angered enthusiasts and local conservationists alike, and they stepped up their lobbying for the line to be included on the Government's revised tentative list, due for submission in 2011.

Class 153 single railcar No 153373 moves out of its depot at Exeter St David's. ROBIN JONES

A pair of First Great Western HSTs line up at Paddington. ROBIN JONES

2000
WR pannier tank No 9682 becomes 100th Barry scrapyard locomotive returned to steam.
STEAM – Museum of the Great Western Railway opens in part of Swindon Works.
Railway Heritage Committee designates Vale of Rheidol Railway for preservation.
Pendennis Castle repatriated.
Warwick Parkway station north of Warwick opened. Owned by Chiltern Railways, it is one of the few stations on the national network not owned by Network Rail.

2001
Wessex Trains came into being when the former Wales and West and Valley Lines franchises were reorganised. Wales and West Passenger Trains Ltd took on the trading name of Wessex Trains and the operation of services in south-west England. The company was owned by National Express Group.
GWR No 5972 *Olton Hall* appears in first Harry Potter film as Hogwarts Castle.
14 October: Plym Valley Railway runs first passenger trains.

2002
3 June: Passenger trains return to Corris Railway.

2003
7 April: Gloucestershire Warwickshire Railway extension to Cheltenham Racecourse station opened by Princess Anne.

2004
Welshpool & Llanfair takes delivery of replica Pickering carriage to start replacing original set scrapped by GWR in 1931.
April: First Group takes over Thames Trains franchise from Go-Ahead Group and runs it as First Great Western Link providing services from Paddington Station to destinations such as Slough, Reading, Didcot, Oxford, Goring and Streatley, Henley-on-Thames, Newbury, Bedwyn, Hereford, Worcester and Banbury. Services are also provided from Reading to Gatwick Airport (via Guildford and Dorking), and from Reading to Basingstoke.
May: *City of Truro* returns to main line to mark centenary of unofficial recordbreaking run over Wellington Bank.

The spirit of Brunel lives on!

Many heritage railways occupying former Great Western branches and routes organised celebrations to mark the 175th anniversary of the GWR in 2010.

Splendid as they all were, for many different reasons, it was a classic named train run over Isambard Brunel's original main line that stole the show.

The rerun by Vintage Trains of 'The Bristolian' from Paddington to Temple Meads and back on Saturday 17 April was remarkable for far more than the performance by the recently-restored former Barry scrapyard wreck GWR 4-6-0 No 5043 *Earl of Mount Edgcumbe*, which, thanks to its expert rebuild and maintenance at Tyseley Locomotive works, proved that it could maintain high-speed running on the modern main line without any difficulty.

It also highlighted the spirit of the ingenuity that Brunel showed back in 1835, when he was busy rewriting the rulebook to make the unimaginable reality.

A core element of the eagerly-awaited run, which began at 11.30am when No 5043 moved the eight-coach train out of platform 3 at Paddington, was a General Utility Van owned by train operating company West Coast Railways and specially adapted by Tyseley.

Tanks contained in the van allowed around 3000 gallons of water to supplement the 4000 in the Castle's tender.

The plastic tanks inside the GUV each held around 220 gallons, meaning that the weight was evenly distributed inside the vehicle, while staying inside the weight limit.

The availability of the GUV overcome issues that have beset high-speed running of steam in the preservation era, when the infrastructure of the steam age such as water columns and troughs have long since been removed, leading to the need for regular breaks to take on water.

Triumph over adversity: following in the footsteps of Brunel's building of the line between Bristol and London, another hurdle had been conquered 175 years later!

The GWR introduced the train to mark the centenary of the opening of the route in 1935.

'The Bristolian' was one of the three top GWR named expresses, the others being the 'Cornish Riviera Express' and the 'Cheltenham Spa Express'. It was hauled by Kings and Castles until 1959, when Warship diesel-hydraulics took over.

The name 'The Bristolian' retained by British Rail, is still used by its successor on the route, First Great Western.

On 12 December 2009, a commemorative train, also called 'The Bristolian', was hauled GWR 4-6-0 No 6024 *King Edward I*.

However, GUV in hand, the run of 17 April was to be something that little bit special.

When the GWR launched 'The Bristolian', officials set a timing of 105 minutes in each direction.

That involved a slightly higher average speed on the Down journey, 118.3miles via Swindon, Chippenham and Bath compared with the Up train running via Filton Junction and Badminton, 117.6 miles from start to stop.

Of the two, the Down 'Bristolian'- given the more favourable gradients at Dauntsey and through Box Tunnel - was booked for an average speed of 67.6mph.

The Up train, faced with 2.25 miles of 1-in-75 up Ashley Hill bank and the long 1-in-300 climb to Badminton, was reduced marginally to 67.2mph.

These timings lasted until 1959 when the Warships cut them to 100 minutes.

On Saturday 17 April, *Earl of Mount Edgcumbe* took the Up journey by storm,

GWR 4-6-0 No 5043 *Earl of Mount Edgcumbe* at Bristol Temple Meads with Vintage Trains' 'The Bristolian' on 17 April 2010. GEOFF SILCOCK

No 5043 was not the only non-stop Castle on 'The Bristolian' on 17 April: restorer and fireman Bob Meanley's 1957 Christmas present, Hornby Dublo No 7013 *Bristol Castle*, hitched a ride on the footplate for the run. All three are seen at Paddington after arrival.
JAMES SHUTTLEWORTH

taking 110 minutes for an end-to-end average speed of 64.2mph!

By any standard, this was an incredible performance by a locomotive sold for scrap in 1963.

Not only that, but it has to be remembered that while 213 locomotives were saved from Barry scrapyard by the preservation movement, not all of them were destined to run again. Indeed, No 5043 was bought by 7029 Clun Castle Limited in September 1973 only as a source of spares for No 7029 *Clun Castle*. It was moved to Tyseley where many parts were removed for safekeeping.

Built at Swindon in March 1936, a year after the 'Bristolian' appeared, No 5043 was first named *Barbury Castle*. At the same, the GWR board decided to transfer the nameplates from its ageing 4-4-0s to modern types, and so it September 1937, the locomotive was renamed *Earl of Mount Edgcumbe*, after a company director.

It was first allocated to Old Oak Common and appeared on the 'Cheltenham Flyer' as well as the Paddington-Wolverhampton services.

In June 1952 it was switched to South Wales, based at Carmarthen and Swansea

Tackling the 1-in-75 climb north of Temple Meads towards Bristol Parkway on the return, No 5043 passes Narroways. PHIL WATERFIELD

(Landore). There, it handled named Welsh expressed such as 'The Capitals United' and 'The Red Dragon'.

No 5043 returned to Old Oak in February 1956 and resumed its duties on top-link trains, being relegated to semi-fasts to Reading and Didcot as more diesels took over.

In May 1958, it was fitted with a double chimney and revised draughting arrangements, which great improved the engine's efficiency. On 5 June 1958, it was recorded as reaching 98 mph on the Up 'The Bristolian'.

In April 1962 it was relocated to Cardiff Canton and then Cardiff East Dock, for secondary duties. Withdrawn in December 1963, it reached Dai Woodham's scrapyard in June 1964.

At Tyseley, little thought was given to the future of No 5043 for many years, but as the preservation movement developed, and the steam centres resources and capabilities expanded, there were many who came to the view that No 5043 should be restored in its own right.

In 1997, the Birmingham Railway Museum Trust launches its project to restore *Earl of Mount Edgcumbe* to main line running condition, in late 1950s condition with Hawksworth tender and BR double chimney. The 5043 Restoration Fund was set up to finance the work and so its future was guaranteed at last.

A Hawksworth tender tank was manufactured and Hawksworth tender frames acquired.

The rusting hulk was moved into Tyseley Locomotive Works in 2000 for restoration to begin.

In 2007, the boiler was hydraulically steam tested and returned to the frames, the first fire having been lit for 44 years.

The nearly-complete locomotive was exhibited at the Tyseley 100 Open Weekend in 2008. On 3 October that year, No 5043 returned to steam and moved under its own power again.

It returned to the national network on 16 October 2008, making a light engine run from Tyseley to Shirley. Three days later, it made a loaded trip from Birmingham Snow Hill to Stratford-upon-Avon. A warm axlebox problem was rectified in time for it to appear in steam, in action as the star of the show at the Tyseley Open Day on 26 October when it was publicly recommissioned.

Its first three revenue-earning main line trips following rebirth included a run to Didcot with Tyseley's No 4965 *Rood Ashton Hall*, then on its own to Melton Mowbray and then a jaunt to London's Kensington Olympia and Clapham Junction.

Its finest hour, however, came at the start of the second decade of 21st century – nearly half a century after it would have been cup up from scrap if it had been bought by any scrapman other than Dai Woodham.

The other major factor in the success of the 17 April run was the close co-operation of Network Rail and First Great Western, and careful preplanning which made sure that the train's progress was not checked by signals on an intensively used high speed route to and from London.

Officials of both Network Rail and FGW rode on the train and maintained constant telephone contact with both the footplate crew and signal controllers. In effect, they were all but making the road as the train sped through the countryside.

Meanwhile, everyone was wondering would today's steam speed restriction of 75mph prevent the train attaining the GWR and Western Region' end to end 110-minute schedule?

Earl of Mount Edgcumbe answered that question with the Up 'Bristolian'.

With driver Andy Taylor on the regulator, speed rose quickly after Bristol Parkway and having climbed up to Badminton, the train was travelling at the maximum (steam) line speed of 75mph.

On-board observers recorded the speed at that point was as near 'Bristolian' standards as was likely to be experienced in modern times, with Swindon being passed 12 minutes early at 72mph.

Gathering pace through the Vale of the White Horse, Didcot was passed 20 minutes ahead of schedule. This was increased by five minutes at Reading.

Running on the Up main under greens, 'The Bristolian' maintained 75mph on most of the remaining 30 miles to Paddington arriving very slightly under 110 minutes start to stop, averaging an end-to-end speed of 64.2mph, just five minutes adrift of the Great Western's original timing.

In the year of GWR 175, that cannot but be described as anything less than absolutely magnificent.

Credit must go to Tyseley's Bob Meanley, his son Alastair and the rest of the locomotive restoration team at Tyseley, West Coast Railways for operating the train and coming up with the GUV water carrier and, of course, FGW and Network Rail for reasons stated above.

Drivers Ray Poole and Andy Taylor together with firemen Alastair and Bob Meanley showed that the footplate skills for which all top link Great Western men were renowned, are still alive.

Who on earth now believes that the GWR came to an end on 1 January 1948?

High speed train: No 5043 in full flight at Cholsey on the return to Paddington. ANDREW BELL

Earl of Mount Edgcumbe pulls away from Middle Hill Tunnel with 'The Bristolian'. Less well known than the nearby Box Tunnel, although having equally-attractive Brunellian classical portals, the 198-yard Middle Hill Tunnel was constructed by George Findlater of Brislington. MARK WILKINS

'The Bristolian' heads westwards through Sonning Cutting, Brunel's great earthwork. ANDREW BELL

2005
Didcot Railway Centre completes building of replica GWR broad gauge *Fire Fly*.
December: First Group announced as the operator of the combined Greater Western franchise for a 10-year period.
April: Helston Railway Preservation Company Limited arrived at Trevarno Gardens to lay first track.
26 December 2005. Dean Forest Railway runs first public DMU trips to Parkend terminus.

2006
1 April: First Great Western, First Great Western Link and Wessex Trains combined into the new Greater Western franchise. All services rebranded First Great Western.
19 May: Parkend officially opened by Princess Anne.

2007
27 May: New Corris steam engine, replica Kerr Stuart 0-4-2ST No 7, hauls first train.

2008
New Minehead turntable becomes operational.
6 Feb: Ebbw Vale Parkway station opened, when services to and from Cardiff Central recommenced after 46 years of being a freight-only line.
10 June: No 6024 *King Edward I* hauled the Royal Train, with Prince Charles and Camilla on board, over the Severn Valley Railway.

2009
West Somerset opens new station at Norton Fitzwarren.
23 July: The Labour government announces electrification of the GWR main line between London, Reading, - Oxford, Newbury, Bath, Bristol, Cardiff and Swansea, "to be completed within eight years".
21 October; Severn Valley Railway's Engine House museum at Highley officially opened by the Duke of Gloucester.

GWR engineering? It never stopped!

One of the big points of GWR 175 year is that it is exactly that – 175 years of Great Western tradition…and still going.

While swathes of rural routes were lost to the closures of the 50s, 60s and 70s, most of the company's main line network is still very much in operation, playing a vital role in Britain's daily transport needs.

Not only can you see a now award-winning modern-day train operator incorporating the GW title, but thanks to the likes of Bob Meanley and Tyseley Locomotive Works, you can see Brunswick green-liveried locomotives running on the national network, in one case hauling timetabled services. That is not to forget the magnificent portfolio of GWR branch lines and cross-country routes reborn as heritage lines; and venues like the National Railway Museum at York, STEAM at Swindon and Didcot Railway Centre where you can view the company's locomotives and coaches close up.

Swindon Works has been closed, but GWR engineering carries on regardless.

I am not referring just to maintenance of steam locomotives and the ongoing restoration of Barry hulks, but the building of new GWR engines.

The NRM's broad gauge *Iron Duke* replica, largely based on spare parts from two much later Austerity saddle tanks, led the way in 1985, and in 2005 we saw the all-new *Fire Fly* launched at Didcot. Yet what about types that could run again on the GWR network as it is today?

Barry scrapyard was a godsend to the heritage railway movement, with GWR types now in regular services on lines across the country they would never have visited in the steam era. However, just as its geographical location meant that its contents were heavily weighted towards the GWR and Southern, so many individual classes like the Halls and Churchward heavy freight 2-8-0s were represented in large numbers, and others not at all. So the GWR heritage steam fleet we inherited, superb as it is, is to some extent an arbitrary rather than planned selection, with many gaps.

In 2009, the new £3-million Peppercorn A1 Pacific No 60163 *Tornado* took to the main line and created a media storm, generating countless headlines and making frequent TV appearances. The public loved it, and there is every reason why what its builder the A1 Steam Locomotive Trust did for LNER designs and apple greens can also be done for the GWR and Brunswick green.

The key to new-build GWR projects is Churchward's policy of standardisation regarding parts. It means that spares from one type can be used on several others.

For the preservation movement waiting to create replicas, it gives them a head start. Rather than having to build every component from scratch, as with *Tornado*, parts from existing locomotives can be used in new ones…or even the bulk of a locomotive can be authentically converted into another type.

The preservation movement was left with an arbitrary assortment of locomotives, many of them acquired by chance rather than choice.

In an ideal world, it would be ideal if at least one of every type had been saved. However, because the early preserved railways did not have the financial resources to pick and choose at the time that key locomotive classes were becoming extinct, or more fittingly, because there were no preservation schemes around at the time, we have inherited a steam fleet that is by no means truly representative of British railway history.

Therefore, the only way to tell the whole story, apart from using models and photographic records, is to build new locomotives to fill in the missing gaps.

In 1979, the Ffestiniog Railway unveiled *Earl of Merioneth*, a new 'double Fairlie' locomotive, based on a century-old design and built at its Boston Lodge works, but produced with a modernish outline with the purpose of supplementing the steam fleet rather than filling any historical void. The same year, the National Railway Museum at York commissioned a working replica of Stephenson's *Rocket* for the Liverpool and Manchester Railway's 150th anniversary in 1980. This locomotive has since acted as an ambassador for the museum at events around the world.

It was Swindon technology's turn next to be replicated. For the 1985 GW150 celebrations to mark the 150th anniversary of Brunel's railway, the museum decided to build a fully working replica of broad gauge 4-2-2 *Iron Duke*.

It was made largely using second-hand parts from two Hunslet Austerity 0-6-0 saddle tanks, and cannot therefore be described as a total new build. However, for the first time since June 1893, when the last original broad gauge engines ran (in the form of South Devon Railway 4-4-0 saddle tanks *Leopard* and *Stag*, used at Swindon for shunting stock into the cutting shop for scrapping), we had the opportunity to see and ride behind one of the behemoths of Brunel's 7ft 0¼in gauge system.

The new *Iron Duke* was built using modern materials and methods to exactly resemble the 1847 drawings. The most obvious feature placing it in 1847 is the exposed wooden lagging: from 1848 sheet iron was added over the lagging and painted to match the tender.

A carriage was built to run behind it, and a short demonstration broad gauge line laid outside the museum so visitors could take a trip back in time to those heady pioneering days and ride behind it.

Tornado was not the first all new main line steam locomotive built in Britain since *Evening Star* was rolled out of Swindon works in 1960, unless you conveniently forget broad gauge.

It was at Didcot Railway Centre, home of the Great Western Society, on 30 April that the 63rd member of Gooch's ground-breaking Firefly class was launched into service, on the venue's own 7ft 0¼in gauge running line.

The locomotive, a replica of the original *Fire Fly* of March 1840, was the culmination of a project begun by the later Royal Navy Commander John Mosse in Bristol in 1981, using original Gooch drawings from 1839 found in an office in Paddington station. Cdr Mosse had been working as consultant architect to British Rail on the restoration of Brunel's old station at the time. In 1982, the Firefly Trust was established to build it, and the job was done for less than £200,000, after the project moved by necessity from its headquarters in Bristol to Didcot where construction took place.

The art of the possible: Churchward and Collett considered the idea of a small mogul, but the West Somerset Railway finally built it! No 9351 is seen passing Watersmeet. WSR COLLECTION

The original 62 members of the class were not built by Swindon, but they paved the way for the GWR to have its own works to turn Gooch's designs into reality under his direct jurisdiction, and were maintained and repaired there. The new *Fire Fly* also perfectly captures the spirit and ambience of the broad gauge era, with its enormous driving wheel, oversize copper domes, stovepipe chimney and wooden boiler cladding. It may look decidedly antiquated, but it was the supersonic jet of its day!

At Didcot, the Firefly Trust has plans to build a dedicated engine house on the site complete with water tank, coal stage and pit.

The most advanced of the GWR new-build projects is to be found at Didcot Railway Centre. We have already seen the recreation by the Great Western Society of an original railmotor, using the surviving coach body, but with an all-new steam motor bogie to power it.

Also well advanced in 2010 is the project to recreate a Churchward Saint by back-converting an example of the later Hall class, No 4942 *Maindy Hall*, obtained from Barry scrapyard in 1973, just as Collett turned No 2925 *Saint Martin* into his prototype Hall in 1924.

The idea of recreating a Saint class was conceived by Great Western Society member Peter Rich more than 30 years ago, while he was rebuilding Churchward mogul No 5322 at Caerphilly. Furthermore, there would be the possibility of converting the Saint from time to time to run as a similar Churchward Atlantic 4-4-2.

However, many components would still need to be made from new. A major appeal for funding was launched by the society in 1995, with the new locomotive named No 2999 *Lady of Legend*, the first new Saint class to be built since 1913.

The major engineering tasks involved in creating the new 'Saint' have been completed at Ian Riley's engineering works in Bury, Lancashire, and the locomotive has now returned to Didcot.

The project has included extensive modifications to the mainframes of the donor locomotive, the manufacture and fitting of new front extension frames, a new running plate with 'square' front drop-end, and a new cab and cab step assemblies.

The new cylinders and motion brackets were fitted and the locomotive was wheeled with the 6ft 8½in driving wheelsets which were completed in 1999. The refurbished bogie with new 3ft 2in wheelsets was also united with the 'Saint'. For the journey back to Didcot, the boiler was mounted in the rebuilt frames.

In GWR 175 year, work was progressing on the boiler as well as the restoration of the 3500-gallon tender.

The other GWR new-build schemes have also been made possible by the Barry scrapyard legacy.

Ten of the last locomotives in Dai Woodham's scrapyard remained together after being bought with public money for an abortive museum scheme in Cardiff, and were inherited by Vale of Glamorgan Council, which has agreed to allow them to be either restored in their own right or dismantled with the parts being used for new-build of extinct GWR classes.

John Buxton of Cambrian Transport Ltd, consultant to both the council and the Welsh Development Agency, produced a report that said that sufficient components could be retrieved to build not only a Hawksworth County 4-6-0, but also the earlier Churchward County 4-4-0 and a largely forgotten design, the 4-4-2 tank engine, in what has become known as the 'Three Counties Project.'

The first Barry 10 donor locomotive was Hawksworth Modified Hall 4-6-0 No 7927 *Willington Hall*, which on 3 November 2006 was taken by low loader to the Llangollen Railway, home of the 6880 Betton Grange project, which had been formed in 1998 with the sole intention of recreating the 81st Collett Grange class 4-6-0, and which had cut a new set of frames, built a cab and had obtained many other parts.

Project members had already developed skills and knowledge from the successful restoration of Barry scrapyard large prairie No 5199, now a regular member of the Llangollen locomotive fleet.

At Llangollen, the Hall's boiler was lifted off and donated to the Grange project. The chassis was then taken away, the frames to be used by the Great Western Society at Didcot to build a new Hawksworth County, for which a new set of appropriate driving wheels were cast in spring 2007.

The new County 4-6-0 will replicate No 1014 *County of Glamorgan*, honouring the origin of the frames and boiler, which is being provided by another of the 'Barry 10', Doncaster-built LMS Stanier 8F 2-8-0 No 48518. Hawksworth studied the 8Fs under his auspices being built at Swindon during World War Two, as he designed his Counties, and so the boilers to the two types were very similar.

The Grange team organised two widely praised Steel, Steam & Stars gala events at the Llangollen Railway in 2007 and 2009, the latter raising money for the cylinder block to be cast.

New Saint No 2999 *Lady of Legend* takes shape at Didcot Railway Centre. GWS

2010

GWR 175 galas held at many heritage venues, including Didcot Railway Centre, Gloucestershire & Warwickshire Railway, Swindon & Cricklade Railway & STEAM Museum. Paignton & Dartmouth Steam Railway rebranded as Dartmouth Steam Railway & Riverboat Company.

February: First Great Western named Train Operator of the Year at the National Rail Business awards.

8 Feb: South Devon Railway buys freehold of line for £1 from Dart Valley Railway plc.

17 April: No 5043 *Earl of Mount Edgcumbe* heading Vintage Trains 'The Bristolian' completes Bristol-Paddington in just under 110 minutes using new water carrier.

May: Gloucestershire Warwickshire Railway runs first public passenger trains over Stanway Viaduct.

23 May: Severn Valley 40th anniversary train.

2013

The new Hitachi Super Express trains scheduled to be delivered as replacements for HSTs. They will have the same top speed of 125 mph but will be capable of 140mph with minor modifications.

2016

Thames Valley commuter services from Paddington to Reading and Oxford, currently served by a combination of Class 165 Network Turbo and Class 166 Network Express Turbo three-car 90mph DMUs, will be replaced by Class 319 four-car 100mph trains currently used on Thameslink after refurbishment.

In 2009, the team bought unrestored Barry 4-6-0 No 5952 *Cogan Hall*, which had been stored at Oswestry, and it will initially aid the new-build project.

The front bogie will be removed and used on Betton Grange. The tender from *Cogan Hall* will then be restored for use behind No 6880.

However, the 6880 Society has promised to restore *Cogan Hall* in its own right and its long-term aim is to have both Nos 6880 and 5952 working together, with a new front bogie built for *Cogan Hall* along with a tender.

In May 2010, the Great Western Society officially launched a nationwide appeal for its long-mooted project to use other 'Barry 10' parts to build a new Churchward 4700 class 2-8-0.

The project team negotiated with the council to obtain GWR prairie tank No 4115 as a parts donor for the new 4700, providing three of the four necessary 5ft 8in driving wheel sets and the extension frame assembly; while another of the rusting hulks, No 2861, would provide the outside-steam-pipe cylinder block which can be modified to suit the 4700, as well as the pony truck. The 4000-gallon tender which came to the society with *Maindy Hall* could be used with a 4700 following overhaul, but many other parts, including the boiler, will have to be manufactured.

When Churchward entered No 4700 into traffic, it carried a standard Swindon No 1 boiler, the same type used by the 2800s, Halls and Granges. However, testing soon showed that a larger boiler was needed for these engines and a new and unique No 7 was created specially for the class. The society hopes to have one of these built from new.

Meanwhile, a group of Severn Valley Railway footplatemen are making progress with producing what many believe is the ideal locomotive for the average heritage railway, the extinct British Railways Robert Riddles Standard 3MT 82000 class 2-6-2 tank engine.

The design work on the type was carried out at Swindon, and all 45 were built there between 1952-55, numbered 82000–82044. The chassis was closely based on the LMS Ivatt Class 4, while the boiler blueprint was derived from a GWR No 2 boiler as fitted to the large prairie and 5600 class 0-6-2Ts.

They were considered an ideal and economical locomotive for short branch lines, but the type had a short life because they were soon replaced by diesel multiple units, or these routes closed altogether.

The last four were scrapped at Cashmore's yard in Newport, South Wales, in October 1968.

The new-build project, originally launched by Buckfastleigh engineman John Besley in 1998, received a boost in 2003 when Stoke-on-Trent City Council agreed to donate a pair of 5ft 3ins centre driving wheels from scrapped BR Standard 4MT 4-6-0 No 76080, identical to those used on the Standard 3MTs.

In spring 2007, the 82045 Locomotive Fund, as the group is known, took delivery of a new set of machined frames, the first major component. Volunteers laid a reinforced concrete base for the fund's site at Bridgnorth in June 2008, and in November the frame plates were delivered to Bridgnorth after drilling at Boro' Foundry in Lye (Stourbridge).

Other large components inherited from John Besley, including two pairs of correct buffers and the chimney from Class 3 mogul No 77014, are now on site, along with a sizeable collection of smaller parts, including driver's brake valve and brake valve pedestal, sanding gear, firehole doors, lamp brackets and the bunker steps.

The fund has also built up a large library of BR drawings of the 82000 class, and these have already been used to construct the frames, buffer beams and buffer beam gusset brackets, and final frame stretcher, the firebox support bracket, was cast in spring 2010. The copper for the inner firebox and firebox tubeplate was purchased at a knockdown price from a German supplier in May 2009, giving the project a massive boost as they raise funds for the biggest component, a new boiler.

Finally, another Barry-based conversion did not fill a gap created by the extinction of a GWR class – but gave us a Swindon 'might have been'!

The West Somerset Railway had acquired an unrestored Barry hulk, 1934-built prairie tank No 5193, from the defunct Steamport museum at Southport; but rather than restore "yet another" 2-6-2T, it was decided to add a tender and create a 2-6-0, similar to the GWR 4300 and 9300 class types which regularly worked the Minehead branch.

While the engine looks at a glance to be exactly like a GWR mogul, with outside steam pipes, lever reverse and flanged motion bracket, it is a new class of locomotive – one which was considered on more than one occasion by the GWR but which never reached the detailed design stage.

While the chassis forward of the cab is identical to a traditional GWR mogul, the standard No 2 boiler of the large prairie is 5½in smaller and has lower pitch than the No 4 boiler fitted to the 4300s.

Other minor detail changes from the original moguls include the position of the curve on the front footplate, the forward-facing flange on the motion plate, the spring type and the compensating beam type. Also, while the cab design will have the larger side windows of the 9300s, lever reverse follows the format of the 4300 so as to offer the greatest level of crew protection.

The conversion was carried out in a way that the locomotive could be reconverted to a large prairie in the future.

Both Churchward and Collett considered building a small-boilered mogul as a lighter version of the 4300 and 9300 classes, but the weight saving was not considered sufficient to take the idea further.

However, several decades afterwards, the West Somerset officials decided that not only would a 'new' type of GWR mogul be in line with the aim of recreating the Minehead branch as it was in the days of steam, but it would also be popular with the general public who prefer to see tender engines on services.

The cost of building the mogul was found to be not much more than restoring it as a 5101 class prairie, of which 10 survive into preservation.

Project spokesman Andrew Forster, the heritage line's locomotive engineer, said: "It is not a new GWR class but a West Somerset Railway class. The GWR just drew up an outline design of what it may have been like."

Unveiled in 2004, the new mogul, No 9351 – an anagram of its original number – proved that the GWR tradition of innovation did not die with Charles Collett.

*Anyone seeking further information on the new Saint, Hawksworth County, railmotor or 4700 projects or would like to help out is asked to contact: Richard Croucher, Great Western Society, Didcot Railway Centre, Didcot, Oxfordshire OX11 7NJ, telephone 01235 817200 or email info@didcotrailwaycentre.org.uk

*Similarly, anyone wishing to contribute to the Betton Grange project or to join the restoration team is asked to write to The 6880 Betton Grange (Society) Ltd, 14 Newborough Road, Shirley, Solihull, West Midlands B90 2HA, or contact the group via its website: www.6880.co.uk.

*The new Standard 3MT project team can be contacted via Chris Proudfoot at Woodford, School Bank, Norley, Frodsham, Cheshire WA6 8JY, telephone 01928 787255 or email: chris.proudfoot045@btinternet.com

British Railways Standard 3MT 2-6-2T No 82000: the 46th example of this Swindon-built class is being built at Bridgnorth on the Severn Valley Railway. BRITISH RAILWAYS

DVD Releases from
BRITAIN'S LEADING RAILWAY PROGRAMME PUBLISHER

An Archive History of GREAT WESTERN STEAM

Volume One - 1923 to 1963

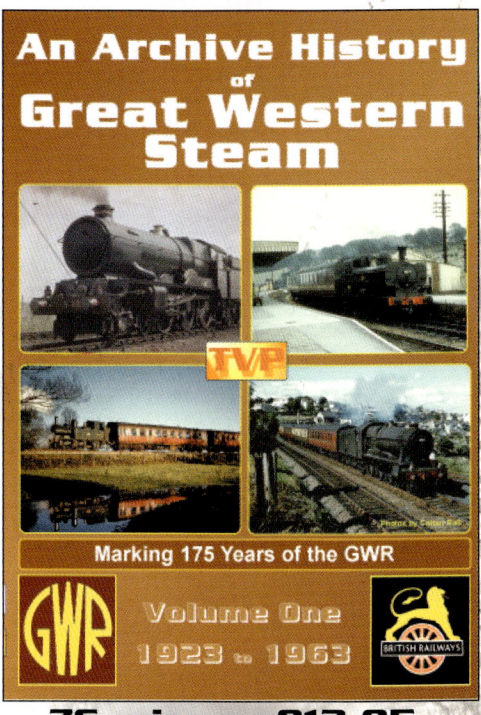

The Definitive Archive History of Great Western Steam from grouping through to the preservation era. Volume 1 traces the development of steam on the Great Western Railway in the 1920s through to Nationalisation in the 1950s and the decline of steam in the 1960s.

The Great Western Railway in the 1920s - The Introduction of the Kings - Centenary Stock - GWR 10 - The World's Fastest Train - Streamlining - The War Years - The Formation of British Railways - Great Western locos produced in the BR Era with 'Castles', Modified Halls, Manors and Panniers - Great Western By-Ways in the 1950s with the Marlow Branch, the Lambourne Branch, Newbury - Winchester, Totnes to Ashburton, Liskeard to Looe, the Fowey branch, Brecon and Cambrian Coast - A journey along the Devon Coast in the early 1950s - the Devon Banks - Plymouth & the Saltash Bridge - Cross country steam in Worcestershire in the early 1950s - Steam Sheds in the 1950s including Stafford Road, Cardiff Canton, Old Oak and Reading - City of Truro - Swindon in the 1950s - First Castle Withdrawn - First 9400 withdrawn - Paddington in the 1950s including 6000 King George V - The Tetbury branch dieselised - The end of the 'Dukedogs - The Last Suburban Steam from Paddington - Western Steam in 1962 - First '5205' withdrawn - First 'Grange' withdrawn - Last of the Kings - 1962 last year for the West Country - Marlow Donkey dieselised - 'Dukedog' arrives on the Bluebell - South Wales Closure - The Steam Scene in 1963 - Farewell 'King' Railtour - Brixham Branch closure - Special trains in 1963 - Western steam to the South Coast - and Paddington Panniers.

76 mins   £12.95

Volume Two - 1964 to 1970

The Definitive Archive History of Great Western Steam from grouping through to the preservation era using mainly film unpublished on DVD. Volume 2 traces the development of steam from 1964 through the end of steam and the fledgling preservation era.

4079 'Pendennis Castle' on Tour - Castles in 1965 - Special trains in 1965 - Last steam on the Lickey - Special in South Wales - Last GWR steam to the South Coast - Scrap gathers at Barry - County Finale - Autumn of Western steam at Chester and in South Wales - Along the Cambrian Coast - Hereford to Gloucester closure - Last push pulls to Chalford with panniers and 14xx - The final year 1965 - 'Clun Castle' on tour - Pendennis at Swindon - Stronghold of steam at Chester and Wrexham with Panniers, 56XX and 2-8-0s - Pendennis on tour in 1965 - Last scheduled steam departure from Paddington - Last Manors on the Cambrian - Branch line special in 1965 - Variety at Bath Road shed in 1965 - Panniers in West Wales in 1965 - Oxley Shed with Manors, Halls, Prairies and Panniers - Special to Severn Valley Railway with 4555 and 1420 - Welsh Special - Stock moves to the Dart Valley Railway - Last Autumn of Western steam with specials and scenes at Oxford - Countdown to the end - Dart Valley steam - Gloucester shed - End of steam special with 7029 - Final workings in 1965 - Scrap at Severn Tunnel & Barry - 1966 survivors on S & D - Panniers at Wrexham in 1966 - Panniers special - Vale of Rheidol - Bath Road Open Day - 1967 'The Zulu' to Chester - 'Clun Castle' on the East Coast Main Line and in the North - Stock moves - 1968 at Didcot - 1969 on Dart Valley - Panniers on London Transport.

80 mins   £12.95

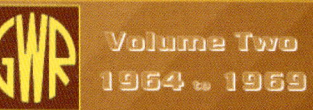

Series Produced to mark the 175th Anniversary of the Great Western Railway

Telephone 01582 833807 (24 hour) or 01582 834319
Order via our web site   www.transportvideo.com

Please send cheque or postal order with order. Most major credit cards accepted
All prices include post & packing for the UK

TRANSPORT VIDEO PUBLISHING. 19 High Street, Wheathampstead, Herts AL4 8BB

Rail Holidays

Escorted tours and full tailor made service to Europe and Worldwide destinations

OF THE WORLD

Holidays to Treasure on Scenic Routes Throughout the World

We focus on travelling by train and combine stunning scenery with exciting places to visit and discovery time. Sit back and relax whilst the scenery, culture and wildlife unfold before your eyes. From classic journeys in Switzerland to awesome routes in Peru.

Made-to-measure holidays with a full personal service to amazing destinations. Train tickets for Eurostar, UK rail, European rail and far away places too.

Dream Journeys on:

Rocky Mountaineer
The Legendary Ghan
The Blue Train
Plus many other routes

Call us for a brochure: 01766 772030

Ffestiniog Travel

Tel: 01766 772030
Fax: 01766 772049
Email: info@ffestiniogtravel.co.uk
www.festtravel.co.uk

Ffestiniog Travel,
First Floor Unit 6,
Snowdonia Business Park,
Penrhyndeudraeth,
Gwynedd, LL48 6LD.